RETHINKING AMERICAN WOMEN'S ACTIVISM

In this enthralling narrative, Annelise Orleck chronicles the history of the American women's movement from the 19th century to the present. Starting with an incisive introduction that calls for a reconceptualization of American feminist history to encompass multiple streams of women's activism, she weaves the personal with the political, vividly evoking the events and people who participated in our era's most far-reaching social revolutions.

In short, thematic chapters, Orleck enables readers to understand the impact of women's activism, and highlights how feminism has flourished through much of the past century within social movements that have too often been treated as completely separate. Showing that women's activism has taken many forms, has intersected with issues of class and race, and has continued during periods of backlash, *Rethinking American Women's Activism* is a perfect introduction to the subject for anyone interested in women's history and social movements.

Annelise Orleck is Professor of History at Dartmouth College. She is the author of *Common Sense and a Little Fire: Women and Working Class Politics in the United States, 1900–1965* and *Storming Caesar's Palace: How Black Mothers Fought Their Own War on Poverty.*

American Social and Political Movements of the Twentieth Century

Series Editor: Heather Ann Thompson,
Temple University

Rethinking the American Anti-War Movement
Simon Hall

Rethinking the Asian American Movement
Daryl J. Maeda

Rethinking the Welfare Rights Movement
Premilla Nadasen

Rethinking the Gay and Lesbian Movement
Marc Stein

Rethinking American Women's Activism
Annelise Orleck

RETHINKING AMERICAN WOMEN'S ACTIVISM

Annelise Orleck

Routledge
Taylor & Francis Group

NEW YORK AND LONDON

First published 2015
by Routledge
711 Third Avenue, New York, NY 10017

And by Routledge
2 Park Square, Milton Park, Abingdon, Oxon OX14 4RN

Routledge is an imprint of the Taylor & Francis Group, an informa business

© 2015 Taylor & Francis

The right of Annelise Orleck to be identified as author of this work has been asserted by him in accordance with sections 77 and 78 of the Copyright, Designs and Patents Act 1988.

Library of Congress Cataloging-in-Publication Data
Orleck, Annelise.
    Rethinking American women's activism / Annelise Orleck.
        pages cm — (American social and political movements of the twentieth century)
    Includes bibliographical references and index.
    1. Feminism—United States—History.   2. Women—Political activity—United States—History.   3. Women's rights—United States—History.
4. Social movements—United States—History.   5. United States—Social conditions.   6. United States—Politics and government.   I. Title.
    HQ1410.O75 2014
    320.0820973—dc23
    2014008522

ISBN: 978-0-415-81172-9 (hbk)
ISBN: 978-0-415-81173-6 (pbk)
ISBN: 978-0-203-06991-2 (ebk)

Typeset in Bembo
by Apex CoVantage, LLC

Printed and bound in the United States of America by Publishers Graphics, LLC on sustainably sourced paper.

CONTENTS

Series Editor's Introduction   *vii*
Prologue: Reflecting on the Wave Metaphor and the Myth of
Monolithic Feminism   *ix*

1   Rethinking the So-Called First Wave – An Extremely
    Brief History of Women's Rights Activism in
    the U.S. Before 1920   1

2   Civil Rights, Labor Feminism and Mother Activism
    From 1920 Through the 1940s   29

3   Varieties of Feminism in a Conservative Age   52

4   Equality NOW! – Feminism and the Law   77

5   Raising Consciousness, Venting Anger, Finding Sisterhood:
    "The Revolution is What is Happening in Every
    Woman's Mind"   105

6   Women's Movements for Redistributive and Social
    Justice: Other Faces of Radical Feminism   137

7   Lesbian Lives, Lesbian Rights, Lesbian Feminism   166

8   Anti-Feminist Backlash and Feminism Reborn:
    The 1970s Through 2013   199

Index   *221*

SERIES EDITOR'S INTRODUCTION

Welcome to the *American Social and Political Movements of the 20th Century* series at Routledge. This collection of works by top historians from around the nation and world introduces students to the myriad movements that came together in the United States during the 20th century to expand democracy, to reshape the political economy, and to increase social justice.

Each book in this series explores a particular movement's origins, its central goals, its leading as well as grassroots figures, its actions as well as ideas, and its most important accomplishments as well as serious missteps.

With this series of concise yet synthetic overviews and reassessments, students not only will gain a richer understanding of the many human rights and civil liberties that they take for granted today, but they will also newly appreciate how recent, how deeply contested, and thus how inherently fragile, are these same elements of American citizenship.

Heather Ann Thompson
Temple University

PROLOGUE

Reflecting on the Wave Metaphor and the Myth of Monolithic Feminism

Wrestling With the F Word

Since the 1980s, feminism – the word, the idea and its history – has carried something of a bad odor in American popular culture. Some of that stems from genuine fear of the dangerous power of female anger. Some of it arises out of the backwash from pundits' purposely distorting stereotypes. Anyone who has listened to radio for the past 35 years has heard the crude characterizations – man-hating, bra-burning, hairy-legged, chanting, marching women, "FEMINAZIS!"

Most high school and college students will run hard to distance themselves from anything that might associate them with such vestigial creatures. Even for most older people, the images generated by the word feminism are unsavory. And so feminists remain, for many, historic figures trapped in amber – tiny, hairy cave women waving their clubs as they march through the mists of recent history. We can see the angry expressions on their faces and tell from the movement of their mouths that they are shouting. But we can't quite hear what they are saying.

Feminism is best left that way, many young people feel. Even enrolling in a women's history course, or a women's and gender studies class is enough to elicit suspicious comments from other students who wonder aloud: "What do you learn in those classes? You're not a feminist are you?"

One purpose of this book is to make the "f word" – feminism – less frightening. What follows is a history of American women's activism in the 19th and 20th centuries that makes clear that there has never been a single or unitary American feminism. Rather there have been diverse and often conflicting expressions of women's desire for greater freedoms, for political and economic equality, for change in the home and in the boardroom. Women's desires for social and political change have not been limited to any time or place. Women's activism can be found everywhere in American social, cultural and political history. One need only look beyond the headlines and the stereotypes.

This book will not shy away from use of the word Feminism with a capital F, or from examining explicitly feminist struggles for legal and economic equality, sexual and political equality. But it will situate feminist identities, thoughts and activisms broadly. It will focus not only on the campaigns of the National American Woman Suffrage Association (the driving force in getting women the right to vote), or the National Organization for Women (founded in 1966 to promote legal equality for women). It will identify feminist ideas not only in arguments for an Equal Rights Amendment to the Constitution or in the famous books most often associated with advances in women's rights. Instead, it will trace and weave together multiple, intersecting streams of women's activism. Some of these have focused only on gender but others have also highlighted race, class, sexuality, motherhood and the struggle for subsistence.

In seeking to "redefine" American women's activism, this book creates a history not of Feminism but of feminisms. It recounts the story not of one women's movement but of women's activism in the abolitionist, labor, civil rights, welfare rights, lesbian and gay rights struggles – and elsewhere. Strands of feminism can be found in many movements if we look closely – in peace and environmental justice movements, among the Riot Grrrls of 1990s rock music, in the military and in the Women's National Basketball Association. There is not enough space in this book to explore all of these expressions of feminism in any depth. Still, this book will make clear that American women's activism has involved much more than a burst of fierce anger that flamed up in the 1960s and 1970s, then died an ignominious death in the 1980s.

Feminism's demise has been regularly reported and celebrated ever since the 19th century. But, to paraphrase Mark Twain, reports of the death of American feminism have usually been greatly exaggerated. It is true that, in some eras, it has been difficult to see women organized en masse. At other times, women's activism has been impossible to ignore. There has been no linear path toward women's progress. Still, if we see American women's activism as a tangle of currents, running through the 19th and 20th centuries – overlapping, diverging, running underground and re-emerging, one can see that it has always been there. Throughout American history, varied forms of feminism can be found at the intersections of social movements that historians have sometimes seen as completely separate. This book will argue that they were not so separate after all. And it will mark moments when, for a time, different streams, disparate movements, have come together. And, as the waters rose, women's discontent became visible.

Uprisings and the Painstaking Labor of Making Change

Historians of social movements, and I am no exception, have been drawn to moments of turbulent unrest that, for lack of a better term, may be described as "uprisings." They are romantic, exciting. They sweep up tens, even hundreds, of thousands of people intoxicated by the prospects for imminent change. But uprisings are rarely if ever truly spontaneous. Not simply the upwelling of long-suppressed frustrations – as they are frequently characterized by pundits at the time – most periods of protest and mass unrest arise out of, and give rise to, longer, quieter times of painstaking and sustained activism.

Fewer people are moved to engage in political action during these in-between times but those who do are women and men whose lives are defined by activism. Often, they have a clear vision of the kinds of changes they hope to bring and they are in the struggle for the long haul. These are the activists who labor in the trenches lobbying and organizing to pass and enforce legislation. They are in the streets – and more recently on the internet – getting petitions signed. They stay up late in crowded storefront offices making phone calls, or in softly lit rooms researching and writing op-eds, political manifestos and legal briefs. It will be difficult in a short book such as this to capture the many kinds of political labor that women activists have performed in the quiet, interstitial years. But this volume will try to convey some sense of the crucial work being done at times when most journalists and historians were looking elsewhere.

Let's consider the dominant metaphor of feminist history that sees American women's activism and advances in women's rights as having come in two major waves – from the mid-19th century to the early 20th, then rising again in the 1960s and 1970s. That framing has resulted in American history too often being taught as if women had little to do with American politics or social change at any other times. This book asks what happens if we describe periods of feminist uprising as wave crests or peaks and the in-between times as troughs?

Waves are defined by their peaks, but the troughs are just as important to the ebb and flow of any political movement. This book will try to make visible some of the troughs in American women's activism as well as the peaks. It will trace not only the inspiring moments of mass uprising but also the years of painstaking work, the less glamorous but equally essential forms of activism that have come before and between and after the peaks.

The New York-born writer, peace activist and feminist Grace Paley – whose political work continued unabated from the 1930s into the 21st century – never minded laboring quietly in the troughs. She knew that she had contributed to change by protesting, speaking out and writing. But she insisted that the unglamorous work was just as important. "You still have to stuff envelopes," she quietly told a group of younger women writers at a 1990s gathering to consider the ways that writing can be a form of political activism.

Paley also reminded younger activists that it can take a very long time to make change. After Paley spoke to a group of U.S. history students about her efforts to end the war in Vietnam, one young woman asked whether she had ever grown so frustrated that she was tempted to engage in armed struggle. "Political violence is nothing more than a form of laziness," she answered. "Making change is hard work. You have to have patience to do the work it takes to bring real change."[1] One theme of this book is inspired by those words. Without the hard, unromantic work that women activists have done in the trough years, there would never have been those dramatic peak moments when enormous changes have seemed to come rapidly and almost magically.

Cresting waves catch the sunlight and then crash on the shore dramatically. It's hard to miss them. They are compelling and beautiful and sometimes a bit dangerous if you get caught up in the wrong parts of the break. But troughs are parts of the same oceanic currents. One cannot understand waves without also probing their depths. Change is constant and currents crisscross. And the water is always moving.

Sex, Gender and Shifting Coalitions

The tides of political activism, just like oceanic tides, are ceaselessly changing, shifting, turning, splitting into rip currents. Extending the wave metaphor to include cross-currents and rip currents is one more way that this book attempts to redefine the history of American women's activism. Borrowing from some of the pioneering historians of American women, this book will argue that women's politics have always been, of necessity, coalition politics. And those coalitions – hard as many different people worked to build them – have inevitably been temporary, unstable and shifting.[2]

Women, like men, are unified by certain physical realities of biological sex, and they also share the gender norms of their culture and generation. Gender norms are socially constructed and historically evolving ideas about what constitutes acceptable behavior for men and for women. What kinds of clothing are men and women allowed to wear? How should our bodies look? May we speak in public settings? Are we allowed to express anger? Ideas about gender have been powerful organizing forces in every era of human history. They have shaped family relationships, political power distribution, workforce participation and economic class formation. They have often united women as a political force, especially at times when gender norms have denied women basic political and economic equality.

But women are as riven by differences of class, race, sexuality, politics, region, religion and age as men are. It has therefore been difficult to sustain political coalitions around women's issues for more than a few years at a time. The history of American women's activism then, is a history of shifting coalitions, constantly forming, dissolving and reforming.

There have been times in U.S. history when significant numbers of women have been able to come together with men and with each other – across lines of difference – to change laws that discriminated against women, to improve access to education and the professions, to win the right to control their bodies, to enhance their economic or political power. But the kinds of broad coalitions women activists had to build to accomplish these changes could hold only for so long. They inevitably crashed and broke up on the rocks of their differences. Writing about such moments of dissolution is also necessary if we are to understand the history of American women's activism.

So this is a story of crests and peaks, of troughs and painstaking labor in the shadows, and it is also a history of break-up and betrayal, of the painful disintegration of carefully tended coalitions, of human conflict, the ends of friendships and loss of trust.

Such painful moments in the history of social and political movements are delicate to write and sometimes difficult to confront. But no history of organizing for political, social and/or economic change is accurate that ignores the painful side of the story. For if "sisterhood is powerful," as some 1970s feminists argued, sisterhood can also be quite painful. This book argues that, in the history of American women's activism, more often than not, it was both at the same time.

Thinking About Women's Activism As Multi-Cultural, Multi-Racial, Cross-Class

That painful instability stemmed largely from the fact that the history of American women's activism, like American history writ large, has been multi-racial, multi-class and multi-cultural. One of the most enduring myths of American feminist history is the idea that activism around gender issues has been of interest only to a small slice of the overall population: white middle-class women. Nothing could be further from the truth. Working-class women have always been active in American politics. African-American and Chicana women have been vocal and visible activists. So too have Jewish women.

Since the 1960s, activism among these women has been the subject of a fair number of historical studies. The historical literature on activism by Chinese women, Italian-Americans, Korean and Puerto Rican women activists is newer but it makes clear that historians have only begun to explore the full range of people involved in American women's movements. These varied groups of women brought multiple and often conflicting strategies and political goals to their movement work, infusing gender consciousness with a range of perspectives on class, race, ethnicity and religion.

A brief study such as this can only touch lightly on the diversity and complexity of American women's movements. Still it is central to this book's purpose to convey the idea that the history of American women's activism has been anything but narrow or simple, anything but exclusively white and middle class. It is that, of course, but it is far more complicated, far more textured, far more conflicted and far more colorful.

Notes

1 Grace Paley, "Comments at the Books and Other Acts Conference," Dartmouth College, April 7–9, 1995.
2 Meredith Tax, *The Rising of the Women: Feminist Solidarity and Class Conflict, 1880–1917* (New York: Monthly Review Press, 1980).

1

RETHINKING THE SO-CALLED FIRST WAVE – AN EXTREMELY BRIEF HISTORY OF WOMEN'S RIGHTS ACTIVISM IN THE U.S. BEFORE 1920

Creation Myths and Realities

The period of women's rights activism that is commonly referred to as the First Wave of American feminism lasted an awfully long time – nearly 90 years – from the first organized expressions of women's discontent in the 19th century to the achievement of woman suffrage in 1920. Many crests and troughs broke up that long period of change. Many waves rose and fell in that time. None of the most famous of the 19th-century women's movement leaders – Susan B. Anthony, Elizabeth Cady Stanton or Sojourner Truth – lived to see American women receive the vote as a right of national citizenship. By the time that right was won, several generations of activists had contributed to the struggle. Their activist roots, their ideologies and their strategies differed – sometimes in fundamental ways. To understand American women's activism in the 20th century, it is crucial to understand that this long "first wave" was really numerous waves. So, before this book ventures into the 20th century, it will briefly ride some of those crests, crash into some of the troughs, and evoke some painful moments of unraveling when the elation of unity was undone by divisions over race, class, gender and generation.

Histories of American women's rights activism have most often begun with the event that has come to be seen as the symbolic creation moment of American feminism, the Seneca Falls Convention of 1848, where delegates composed the first full-blown women's rights manifesto to come out of the still-young United States. In fact, women's rights rhetoric had been part of struggles before Seneca, going at least as far back as the American Revolution when the language of "self-evident" equality captured the imagination of women as well as men, enslaved as well as free people. But organized women's activism on a mass scale first appeared in the decade leading up to Seneca, arising out of the industrial labor movement, the temperance movement, and, perhaps most importantly, the anti-slavery movement.[1]

Women were heavily involved in each of these struggles in the first half of the 19th century. But, at least at first, they were not moved by what we might see as overtly "feminist" sentiments. Rather they were concerned with the issues those movements foregrounded – shorter work days, safer factory conditions, a living wage, combating alcohol abuse in the hard-drinking early republic, and fighting the pervasive moral and political evil of human slavery. Women abolitionists, labor activists and temperance advocates began to think explicitly about the issue of women's political equality partly because they were inspired by the egalitarian rhetoric and culture of those movements, and partly because of the hostility they encountered from people who did not believe that women should be engaging in politics.

The 1830s was a particularly turbulent decade in American history – marked by religious and political mass movements, utopian community-building and the first stirrings of industrial labor activism. Women mill workers – Yankee farm daughters laboring in Lawrence and Lowell, Massachusetts – were very much at the center of that era of political and cultural unrest. They struck in 1834 and 1836 to protest wage cuts. They marched and paraded through Lowell in what one mill agent called an "amizonian (sic) display." They circulated strike petitions, made speeches and urged other women workers to walk out of the mills in support of the strike.

Amused and also annoyed at being compared to the mythical one-breasted army of women warriors, these militant young women decided that they needed to speak for themselves. They feared that their movement would be slandered by biased bosses with greater access to print media. And so they decided to tell their own story. Beginning in 1841, New England mill workers began chronicling their activism and their lives in a newspaper called *The Lowell Offering: a Repository of Original Articles Written by Factory Girls*. The "Offering" reflected a politics forged on the mill floor and in mass street meetings, but also infused by the spirit of the more leisurely evening hours they spent together in workers' dormitories. These young women had a great deal to say. In the *Lowell Offering* and a more radical journal called *Voice of Industry*, they published young mill workers' first attempts to articulate a political theory of industrial feminism – grounded in their sense of how gender and class shaped and limited their lives.[2]

Mixing pragmatic demands for change with reflections on the social position of industrial woman workers, Lowell activists created the Lowell Female Labor Reform Association – the first political organization for women workers. They circulated petitions, marched on the state capitol in Boston, and testified before state legislators, demanding safer workplace conditions and a ten-hour day. Positing a relationship between free and un-free labor in the U.S., they referred to themselves as "wage slaves."[3]

That new phrase could be found in their published poetry, in the songs they sang as they marched and protested, and in their public testimonies. It was a knife's edge position they carved out – both asserting a sense of sisterhood with enslaved African-American women in the South and expressing a measure of outrage that they – Yankee daughters – should be treated as badly as slaves. They both condemned the institution of slavery and distanced themselves from it. "I cannot be a slave," they sang as they marched. "I will not be a slave."[4]

But, time and again, for all of the attention they received, these militant factory workers were brought up short by the fact that their political leverage was minimal. As free workers, they could choose which masters they worked for but they could not choose to be free of all masters because their economic circumstances required them to work. They needed the money. The class status of their families forced them to labor. And yet they were unlike laboring men because of their sex. They had little ability to pressure elected officials to pass safety or hours legislation. For, though they were white and free born, they were women. And – as women – they did not have the right to vote.[5]

Even as women mill workers came to this dispiriting and galvanizing recognition, middle-class women abolitionists were grappling with the same issue. The 1830s was a period of intense activity by those who opposed slavery. Hundreds of middle-class women's anti-slavery organizations were formed during those years, many of them in the Northeast. In 1837, to foster broader social and political networks, abolitionists convened the first Anti-Slavery Convention of American Women, held in New York. It attracted women delegates from eight states.

The movement gained momentum and attracted more women every year. But, as strong as anti-slavery sentiment was in the Northeast, women faced strong resistance to their playing leading roles in the abolition movement, especially from religious authorities. Militant women abolitionists represented a counter-culture and their views on sex and gender, together with their views on race, marked them as radical – truly different from most of their neighbors, even in the North.

The most famous example of abolitionist women flouting the gender norms of their day was the 1837 speaking tour of two South Carolina sisters, Sara and Angelina Grimké. When the two traveled north to bring a Southern white woman's perspective to the movement against slavery, they were lauded by abolitionist organizer Theodore Weld. Because they were from a slave-holding family, he wrote, the sisters "could do more at convincing the north than twenty northern Females." Fearful of those powers of persuasion, Boston's pro-slavery ministers urged congregants to boycott the women.[6]

In June 1837, the Congregationalist Ministers' Association of Massachusetts issued a pastoral letter asserting that "the power of woman is in her dependence" and condemning "any of that sex who so far forget themselves as to itinerate in the character of public lecturers and teachers." Women were like vines, the ministers opined, "whose strength and beauty is to lean upon the trellis-work" of home. But when a woman "thinks to assume the independence and overshadowing nature of the elm . . . (she) will not only cease to bear fruit but will fall in shame and dishonor into the dust."[7]

Insisting on their right to speak publicly about the evils of slavery, the Grimkés challenged conventional views of "true womanhood." Sara began publishing "Letters on the Equality of the Sexes," much to the chagrin even of staunch supporters like Weld who feared that taking on "the woman question" would lessen her effectiveness as an abolitionist. He urged the sisters to wait before taking up the cause of women's rights. "Can you not see," Angelina asked him, "women could do, and *would* do, a hundred times more for the slave if we were not fettered?" She concluded: "The time to assert a right is the time when that right is denied."[8]

At the end of the sisters' nine-month tour, Angelina Grimké was invited to share her views on slavery before the Massachusetts legislature. It was the first time a woman had been asked to address a legislative body anywhere in the U.S. Entering the state house in Boston, she was greeted both with cheers and loud boos. Grimké later wrote to her friend Sarah Douglass to describe the uproar. All the furor she and her sister had caused could not "but have an important bearing on the Woman Question," she mused. Angelina and Sara Grimké had not been moved to activism by concern for women's rights. Slavery was their issue. But, by the end of the 1830s, they had come to believe that "manumission of the slave and the elevation of woman" were inextricably tied together."[9]

The most commonly taught narratives of 19th-century American feminism move from the Grimkés to the World Anti-Slavery Convention in London in 1840. There, two American delegates – Quaker activist Lucretia Mott and New York social reformer Elizabeth Cady Stanton – were denied the right to speak because of their sex. As a compromise, they were seated behind a barrier so that male delegates could not see them. Mott and Stanton's humiliation in London left them determined to organize the first convention of women's rights supporters in the U.S. Or so the story is usually told. While it is true that the experience angered them, the flame of their interest in women's rights was lit long before. Mott would later say that the idea for a women's rights convention first occurred to her in 1837 at a multi-state gathering of women abolitionists. The campaign for women's rights flowed naturally, she argued, from the "universal conception of liberty" these activists shared.[10]

Between 1837 and 1848, women's rights became a primary goal for Mott, Stanton and other social reformers, but it was far from their only cause. Women's rights activism did not spring forth suddenly. It arose over time, sparked by the deep discussions about liberty and equality that were part of every-day life in the reform communities that dotted the U.S., England, France and Germany in the 1830s and 1840s. Mid-19th-century reformers espoused a broad, internationalist social justice vision that embraced rights for women but also peace, racial justice, temperance and labor activism. These goals and movements overlapped. In an era of evangelical awakening, communal experimentation and the first utopian ideologies of the industrial age, visions of change were rampant. And "all these subjects of reform," Lucretia Mott wrote in 1848, "are kindred in nature."[11]

Still "the woman question" was definitely on the front burner for mid-19th-century social justice activists. From the late 1830s through the 1840s, members of anti-slavery societies, radical Quaker meetings and labor organizations frequently debated women's proper role in the public sphere. Finally, in 1848, a group of committed activists gathered for the first major American women's rights convention.

Held in Seneca Falls, New York on July 19–20, 1848, it brought together men and women, white and black, including former slave Frederick Douglass, perhaps the leading 19th-century male exponent of woman suffrage. Out of that convention came the Declaration of Sentiments, signed by 68 women and 32 men. Echoing the American Declaration of Independence, it began: "We hold these truths to be self-evident, that all men and women are created equal, that they are endowed by their creator with certain inalienable rights, that among these are life, liberty and the pursuit of happiness."

The language of the Declaration of Independence, still vivid and alive for these activists, formed a common sense frame for their exposition of women's rights. And it encouraged them to claim divine blessing for their cause. What rights God has conferred, man cannot take away. Like the founding fathers before them, they listed their grievances and goals – clearly stated and unapologetically demanded. Women, the Declaration averred, wanted access to education and to the professions, control of their own wages and property, freedom from physical abuse by husbands, the right to sue for divorce, and to custody of their children when marriages did break up. And they wanted the power to bring all of this about through exercise of the vote.

Indeed they argued that "all laws which prevent woman from occupying such a station in society as her conscience shall dictate, or which place her in a position inferior to that of man, are contrary to the great precept of nature, and therefore of no force or authority." In other words, it was women's right to disobey those laws and the government that made them. Once again, using the language and form of the Declaration of Independence, they called for a woman's revolution: "When a long train of abuses and usurpations . . . evinces a design to reduce them under absolute despotism, it is their duty to throw off such a government . . . Such has been the patient sufferance of the women under this government, and such is now the necessity which constrains them to demand the equal station to which they are entitled."[12]

The modernity of their demands is striking. They asked not only for legal equality for women, but for the right to control their bodies, property, and relationships. It is clear that they understood the revolutionary nature of what they were asking for. As Lucretia Mott said five years later at one of the less famous woman's rights conventions that followed Seneca: "Any great change must expect opposition, because it shakes the very foundation of privilege."[13]

Those who gathered at Seneca also understood the painstaking work that it would require to "shake the very foundation of privilege." Over the next ten years, they organized numerous women's rights conventions – including one only two weeks after Seneca Falls – to strategize about how to bring some of the deep and lasting changes they had just demanded. The first national woman's rights convention in 1850 in Worcester, Massachusetts attracted 1,000 people. National conventions were convened annually after that, except for 1857. These later gatherings are far less well known than the Seneca Falls Convention, though they attracted thousands of participants overall. They are little discussed in popular narratives of American feminism, because these were parts of the unglamorous process of ongoing organizing that it took to slowly bring change in all of the areas that the signers of the 1848 Declaration had first laid out – education, property, marriage, bodily integrity, the vote. These were the waves that followed the first crest – less thrilling, less surprising. But without their steady rise and fall, the foundations of privilege would never have eroded and finally washed away.

"Arn't I a Woman": Isabella Bomefree Complicates the Story

One of the reasons that it is easier to focus on the crests, the moments of uprising, is that coalition is complicated. The grievances and goals listed in the Declaration of Sentiments highlighted clear legal and customary inequalities rooted in sex, and thus were able to unify disparate constituencies under the banner of legal and economic equality for women. But power differentials and differences in perspective arising from class and race also divided advocates for women's rights. The history of 19th-century American women's activism is a long story of both.

No figure in the history of the 19th-century American women's movement has come to represent both those fissures and the persistence of unlikely coalitions more vividly than Sojourner Truth. In the years after Seneca Falls, Truth, whose given name was Isabella Bomefree, did a series of stump speeches against slavery and for women's rights that became the source of her enduring fame. The substance of her arguments was consistent through all of these speeches. But the one that made her famous was delivered at an Ohio women's rights convention in 1851. Reporters and suffrage movement historians reprinted it over the next few decades in enough different versions that we cannot be sure exactly what words she used. But the essence of Truth's point was crystal clear – that popular understandings of womanhood itself were grounded in race and class stereotypes. "Arn't I A Woman" – the speech she allegedly gave in Ohio that day – was to become one of the most famous texts in the history of American feminism.[14]

Truth, a poor, illiterate mother, domestic worker and former slave, argued with those who insisted that women were pious, sheltered and fragile – in need of protection by men. "Nobody ever helps me into carriages, or over mud-puddles, or gives me any best place!," she is supposed to have said that day in Akron.

> And arn't I a woman? Look at me! Look at my arm! I have ploughed, and planted and gathered into barns, and no man could head me! And arn't I woman? I could work as much and eat as much as a man – when I could get it – and bear the lash as well! And arn't I a woman?[15]

Truth reminded listeners that enslaved women's experience of motherhood, far from being sanctified, was commodified. Truth's own children were sold away as chattel. "And when I cried out in my mother's grief, none but Jesus heard me. And arn't I a woman?" she famously challenged listeners. As late as 1858, Truth faced down members of her own audiences who insisted that, with her six-foot frame, muscular arms and deep voice, she must actually be a man. During one such instance, she allegedly tore open her shirt and bared her breasts.[16]

Such brazenness has become the stuff of Truth's legend as a larger-than-life founding mother of the American women's movement. Truth was cast as a curiosity and an exotic in a movement dominated by white, middle-class women. She was in many ways anomalous – a former slave among free people, an illiterate woman among the book-learned, a poor woman among comfortable and even affluent activists. And yet, her activist history was in other ways quite typical for social reformers of her day.[17]

Her early history certainly distinguished her both from privileged white women's rights activists and more affluent, educated black women in the movement. Born into slavery in Duchess County, New York in 1797, she was the victim of harsh beatings, and was torn away from her first love, the father of her first child. She later married an older man on her plantation with whom she had four more children, the eldest of whom was sold away from her to a plantation in Alabama in 1826. Bomefree ran away – or as she put it "walked off" – with her infant daughter and was taken in by a Quaker couple who bought out the remaining time she owed her master. The Quaker community helped Bomefree to sue in court for the return of her son. He was brought back to her alive but scarred and bruised from beatings. Slavery became illegal in New York in 1827.[18]

At about this time, like so many Americans in that era of religious awakening, Bomefree underwent a spiritual conversion and changed her name to Sojourner Truth. She would later say that she abandoned her childhood name because she wanted to leave all vestiges of her slave life behind her and to make clear that her life would now be devoted to preaching God's truth.

Like other religious searchers in the first decades of the 19th century, Truth joined a commune built around a charismatic leader. This community was called the Kingdom, and it followed a leader who preached strict observance of Old Testament laws. The group disbanded at his death several years later, and Truth, penniless, moved to New York City where she earned her keep as a domestic worker. In the early 1840s, Truth decided to try to support herself as an itinerant speaker. For the next few years, she traveled through Brooklyn and Long Island preaching.[19]

Truth's preaching brought her in 1844 to Northampton, Massachusetts, a center of free-thinkers and utopian dreamers. She liked what she found and decided to settle there in another commune called the Northampton Association of Education and Industry – 200 people, almost all white, who collectively farmed, raised livestock and ran a silk factory. Northampton was quite different from her prior experience in collective living. Abolitionist, pro-women's rights and agrarian socialist in nature, the community attracted many of the era's most notable reformers, including abolitionist publisher William Lloyd Garrison (brother-in-law of the commune's founder), Frederick Douglass and some abolitionist members of Britain's Parliament.

Truth – with her experience of slavery and her powerful critiques of race and gender norms – added a unique dimension to the spirited discussions already raging in Northampton when she arrived. Her arguments for women's rights, abolition, collective living and pacifism had deepened and become quite sophisticated during her years in New York City. Now she was engaged in conversation with writers and publishers, philosophers and intellectuals who were at the heart of American dissent and reform activism. They were keen to promote her ideas.

Truth dictated a memoir of her early life to commune member Olive Gilbert. William Lloyd Garrison, publisher of the radical abolitionist newspaper, *The Liberator*, printed it in 1850. *The Narrative of Sojourner Truth* enhanced her fame, provided some income and increased demand for Truth to speak at women's rights, peace and anti-slavery gatherings. By the early 1850s, she was widely known among reformers for her oratorical power and clarity.[20]

Ironically, Truth's fame caught her up in the very fabric of stereotype and distortion that she challenged. This was even true among the movement activists who helped to make Truth famous. Harriet Beecher Stowe, author of the bestselling anti-slavery novel *Uncle Tom's Cabin,* called Truth "the Libyan sibyl." Stowe both idealized Truth and exoticized her – describing a physically powerful African, almost unnaturally strong and dignified, an illiterate, charismatic religious fanatic who believed she could talk to God. According to many popular narratives of Truth's life, that belief in her direct connection to God gave Truth a moral authority that emboldened her to speak assertively to powerful men – most notably Brooklyn's famed reform preacher Henry Ward Beecher and President of the United States, Abraham Lincoln. Better-educated and more affluent black advocates for women's equality attracted less attention in the press of the day and have appeared much less frequently in popular histories of early American feminism. Perhaps this is because they were less easily cast as exotic counterpoints to the middle-class white women whose image and rhetoric came to define the movement.[21]

And yet, as distinctive and extraordinary as she was, Truth's life path and beliefs were not all that different from those of other reformers among whom she traveled in those years. Even the belief that she spoke directly to God was typical of the Spiritualism movement of that time. The Progressive Friends, a splinter group of Quakers in which she was active for a while, sought to make contact with supernatural spirits. This was not simply an idiosyncratic belief of the colorful Isabella Bomefree.[22]

The legend of Sojourner Truth is forever caught in that peak moment of women's activism before the Civil War, but Isabella Bomefree continued her work in the trough years. During and after the Civil War, Truth continued to advocate for freed slaves. She worked at refugee camps, where she cared for people who had escaped from slavery, and she helped to establish a Freedman's Hospital to treat their injuries. It was in the context of her work for the National Freedman's Relief Bureau in Washington, D.C. that she met Lincoln in 1864. For years after the war, Truth lobbied to convince federal officials to provide land and financial compensation to former slaves. At the same time, she raised money on her own. Drawing large audiences to her talks, she donated the proceeds to the "Exodusters" – former slaves who left the South in the 1870s – helping them to purchase farmland in the Midwest. When illness finally curtailed her activities, Truth checked herself into one last famous reform community – the Battle Creek Sanatorium founded by healthy living activist Dr. John Harvey Kellogg. Truth died in Michigan in 1883.[23]

A House Divided – Race, Class and Women's Suffrage After the Civil War

With the end of the Civil War, the First Wave crashed on the rocks of racial difference in a painful and visible way. In 1869, Congress passed the 15th Amendment to the U.S. Constitution, granting African-American men, but not women of any race or class, the right to vote. It was a bitter moment for many women activists who had struggled for a broader social justice agenda – assuming that woman suffrage would come with the end of slavery. Over the next year, as the amendment went to the states for ratification, deep fissures opened up in the prewar reform coalition. Long-time friends and allies began to doubt each other. Veterans in the struggle for social equality now extolled racism, xenophobia and class power in the name of women's rights.

The broad coalition of abolitionists and suffragists, working people and temperance advocates reached one of its most painful moments of reckoning in New York City in the spring of 1869 at the annual meeting of the American Equal Rights Association. The association was only three years old, founded in 1866 by Elizabeth Cady Stanton, Frederick Douglass, Susan B. Anthony and Lucy Stone.

The new group was founded to formalize the relationship between the abolitionist and woman's rights movements and to take them into the next phase following the end of slavery. On January 29, 1866, radical Republican Senator, Thaddeus Stevens, accepted a petition for "universal suffrage" – a plea to enfranchise women and black men all at once – submitted by Stanton, Anthony, Stone and other New York activists. Optimism was widespread.[24]

But the new coalition, committed to struggling for equality of opportunity and legal rights regardless of race or sex, quickly hit its first rocky moments. The 14th Amendment to the U.S. Constitution, passed by Congress in the summer of 1866 and ratified in 1868, was supposed to guarantee equal treatment under the law for all Americans. But section 2 guaranteed the right to vote only to "male" citizens. The 15th Amendment, passed in February 1869, specified that the right to vote could not be denied on the basis of race, color or condition of previous servitude. Taken together, the language of the two amendments virtually guaranteed that women would be denied the right to vote. Many long-time woman suffrage advocates were enraged. They felt abandoned and betrayed by their allies.[25]

That feeling had begun to fester with the passage of the 14th amendment in 1866 and it caused Stanton and Anthony to change their positions in ways that dismayed old friends in the struggle for social justice. Though the two had long opposed restricting the vote to educated people, in 1867 they began to support that idea. Though they had always supported the Republican Party for its views on social equality, they now felt frustrated by allies who prioritized the rights of black men over those of women. In the years after the Civil War, Stanton and Anthony found allies in the Democratic Party who argued that black men should not be elevated above white mothers, daughters and sisters.

Hoping to recruit Irish immigrant workers to the woman suffrage cause, Stanton and Anthony engaged the Democratic railroad and shipping magnate George Francis Train to speak for woman suffrage. Train was a very colorful character. He entertained and charmed audiences sporting floppy curls, a white vest and lavender gloves. But his alliance with Stanton and Anthony was deeply troubling to their old friends in the abolition movement. During the war, Train had battled against immediate abolition of slavery. In 1867, he courted Irish working-class support for woman suffrage by arguing that black men should not get the vote before white women.

Train threw himself into the woman suffrage cause, even offering to fund a suffrage newspaper to be edited by Stanton and Anthony. The first issue was published in January 1868 as voters debated ratifying the 14th amendment. Choosing militance over accommodation, the women called their weekly newspaper *The Revolution*. Its masthead read: "Men, Their Rights and Nothing More. Women, Their Rights and Nothing Less."

Long-time allies challenged the integrity of the publication. Abolitionist newspaperman William Lloyd Garrison wrote Anthony "in all friendliness" to wonder how she and Stanton "should have taken such leave of good sense and departed so far from true self-respect" as to think of "looking to the Democratic Party and not to the Republican to give success to your movement! . . . The Democratic Party is the 'anti-nigger' party, and composed of all that is vile and brutal with very little that is decent and commendable."[26]

Stanton and Anthony would not back down. They published Garrison's letter in *The Revolution,* rejecting its logic. Stanton explained herself in an unapologetic note to her abolitionist former comrade Thomas Wentworth Higginson. "I know we have shocked our old friends who were half asleep on the woman question . . . but time will show that Miss Anthony and myself are neither idiots nor lunatics . . . The position of such men as Garrison . . . proves that we must not trust any of you. No! my dear friends. We are right in our present position. We demand suffrage for all citizens of the republic in the Reconstruction. I would not talk of Negros or women but of citizens."[27]

By 1869, these disagreements over voting rights had turned ugly. In January of that year, Stanton addressed the National Woman Suffrage Convention in Washington, D.C. on the subject of the "infamous 15th amendment" and its promise of suffrage to formerly enslaved men. The speech she made that day would become one of the most controversial speeches of her long career:

> If American women find it hard to bear the oppressions of their own Saxon fathers, the best orders of manhood, what may they not be called to endure when all the lower orders of foreigners now crowding our shores legislate for them and their daughters. Think of Patrick and Sambo and Hans and Yung Tung, who do not know the difference between a monarchy and a republic, who can not read the Declaration of Independence or Webster's spelling-book, making laws for Lucretia Mott, Ernestine L. Rose, and Anna E. Dickinson. Think of jurors and jailors drawn from these ranks . . . to decide the moral code by which the mothers of this Republic shall be governed? This manhood suffrage is an appalling question, and it would be well for thinking women, who seem to consider it so magnanimous to hold their own claims in abeyance until all men are crowned with citizenship, to remember that the most ignorant men are ever the most hostile to the equality of women, as they have known them only in slavery and degradation.[28]

Simmering tensions exploded at the annual meeting of the American Equal Rights Association in New York City in May 1869. Stephen Foster, a delegate from Massachusetts, started things off by rising to say that he would not remain in the organization with Stanton as President if she did not publicly repudiate Train for his scathing disrespect of black men's voting rights. Through her association with Train, he said, she had betrayed the principles of the organization. She asked him which principles and he replied the equality of all people and "universal suffrage." Henry Blackwell stood up to remind listeners that Stanton and Anthony had always been clear and fervent in their support of black suffrage. Then came a moment that riveted the crowd and that has become an indelible part of American woman suffrage history.

Stanton's long-time ally and close friend, Frederick Douglass, challenged the suffrage leader:

> There is no name greater than Elizabeth Cady Stanton in the matter of women's rights and equal rights but . . . I do not see how any one can pretend that there is the same urgency in giving the ballot to the woman as to the Negro . . . When women, because they are women, are hunted down through the cities of New York and New Orleans; when they are dragged from their houses and hung upon lamp-posts; when their children are torn from their arms, and their brains dashed out upon the pavement; when they are objects of insult and outrage at every turn; when they are in danger of having their homes burnt down over their heads; when their children are not allowed to enter schools; then they will have an urgency to obtain the ballot equal to our own."[29]

Douglass' moving and eloquent argument seemed to have ended the debate, but then Stanton's closest comrade Susan B. Anthony rose to speak. What she said shocked many in the room, for the baldness of its arrogance, but it won rousing applause from others. "The old anti-slavery school say women must stand back and wait until the Negroes shall be recognized," she began. "But we say, if you will not give the whole loaf of suffrage to the entire people, give it to the most intelligent first."[30]

This was the moment when women's rights activism came to be associated with racism, ethnocentrism and class privilege. This was the moment when the broad coalition that had spawned and nourished mid-19th-century American feminism broke apart. It was to remain in tatters for several decades. Lucy Stone, representing the "Boston wing" of the suffrage movement took those who felt they could applaud the 15th amendment enfranchisement of black men and formed the American Woman Suffrage Association. Stanton and Anthony – the so-called New York wing of the movement – started the National Woman Suffrage Association. And their short-lived newspaper *The Revolution* – the name of which marked their brand of feminism as the more radical – continued its laser focus on women's rights above all else.

As suffrage history has most often been taught, the AWSA was the "conservative" wing of the post-Civil War American women's suffrage movement. Stanton and Anthony and the New York movement have been seen as the true feminists, architects of the future. But some of these characterizations were shaped by the identity politics of the years when they were written, the years when American women's history emerged as a field. Looking back from the 21st century, one might just as easily see the universalist position of Lucy Stone and the AWSA as the more radical – or at least the more humane.

Though Stone agreed that the influence of women was desperately needed in American government, and even saw the issue of women getting the vote as more pressing than suffrage for freed men, she could not bring herself to pit women against black men at that moment. "Woman has an ocean of wrongs too deep for any plummet," she told the Equal Rights Association delegates,

> and the Negro, too, has an ocean of wrongs that can not be fathomed. There are two great oceans; in the one is the black man, and in the other is the woman. But I thank God for that XV Amendment, and hope that it will be adopted in every State. I will be thankful in my soul if any body can get out of the terrible pit.

Any expansion of political rights, she reasoned, was good for all people who cared about equality.[31]

So how do we understand the position that Stanton and Anthony took in that moment – the embrace of Train, the shift to a campaign for educated suffrage, the resort to racial and class epithets? Some of it stemmed undoubtedly from a sense that the men of the abolition movement and of the Republican Party had betrayed them and they were deeply angry at the snub. Stanton lashed out with the fury of a loved one betrayed.

Even though she was happily married and seemed as close with her male as her female children, Stanton described men as a political class in ways that might make the most militant gender essentialist wince. Arguing in 1869 that women were better suited than men to run the world, she opined: "The male element is a destructive force, stern, selfish, aggrandizing, loving war, violence, conquest, acquisition, breeding in the material and moral world alike discord, disorder, disease, and death. See what a record of blood and cruelty the pages of history reveal!"[32]

Stanton's jaundiced view of male politics notwithstanding, her characterizations of "ignorant" male voters were clearly racist, and tinged by an outraged sense of entitlement denied. Stanton has been described by biographers both as an egalitarian and an elitist. She was deeply and genuinely repelled by slavery but, as a woman of privilege, she was not immune to the racism and ethnocentrism of affluent 19th-century white Protestant Americans. Certainly there is no easy way to explain away her use of the epithet Sambo or her only slightly less derogatory allusions to Irish, German and Chinese immigrant men. But her personality also matters. Biographer Lori Ginsberg describes Stanton as an absolutist in her political vision, and as an intellectually arrogant woman. She was, writes Ginsberg, a bit too sure of herself. She was also someone who grew bored easily and sought the excitement of new paths. One has to wonder if these traits did not contribute to her embrace of the Democratic Party in the years after the Civil War.[33]

And yet, amazingly, the coalition did not stay broken. As dramatic and painful as the breakup of the suffrage coalition was, it did not permanently rupture. Nothing illustrates that more compellingly than the fact that Frederick Douglass, the most-esteemed and best-known African-American man of the 19th century, reconciled with Stanton and Anthony. He remained their friend, and an ally of the women's rights movement, until the end of his life in 1895.

In his old age, Douglass published a fond reminiscence of his first meeting with Stanton –

> Five and forty years ago in Boston, before the snows of time had fallen on the locks of either of us, and long before the cause of women had taken its place among the great reforms of the 19th century, Mrs. Elizabeth Cady Stanton, then just returned from her wedding tour in Europe, did me the honor to sit by my side and, by that logic of which she is master, successfully endeavored to convince me of the wisdom and truth of the then new gospel of women's rights.

Stanton wrote to Douglass to thank him, seeming to be genuinely moved that she was the one who had brought the great man to the suffrage cause: "I have, I know, made many converts to women's suffrage, but I was not aware that I had been so instrumental in adding a black diamond to our suffrage diadem." Stanton visited Douglass shortly before he died and by all accounts the two enjoyed a very warm time together.[34]

On the very day of his death in 1895, Frederick Douglass was the lone man at a women's rights convention in Washington, D.C. His *New York Times* obituary noted that Douglass never missed the opportunity to attend annual conventions of the National Woman Suffrage Association. On that last day of his life he was escorted amidst great applause to a seat on the officers' platform of the Women's National Council, next to its President, Susan B. Anthony. The two had first met at a Boston anti-slavery meeting decades earlier. At that gathering, Stanton and Anthony were denied the right to speak because they were women. According to Douglass' obituary, he had offered to read Stanton's speech aloud. One would imagine, given his legendary oratorical powers, that he did a passable job of it. But Stanton was displeased. As he liked to tell the story, she strode to the stage, took the speech from his hands, and said: "Here, Frederick, let me read it."[35]

At the moment of his sudden death at the age of 78, Douglass was in the midst of re-enacting for his wife the day's discussions and debates at the Women's National Council. He was so enthusiastic, his wife told reporters, so impassioned, so engaged, that it took her a moment to realize that he had died. At first, she thought that his sudden slump to the floor was just another bit of drama, part of his excited recounting of his last day in the woman suffrage movement.

The coalitions that American women's rights activists built during the second half of the 19th century were subject to damaging divisions over questions of race and class, but they were also remarkably durable. In the end, the personal friendship and respect between Douglass, Anthony and Stanton – three of the greatest American social reformers of their time – and Douglass' allegiance to women's rights as a cause proved to be more lasting than the profound disagreements that had torn them apart. Any history of Frederick Douglass' decades-long friendship with Elizabeth Cady Stanton and Susan B. Anthony must include his searing condemnation of the women's immoral embrace of racist stereotypes to further the cause of woman suffrage. But it is also important to record their reconciliation and sustained affection. For these remind us that social justice movements are always personal as well as political, fragile and resilient both, subject to shattering divisions but equally capable of healing and revival.

A Red Record: Lynching and Deepening Divisions Among Women Activists

Race continued to complicate women's activist alliances through the remainder of the 19th century and into the 20th, as gender and class continued to strain and fracture struggles for racial and economic justice. But if these strains were painful and draining, they were at times also productive. At the outer edges of the movements for woman suffrage, racial equality and labor rights, radical women articulated uncompromising views about race, sex and class that angered mainstream movement leaders but also helped to forge new kinds of coalitions. Here the turbulent career of teacher, journalist, anti-lynching crusader and women's suffrage activist Ida B. Wells provides an illuminating illustration.[36]

Born a child of slaves in 1862, raised among black crafts-people, businesspeople, politicians and reformers in the years after the Civil War, Wells trained to be a teacher. Just 21 years old, she refused to give up her seat in a "ladies' car" on the Chesapeake, Southwest and Ohio railroad in 1884. Challenging the just-then hardening strictures of Jim Crow segregation, the young Wells became a public figure.

Moving to Memphis, she became part owner of a newspaper called the *Free Press*. After three friends – black businessmen – were lynched in 1892, Wells did her own investigation of the facts behind the crime. The stories she published were literally explosive. She argued that the myth of the black male rapist, deployed by white supremacists to justify lynchings, was meant to cover over a fact that white southern men were desperate to hide – that some white women entered into consensual relationships with black men. On May 21, 1892 Wells published this:

> Nobody in this section of the country believes the old threadbare lie that Negro men rape white women. If Southern white men are not careful, they will overreach themselves and public sentiment will have a reaction; a

conclusion will then be reached which will be very damaging to the moral reputation of their women.

Wells also stirred rage by commenting on white men's sexual assaults of black women. Her newspaper office was firebombed. Soon thereafter, death threats forced her to leave the South.[37]

Wells toured the U.S. speaking against lynching. In her wake, black women organized chapters of their first national political organization – the National Association of Colored Women. Like abolitionists before them, 19th-century anti-lynching activists were not catalyzed to act by feminism. Still, anti-lynching activism became a forum and a tool through which black and white women proceeded to advocate for women's rights. And it paved the way for increased black women's activism in the suffrage movement.

In 1894, Wells traveled to London where she spoke to large and influential audiences, condemning lynching with characteristic bluntness and raw emotion. She stirred up her usual firestorm when she told British journalists that lynching arose out of white men's rage that white women seemed to enjoy the company of black men. She then proceeded to describe in detail the horror of white women participating in the lynching of their former lovers.[38]

> "You see," she said, "the white man has never allowed his women to hold the sentiment 'black but comely,' on which he has always so freely acted himself . . . White men constantly express an open preference for the society of black women. But it is a sacred convention that white women can never feel passion of any sort, high or low, for a black man . . . If the guilty pair are found out, the thing is christened an outrage at once, and the woman is practically forced to join in hounding down the partner of her shame. Sometimes she rebels, but oftener the overwhelming force of white prejudice is too much for her . . . 'What!' cried out one poor negro at the stake, as the woman applied the torch, egged on by a furious mob . . . 'Have you the heart to do that, when we have been sweethearting so long?'"[39]

The British press – inflamed by Wells' passion – pointedly criticized the morality of white Americans, especially women's rights activists who remained silent about the ongoing violence against African-Americans. One white woman leader drew Wells' attention at that moment because she was also visiting London. Frances Willard – the powerful President of the Women's Christian Temperance Union (WCTU) – then the largest women's organization in the U.S., was also on a speaking tour. In 1890, Willard had declared that Northern states like New York were wrong to give the vote to Asian and European immigrant men and that the measures being taken by Southern states to restrict black men from voting were wise. "We had irreparably wronged ourselves by putting no safeguard on the ballot-box at the North that would sift out alien illiterates," Willard said.

It is not fair that they should vote, nor is it fair that a plantation Negro, who can neither read nor write, whose ideas are bounded by the fence of his own field and the price of his own mule, should be entrusted with the ballot . . . The Anglo-Saxon race will never submit to be dominated by the Negro so long as his altitude reaches no higher than the personal liberty of the saloon.[40]

When Willard made that speech, Wells had held her tongue, "accustomed to the indifference and apathy of the Christian people." However, just before their visit to London, Willard had attacked Wells by name in her presidential address to the WCTU convention in Cleveland. Willard condemned Wells' assertion that white women would voluntarily enter into sexual relationships with black men. This was outrageous, she said, a defamation of white women's character. She called on Wells to apologize. And though the "lawlessness" of lynching was wrong, Willard said, she seemed to affirm "that old threadbare lie," the charge that more than a few black men were guilty of raping white women. Willard called such rapes "atrocities worse than death," and said she understood how white men's emotions could get out of control when faced with such crimes. Finally, she accused Wells of not knowing who her friends were, and of hurting the anti-lynching cause by offending white women.[41]

Wells responded with fury, first in conversations with the press in London in 1894, then in her own 1895 book *A Red Record*. Chapter 7 was entitled "Miss Willard's attitude." Before Wells' book was published, Willard had tried to back-pedal, insisting that she "did not intend a literal interpretation to be given to the words used." Wells was un-mollified. She wrote:

> I desire no quarrel with the W. C. T. U., but my love for the truth is greater than my regard for an alleged friend who, through ignorance or design, misrepresents in the most harmful way the cause of a long suffering race . . . When the lives of men, women and children are at stake, when the inhu-man butchers of innocents attempt to justify their barbarism by fastening upon a whole race the obloque[sic] of the most infamous of crimes, it is little less than criminal to apologize for the butchers today and tomorrow to repudiate the apology by declaring it a figure of speech.[42]

Willard was not the only respectable activist who bristled at Wells' uncompro-mising rage. Wells' insistence on speaking and writing frankly about white men's rape of black women and black women's relations with white men made many middle-class black activists uncomfortable. Some black clubwomen were among Wells' strongest supporters. And many black civil rights activists, male and female, agreed with Wells that Willard was an apologist for the worst kinds of Southern white violence. However, even if they privately applauded Wells' blistering response to Willard, they thought it unwise to engage in a public fight with the leader of the first national reform organization to welcome black women as members. Willard seemed unassailable.

When it came to choosing sides, there were influential black women activists who chose Willard. At the very same Cleveland conference where Willard condemned Wells, a group of black clubwomen presented the WCTU President with a bouquet honoring her contributions to black causes. Five years later, in 1899, Wells was barred from attending the annual convention of the National Association of Colored Women, which she had helped to found. Some members said she made them uncomfortable.

Wells' unflinching 1895 pamphlet, *A Red Record* was, for certain middle-class black activists, a bridge too far. She described rapes of black women and girls. alongside graphic accounts of lynchings. Some black male leaders felt that Wells insulted the race by writing that white Southern men assaulted black women routinely. By the turn of the 20th century, Ida Wells had become, for many people, too hot to handle. A few black ministers even accused Wells of prostituting herself by giving public lectures. It was the same argument that had been made against the Grimkés. Even Wells' racial identity became fair game; critics called her "a sharp yellow woman."[43]

All of this made Wells barely visible in the history books until the 21st century. Her importance in galvanizing public opinion against the barbarism of lynching was second to none. At various points in her life, she collaborated politically with illustrious leaders – Frederick Douglass, W.E.B. Dubois and Susan B. Anthony. Still, she was, for many decades written out of mainstream histories of woman suffrage, the National Association of Colored Women and the National Association for the Advancement of Colored People.

Living in Chicago, married with four children, Wells broadened her focus considerably in the last decades of her life. She worked with Pan-Africanist Marcus Garvey, became active in settlement houses in poor African-American and white immigrant neighborhoods and organized for the Brotherhood of Sleeping Car Porters and Maids. She was a radical and a builder of temporary shifting coalitions with a broad vision of social justice. She was a powerful and passionate speaker who toured widely and inspired the formation of new organizations. But everywhere she went, she left people outraged and uncomfortable. For those reasons, her work has only recently begun to be factored into histories of women's and civil rights activism.[44]

One so uncompromising fits in few places. Fierce and furious, she sought allies where she could find them, jumping between movements but also – through her writings and speeches – forging intellectual and political links between varied movements and their leaders. Like Lucretia Mott before her, Wells described herself simply as a "crusader for justice." And yet, in many ways, Wells must be seen as a foremother of later feminists. She was an idol smasher, using journalism to bring attention to subjects that had previously been considered inappropriate for public discussion. She insisted on probing the links between race, gender, sexuality and violence – and she didn't really care who she made uncomfortable. That was part of her political strategy.

Ida B. Wells-Barnett died in 1931 at the age of 68 – well before the civil rights era, the Black Power years and the feminist resurgence of the 1970s. It would be decades before women's rights activists were again willing to grapple so publicly, and so frankly, with issues of sex and violence and their relationship to political structures of power. Eighty years after her death, Ida B. Wells is finally being rewritten into the history of the struggles for racial equality, against sexual violence and for greater political rights for women. Both the many attempts to silence her and Wells' refusal to be silent about the violent acts performed in the name of white women's sexual purity are central to any rethinking of American women's activism.

The Great Waves of 19th and Early 20th-Century Immigration

The final decades before women earned the right to vote nationwide in 1920 were in many ways the most complicated era for coalition-building and political action. More than 20 million immigrants came to the U.S., from Southern and Eastern Europe, from Asia and the Middle East, from Mexico, the Caribbean and Latin America. They followed 9 million immigrants – mostly from Central and Northern Europe but also from Asia – who had come to American shores between 1840 and 1880. These newcomers brought with them ideologies, perspectives and problems new to North American politics, wrought by experiences of revolution, ethnic and religious violence and rapid industrialization in their home countries. They also brought different gender norms.

These newcomers infused the U.S. struggle for woman suffrage with fresh energy and they greatly expanded the numbers involved in women's rights activism. But they also completely changed the nature of organizing and the texture of women activists' political vision. Below are some snapshots from the new centers of women's activism and the new kinds of networks that were appearing in American cities at the turn of the 20th century.

In California, immigrant Chinese women, though very few in number, made their voices clearly heard in these years. We know what issues concerned them in part because Chinese American journalists, writing in the immigrant press, focused on issues of particular concern to Chinese women. They wrote detailed accounts of women's struggles for social and political rights in China after the 1911 nationalist revolution. Journalists also covered political organizing by Chinese women in the U.S. They described Chinese immigrant women's campaigns for woman suffrage in New York and San Francisco, their work to increase immigrant women's access to education, and their struggles to end the abduction of immigrant girls and women into sex slavery, and to end the centuries-old practice of foot-binding.[45]

Unrest among women across Chinese America continued to grow through the first decades of the 20th century, particularly among those with an education. Xue Jinqin came to study at the University of California at Berkeley. Within a few years, she had become a well-known activist in the Bay Area. Her speeches drew crowds numbering in the hundreds and sometimes the thousands. Xue was impassioned about the need for education for women and for an end to foot-binding. The size and fervor of her audiences reflects the power of those causes in galvanizing Chinese immigrant women.[46]

Chinese immigrant women also worked with white women suffragists and Christian religious activists to fight the traffic in Chinese women who were sold and kept captive as sex slaves. The trade in Chinese women was rampant in California and New York after a series of immigration laws passed in the late 19th century effectively barred Chinese women from entering the U.S. legally. Many dramatic conflicts between brothel-keepers and Chinese captives took place around the Presbyterian Home in San Francisco. There a young immigrant from New Zealand named Donaldina Cameron provided refuge for Chinese women fleeing madams and pimps who had tried to hold them captive.

When a woman named Jinqui ran away from her enslavement and sought asylum, she became a cause celebre among California university students and members of the Chinese immigrant community. They led protests that ultimately freed her. But, because the campaign uncovered the cooperation of various California elected officials who were taking kickbacks from sex traffickers, the protests angered powerful men. Jinqui was freed but, soon after, she was deported.[47]

Feminist and nationalist sentiments reinforced one another in the U.S.-based Chinese community, and also in Korean communities across the U.S. Korean immigrant women mobilized as activists first to protest Japan's colonization of their home country. But, soon they were blaming Korean nationalists for their failure to recognize and educate women – arguing that this lapse weakened the nation. Chinese women activists, too, blamed social problems in the old country on the repression of women. Chinese, Korean and Japanese women in the U.S. rallied in support of women's rights in their home countries, even as they protested for racial, ethnic and gender equality in America.

Chinese immigrant women in California, and Korean immigrant women in various parts of the U.S. also organized to provide relief for victims of war and national disaster at home. Although these women were not initially drawn to activism by a desire to enhance women's social or political rights, their immersion in political organizing did win them greater power and respect in their own communities. Like the abolitionists of 70 years earlier, like the anti-lynching activists of the same era, they found that involvement on behalf of their race made them consider themselves women's rights advocates as well.[48]

At the same time, in industrial cities and towns across the U.S., hundreds of thousands of immigrant women had become part of a burgeoning labor movement. The second decade of the 20th century – the final decade before women got the vote across the U.S. – was a time of unprecedented activism and organizing by women workers. More diverse in its membership than any women's movement in American history, the early 20th-century campaigns to organize women workers in dress, underwear, coat, hat and shoe manufacturing, in textile mills and in canneries, boasted activists who spoke and wrote in three dozen different languages.

It began in New York City, with the great garment workers' "uprising" of 1909 – in which 40,000 shirtwaist makers struck – the largest women's strike to that time in the U.S. The strike was sparked by the impatient militance of a 23-year old dress maker named Clara Lemlich, an immigrant from Ukraine who had been organizing young women workers to protest speed-ups and wage cuts. Listening to one labor leader after another counsel caution, the hot-headed young militant jumped up on to the stage and shouted in Yiddish: "I have something to say! I am one of those girls who suffers from the conditions being described here. No more talk. I move we go on a general strike." The young immigrant women workers exploded in cheers, hurling high the wide brimmed hats they'd made for themselves in imitation of the latest American fashions. By the next morning, the streets of the Lower East Side were crowded with whispering, singing, laughing, picket lines made up mostly of immigrant teenage girls.[49]

Between 1909 and 1919, young immigrant women garment and textile workers – Jews from Eastern Europe, Southern Italian and Irish Catholics, and smaller numbers of Caribbeans, Middle Easterners, white and black native born women – participated in a wave of strikes. What began in New York spread to Philadelphia, then to Boston, Chicago, Cleveland and Kalamazoo, Michigan. The strike spirit also filled mill workers in Lawrence, Massachusetts who launched the famous Bread and Roses strike of 1912 pitting male and female workers, women and girls, housewives and laborers against the mill owners, their hired guards and National Guard troops. Finally, the strike wave came back to Brooklyn, New York in 1913 when 35,000 workers speaking scores of languages shut down the "white goods" trade arguing, among other things, for time to write poetry, away from the relentless hum of sewing machines.[50]

This wave of strikes was a genuine uprising, mostly of girls who were simply tired of being exploited. As journalist Theresa Malkiel put it in *The Call*, New York's Socialist newspaper, these "girl strikers" were responding to "an overflow of abuse and exhaustion." The speed of garment production had doubled between 1900 and 1905. Textile mills, the other major employer of women in industry, had also sped up and become more dangerous. Affluent women, and the first generation of college women, began to pay attention to the fate of their less fortunate sisters.

A wave of scholarly studies and muckraking journalism made vividly clear to affluent readers the disturbing conditions for young women in industry. Women investigators in the shops and mills found teenage workers who peered out at them from "young old faces" with pale, sagging skin and dark circles under their eyes.

These young workers endured brutal hours. Seventy-two-hour weeks were not uncommon. Injuries on the job happened often. Fires broke out regularly. And sexual harassment was rampant. Once electric sewing machines replaced foot pedals, workers were charged for their use of electricity as well as thread. And mistakes came out of their paychecks.[51]

These "girls' strikes" riveted the attention of the nation in an era of rising newspaper circulation and emergent photo-journalism when young reporters flocked to their picket lines and rallies. More than spontaneous responses to miserable working conditions, they were forward-looking protests, expressions of what one woman scholar in 1915 called "industrial feminism." These young workers were expressing a class-specific vision of women's rights.

That vision was shaped by the revolutionary socialism and anarchism that young immigrants had been exposed to in Europe – in the small towns and cities of Russia during the early years of the revolution, in Italian factories and peasant uprisings during the years of ferment around Italian unification. It was fueled by Irish revolutionary nationalism, by the Easter Uprising of 1916. It was shaped by the peasant socialism of the Mexican Revolution. And it was also influenced by American anti-slavery and women's suffrage activism and by the home-grown socialism of railroad union leader Eugene Victor Debs. When young immigrant girl strikers were interviewed by reporters, they cited their rights under the U.S. Constitution and quoted the Declaration of Independence. They also revived 19th-century women mill workers' practice of comparing themselves to plantation field slaves. Girls as young as 12 could be seen on the streets of New York during the 1909 uprising wearing banners that said in Yiddish: "We Are Not Slaves."

Immigrant Women and the Final Push For Woman Suffrage

The lives and careers of Pauline Newman, Clara Lemlich, Rose Schneiderman and Fania Cohn illuminate both the militance of those years and the ways in which a generation of poor, disfranchised immigrant working girls would forever alter the relationship between government and American workers. All born in the Jewish small towns of Eastern Europe – in Lithuania, Belarus, Poland and Ukraine – these young women came to consciousness about gender and ethnicity as young girls. They were denied an education by Jewish religious authorities because they were female and by Russian officials because they were Jews. Fleeing economic hardship and anti-Jewish violence, they all emigrated to New York in the last years of the 19th century, part of a Jewish exodus that brought 2.5 million immigrants to the U.S. between 1881 and 1924.

Once in New York, these young women had hoped to attend free public schools and pursue their dreams of an education. But they found themselves instead swallowed up by long work days in garment shops – feeding the market for the new ready-to-wear clothing industry. Disappointed by the promises of

America denied, they were soon drawn to alternative kinds of education. They found it at places like the Socialist Literary Society and the Women's Trade Union League – a cross-class organization of women reformers dedicated to promoting union membership among working women. Informed as much by the revolutionary Socialism of Russian Jewry as by the suffrage militance of affluent educated New York women, these young immigrants organized both inside and outside their garment shops in the years leading up to the 1909 "uprising."

For these young women workers, the crucible that transformed their movement, their vision, their lives, came on March 25, 1911 when the Triangle Shirtwaist Factory in New York City caught fire. Triangle operated in the heart of Greenwich Village affluence – just one block off of Washington Square with its elegant townhouses, next door to New York University. Headquartered on the 8th, 9th and 10th floors of the Asch Building on Greene St. and Washington Place, Triangle was a modern factory – with high ceilings and tall windows. It boasted a fireproof building with elevators. It was not a sweatshop crammed into some windowless back room, choked by coal smoke. Skilled, experienced workers vied to get jobs there. Those workers were the core organizers of the 1909–1910 shirtwaist makers' strike – fighting for higher wages, shorter hours and safer conditions.

Unlike hundreds of other shirtwaist manufacturers in New York City, Triangle's owners Max Blanck and Isaac Harris had refused to settle with the union in 1909–1910. They increased workers' wages and cut hours but they would not recognize any outside force that constrained in any way how they chose to run their business. One issue that had particularly worried Triangle workers and others throughout the garment industry was never addressed in the strike negotiations. That was the pressing question of fire safety.

Cap maker, suffragist and Women's Trade Union League organizer Rose Schneiderman, had, for years, been warning manufacturers, union officers and government officials about the potential for disastrous fires. In the early 20th century, fashionable clothing was made in shops piled high with shiny grass linen and other flammable fabrics. These tottering piles blocked exits and filled the air with flame-enhancing dust that clung to everything and everybody. Men in the unions did not take this issue seriously. Manufacturers bristled at being told how to run their businesses. And government regulation of factory safety was, in 1911, pretty much toothless.

In November 1910, a devastating fire swept a Newark garment factory – spreading exactly as women trade unionists had warned it would, killing 26 young workers, most of them women. There was the predictable outcry but nothing much changed. Then, on a warm spring afternoon in March 1911, a stray cigar ash ignited the fabric and fabric dust that filled the Triangle Factory and, within minutes, a terrifying fire raged. Most of the workers on the 8th floor were able to escape via stairs and elevator. Heroic elevator operators – Italian immigrant men – rushed up and down to ferry the mostly Jewish and Italian immigrant women workers to safety. They saved at least 150 lives. Scores of workers on the 10th floor climbed to the roof and were helped to the building next door by vigilant New York University students.

For those who worked on the 9th floor, however, what followed was hellish and devastatingly lethal. One door was locked to prevent theft by the workers and the other was blocked by bodies piling up, as young women passed out from smoke inhalation. Panicked workers rushed to the fire escapes, one of which collapsed under their weight. As horrified onlookers watched from below, 26 plunged to their deaths.

Once the fire escape was gone and the doors blocked, the remaining workers faced a horrifying death by fire. Instead young women rushed to the tall arched windows and began stepping out, one by one, and jumping to the streets below. Harried firemen tried to catch them in their nets but the bodies tore through and shattered on scorched and bloody sidewalks. Even in an overcrowded, immigrant-filled city used to occasional outbreaks of violence, this was a horror that seared everyone who saw it.

An estimated 10,000 people watched as 146 workers died in a little over half an hour. Onlookers heard screams and the sounds of bodies thudding to the street. They smelled the blood and smoke and saw the corpses lined against the scorched building. It was all made worse by the fact that most of the victims were young girls and women, the youngest of the dead only 14 years old. The Asch building stood in mute testimony to the tragedy, its fireproof exterior bearing only superficial scorch marks.[52]

The trauma of Triangle permanently altered the relationships of government to labor in the U.S. Triangle eyewitness Frances Perkins, one of the first generation of college-educated women reformers, helped create new state and federal positions to regulate labor and workplace safety. Triangle fueled the rapid emergence of a "maternalist" state, shaped by the notion that the core mission of government was to care for and protect the nation's most vulnerable citizens. In those ways and others, the Triangle tragedy recast the goals and reshaped the contours of American women's rights activism. It dramatically intensified the urgency of the campaign for woman suffrage, heightening the visibility of a sex-segregated labor force and casting in stark relief the potential ramifications of women laboring in industry without political rights.

One year after the fire, the Wage Earner's League for Woman Suffrage held a mass meeting in New York City to answer the "sentimentality of New York Senators" with the "common sense of working women." Diminutive red-haired Rose Schneiderman had, in the aftermath of the Triangle Fire, condemned unregulated industrial workplaces as modern-day torture chambers for workers. Now she skewered the idea that "putting a ballot in a box one day a year" would damage women's femininity more than standing on their feet all day in a dust-choked factory or a fume-filled laundry. She didn't believe it and she didn't believe that New York senators opposed to woman suffrage believed it either. Clara Lemlich, the dressmaker whose speech had sparked the 1909 New York City garment uprising, wondered why men who said they wanted to protect women insisted on arresting prostitutes when their male customers went free. The cheering crowd seemed poised to pass woman suffrage in New York but they needed men's votes to do so. Suffrage initiatives failed several times before one finally succeeded.[53]

New York did not pass woman suffrage until 1917. Votes by working-class men, many of them immigrant, were crucial in finally passing the state law. Nationally, the vote came just a few years later. Congress passed the 19th amendment, giving women the right to vote, in 1919. Women won the votes partly as thanks for their contribution to the World War I war effort. And in part, Congress finally voted for suffrage after Woodrow Wilson came out in favor. Militant suffragists had chained themselves to the White House fence during the war, been imprisoned, gone on hunger strike, been force-fed. It was a dramatic end to the 80-plus-year struggle

It took another year for three-quarters of the states to ratify the amendment. In January 1920, Kentucky became the 23rd state to do so. Fittingly, the bill ratifying the amendment was signed by Governor Edwin Morrow, a man whose political vision had been thoroughly imprinted by the fusion of anti-lynching and women's rights politics pioneered by Ida B. Wells. Morrow had campaigned for office during World War I on a platform both of women's equality and of using government power to quell racial violence. Just a few weeks after he signed the suffrage bill, he would use Kentucky's National Guard troops to prevent the lynching of a black man on trial for murder.[54]

Eighty-two years after the Grimké sisters' speaking tour, 72 years after the Seneca Falls convention, 26 years after Ida B. Well's international anti-lynching tour, 11 years after the "Uprising of the 20,000," American women finally won the vote. Through the 19th and early 20th centuries, women's rights activists had painstakingly built and painfully shattered alliances. There were peaks and troughs, moments of broad coalition and of dramatic dissolution. Women won the vote first in Western states, in part because the rough and ready egalitarian nature of frontier life made change easier to achieve but, more importantly, because state officials sought increased representation in Congress. By 1920, the cause of woman suffrage had been taken up by an incredibly broad, deeply conflicted and unstable alliance: wealthy socialites and poor industrial workers, immigrants and native born, black and white anti-lynching activists, white supremacists and nativists who thought that women's votes would enhance their power.

The unwieldy and unstable nature of the suffrage coalition, and the deeply anti-egalitarian nature of some of its members, strained the coalition to the breaking point. But it held together long enough for three-quarters of the states to ratify the 19th amendment – making it the law of the land. Woman suffrage was revitalized as a cause by an infusion of fresh energy from labor movement activists, most of them new immigrants who harkened back to the Lowell mill workers in their iconography and self-representation. When women finally got the right to vote across the country, the governor who signed the state ratification bill guaranteeing that right was a man whose career epitomized the long interaction of the struggles for gender and race equality. Broad visions of justice – embracing race and class as well as gender – were still there at the end of nearly a century of struggle for woman suffrage. That seems fitting. That the suffrage coalition would again founder after 1920 on the shoals of race and class was perhaps inevitable.

Notes

1 See Nancy Hewitt, "Origin Stories: Remapping First Wave Feminism," *Proceedings of the Third Annual Gilder Lehrman Center International Conference at Yale University,* "Sisterhood and Slavery: Transatlantic Anti-Slavery and Women's Rights, October 25–28, 2001; for a good portrait of the array of early republic American women's organizations, see Anne M. Boylan, *The Origins of Women's Activism, New York and Boston, 1797–1840* (Chapel Hill, NC: University of North Carolina Press, 2002).

2 See Anne Alves, "'My Sisters' Toil': Voice in Anti-Slavery Poetry By White Female Factory Workers," in C. James Trotman, *Multi-Culturalism: Roots and Realities* (Indiana: University Press, 2002), pp. 138–154 for an interesting reading of the race/class/gender perspective of the New England mill girls in this period.

3 Bruce Laurie, *Artisans into Workers: Labor in Nineteenth-Century America* (Urbana-Champaign: University of Illinois Press, 1997).

4 Harriet H. Robinson, *Loom and Spindle or Life Among the Early Mill Girls* (Boston: 1898), p. 51.

5 See Thomas Dublin's classic, "Women, Work and Protest in the Early Lowell Mills: 'The Oppressing Hand of Avarice Would Enslave Us'" *Labor History* 16 (1975): pp. 99–116; see also Thomas Dublin, *Women At Work: The Transformation of Work and Community in Lowell, Massachusetts, 1820–1860* (New York: Columbia University Press, 1981).

6 Theodore Weld to Sara and Angelina Grimké, August 15, 1837. *The Letters of Theodore Weld, Angelina Grimké Weld and Sarah M. Grimké, 1822–1844, Vol. II* (New York: DaCapo Press, 1970), pp. 425–432.

7 "Pastoral Letter of the General Association of Massachusetts," June 18, 1837, reprinted in *American Rhetorical Discourse*, second edition, ed. Ronald Reid (Prospect Heights, IL: Waveland Press, 1995), pp. 363–367.

8 Angelina Grimké to Theodore Weld and John Greenleaf Whittier Brookline [Mass.] 8th Mo 20 – [1837]; *The Letters of Theodore Weld, Angelina Grimké Weld and Sarah M. Grimké, 1822–1844, Vol. II* (New York: DaCapo Press, 1970), pp. 425–432.

9 A.E. Grimké to Sarah Douglass, 2nd month, 25th, 1838. *The Letters of Theodore Weld, Angelina Grimké Weld and Sarah Grimké, 1822–1844, Vol. II* (New York: DeCapo Press, 1970), pp. 572–575; Gerda Lerner, *The Grimké Sisters From South Carolina* (Chapel Hill, NC: University of North Carolina, 2004, reprinted from 1967).

10 Carol Faulkner, *Lucretia Mott's Heresy: Abolition and Women's Rights in Nineteenth Century America* (Philadelphia: University of Pennsylvania Press, 2011).

11 For a deeper understanding of the overlapping and international networks of abolitionist and women's rights activists, see Bonnie Anderson, *Joyous Greetings: The First International Women's Movement, 1830–1860* (New York: Oxford University Press, 2000) and Hewitt, op. cit. Mott quote, cited in Hewitt, is from "Letter," in the radical anti-slavery publication, *The Liberator*, October 6, 1848.

12 "Declarations of Sentiments and Resolutions," Woman's Rights Convention, Held at Seneca Falls, July 19–20, 1848. The Elizabeth Cady Stanton and Susan B. Anthony Papers Project, http://ecssba.rutgers.edu/docs/seneca.html.

13 Cited in Anderson, op. cit., p. 6.

14 Sojourner Truth, *The Narrative of Sojourner Truth, Dictated by Sojourner Truth, edited by Oliver Gilbert* (Boston: Printed for the author, 1850), pp. 133–135.

15 Elizabeth C. Stanton, S.B. Anthony, and Matilda J. Gage, *History of Woman Suffrage*, vol. 1 (Rochester, NY: Charles Mann, 1887), p. 116.

16 Barbara Welter, "The Cult of True Womanhood, 1820–1860," *American Quarterly*, Vol. 18, No. 2, Summer 1966: 151–174.

17 Ann Braude, *Radical Spirits: Spiritualism and Women's Rights in 19th Century America* (Boston: Beacon Press, 1989).

18 Sojourner Truth, *The Narrative of Sojourner Truth, Dictated by Sojourner Truth, edited by Oliver Gilbert* (Boston: Printed for the author, 1850).

19 Braude, op. cit.

20 Truth, *Narrative,* op. cit.

21 George Frederickson, *The Black Image in the White Mind: The Debate on Afro–American Character and Destiny, 1817–1914* (Middletown: Wesleyan University Press, 1987), p. 97.

22 Nell Irvin Painter, "Sojourner Truth in Life and Memory: Writing the Biography of an American Exotic," *Gender and History*, Vol. 2, No. 1, Spring 1990: pp. 3–16; Nell Painter, *Sojourner Truth: A Life, A Symbol* (New York: Norton, 1996); Harriet Beecher Stowe, "Sojourner Truth: The Libyan Sibyl," *Atlantic Monthly* 11, April 1863, pp. 473–481.

23 For Truth's own account of her meeting with Lincoln see her letter to Rowland Johnson, November 17, 1864, reprinted in Truth, *Narrative on Sojourner Truth*, pp. 176–180; Painter, op. cit.

24 "Suffrage Petition, 1866, RG 233, National Archives."

25 The Constitution of the United States, Amendments 11–27. http://www.archives.gov/exhibits/charters/constitution_amendments_11–27.html.

26 *The Revolution*, January 29, 1868; *Letters of William Lloyd Garrison*, Volume VI, eds. Walter Merrill and Louis Ruchames (Cambridge, MA: Belknap Press, 1981), pp. 29–30.

27 ALS, January 13, 1868, Galatea Collection, Department of Rare Books and Manuscripts, Boston Public Library; printed in variant form in *Elizabeth Cady Stanton As Revealed in Her Letters, Diary and Reminiscences*, 2: pp. 120–21. Cited in Patricia G. Holland, "George Francis Train and the Woman Suffrage Movement, 1867–1870" from Books at Iowa 46 (April 1987) http://www.lib.uiowa.edu/spec-coll/bai/holland.htm.

28 Elizabeth Cady Stanton, Susan B. Anthony and Matilda Joslyn Gage, eds. *The History of Woman Suffrage, Volume II, 1861–1876* (New York: Fowler & Wells, 1882; reprinted by New York: Source Book Press, 1970), pp. 348–355.

29 "Debates at the American Equal Rights Association Meeting, New York City, 12–14 May 1869," in Stanton and Gage, eds. op. cit. pp. 381–398.

30 ibid.

31 ibid.

32 ibid., pp. 348–355.

33 Lori Ginsberg, *Elizabeth Cady Stanton: An American Life* (New York: Hill and Wang, 2009).

34 *Elizabeth Cady Stanton as Revealed in Her Letters, Diaries and Reminiscences*, ed., Theodore Stanton and Harriet Stanton Blatch (New York: 1922), p. 229.

35 "Death of Fred Douglass," *New York Times*, February 21, 1895.

36 On Wells' life see, Patricia Schechter, *Ida B. Wells and American Reform, 1890–1930* (Chapel Hill, NC: University of North Carolina Press, 2001); Paula Giddings, *Ida: A Sword Among Lions* (New York: Harper Collins, 2008); and Crystal Feimster, *Southern Horrors: Women and the Politics of Rape and Lynching* (Cambridge, MA: Harvard University Press, 2011).

37 Miss Ida B. Wells, "Lynch Law In All Its Phases," *New York Age,* October 1892.

38 Crystal Feimster, op. cit., offers a moving and nuanced analysis of the horror of white women participating in the lynching and torture of black men, some of whom were former lovers.

39 "Interview with Ida B. Wells," *Westminster Gazette,* May 10, 1894.

40 "Interview with Frances Willard," *The Voice,* October 28, 1890.

41 Ida B. Wells Barnett, A *Red Record* (Chicago: Donahue and Henneberry, 1895), Ch. VII, "Miss Willard's Attitude," pp. 80–82. See Schechter, op. cit., pp. 107–110.

42 Wells, *A Red Record*, pp. 89–90.

43 Wells, *A Red Record*, op. cit.

44 See Giddings, op. cit., pp. 5–7.

45 Judy Yung, "The Social Awakening of Chinese-American Women, as Reported in Chung Sai Yat Po, 1900–1911," in Ellen Dubois and Vicki Ruiz, eds., *Unequal Sisters: A Multicultural Reader in U.S. Women's History*, 1st edition (New York: Routledge, 1990).

46 Yung, op. cit.

47 Yung, op. cit.

48 Yung, op. cit and Alice Yang Murray, "Ilse Women and the Early Korean American Community: Redefining the Origins of Feminist Empowerment," in Dubois and Ruiz, eds., *Unequal Sisters*, 3rd edition (New York: Routledge: 2000).

49 See Annelise Orleck, *Common Sense and a Little Fire: Women and Working Class Politics in the United States 1900–1965* (Chapel Hill, NC: University of North Carolina Press, 1995), Chapter 2, "Audacity."

50 Orleck, op. cit.

51 Annie Marion Maclean, *Wage Earning Women* (New York: Macmillan, 1910), pp. 36, 61. Orleck, op. cit., pp. 31–41.

52 See Orleck, pp. 31–41, David Von Drehle, *Triangle: The Fire That Changed America* (New York: Grove Press, 2004), and Jamila Wignot, "The Triangle Fire," *PBS American Experience*, 2011.

53 "Senators v. Working Women" (Handbill of the Wage Earner's League for Woman Suffrage) Reel 12, Leonora O'Reilly Papers, *Papers of the New York Women's Trade Union League and Its Principal Leaders*. For a full account of the wage earner's suffrage movement see Orleck, op. cit., Chapter 3, "Common Sense: New York City Working Women and the Struggle for Woman Suffrage."

54 "Kentucky Suffrage Bill Signed," *New York Times*, March 31, 1920; Hambleton Tapp and James C. Klotter. *Kentucky: Decades of Discord, 1865–1900* (Lexington: The University Press of Kentucky, 1977).

2

CIVIL RIGHTS, LABOR FEMINISM AND MOTHER ACTIVISM FROM 1920 THROUGH THE 1940S

Riptides

The crash and subsequent splintering of the woman suffrage alliance after 1920 was as predictable as it was traumatic. The peak of the suffrage movement in the late 19th and early 20th centuries had brought together a greater range of people than any other coalition in American history – rich, middle-class and poor people, immigrants and natives, African-Americans, whites, Jews, Catholics and varied Protestant sects, socialists and capitalists, racial progressives and white supremacists. It was perhaps the ultimate example of the role that shifting coalitions have played in the history of American women's activism. To enact a change so expansive as granting voting rights to half of the country's population it was necessary to find ways to rally people in every part of the country and across every kind of social, political and economic divide. Such an expansive coalition could not last. And it didn't.

Still, the outcome was not as simple as some standard narratives of American women's movement history have portrayed it. The "First Wave" of American feminism did not drain away after women won the vote nationally in 1920. Suffragists did not simply lose energy, having achieved the long-sought-after goal. It was, inevitably, somewhat anti-climactic when women did finally get to vote. Despite all the talk of independence, overall, women tended to vote the same ways that their fathers had, that their husbands and brothers did. And, having struggled for so long for one elusive victory, some women suffered a failure of imagination about what should come next.

But, when the vast suffrage alliance shattered spectacularly in the years after 1920 over issues of race and class, its constituent pieces did not simply sink into the earth. They remained very much alive and active. Riptides pulled women's activism into divergent political currents; rivulets carved channels for political change around many different issues – women's rights, labor rights, the ongoing struggle for racial equality. On the other side, some former suffragists organized to fight those movements, to promote patriotism, to ferret out radicalism – creating in 1926 a Spider Web chart that purported to tie American women radicals to one another and all of them to revolutionary Moscow. Across the country, hundreds of thousands of white women even became active in racial supremacist movements. Far from a quiescent era, the 1920s were a boiling time for women's activism. But there was no visible, singular movement as there had been in the pre-suffrage days. Wavelets deposited sands in new ways, built new structures. American women's activism welcomed the 20th century.[1]

Crashing Waves – How Different Suffrage Constituencies Came into Conflict

The woman suffrage movement had contracted, then expanded rapidly after the turn of the 20th century. As the first generation of suffrage movement leaders began to die off, toward the end of the 19th century, the cause had seemed to many to be growing stale. The new century had brought infusions of fresh energy from a variety of sources – some radical, some progressive and some decidedly not. Self-supporting women, from industrial workers to professionals, from the country's first women nurses and teachers, to clubwomen and bohemians rallied to the cause of woman suffrage in the early 20th century. So did nativists and white supremacists.

Harriet Stanton Blatch, daughter of Elizabeth Cady Stanton, returned to the U.S. after 20 years of living in Britain and she helped to cement ties between the American movement and the more militant British suffragists. Blatch started the Equality League for Self-Supporting Women in 1907, which helped to bring thousands of working women into the movement. Blatch argued that "it is the women of the industrial class . . . who have been the means of bringing about the altered attitude of public opinion toward women's work in every sphere of life." British suffrage leader Emmeline Pankhurst toured the U.S. to raise awareness of her cause, and these speaking tours also helped to infuse American suffragism with the electricity and militance of the most radical civil disobedience-oriented wing of the British movement.[2]

But there were also decidedly anti-progressive constituencies who rallied to woman suffrage in the early 20th century, including white Southern women determined to fight attempts by African-Americans to vote and run for office. Women's Ku Klux Klan activists in places like Indiana and Oregon touted suffrage as a tool to fight unrestricted immigration. Women determined to ban the sale of alcohol, and nativists hoping to limit the political influence of anyone not white, native-born and Christian also saw woman suffrage as a means to their particular ends. In the years leading up to 1920, these arguments for suffrage conflicted sharply with those of working-class, immigrant and African-American women. Groups like the Women's KKK sought to achieve post-suffrage goals that were clearly and profoundly exclusionary and anti-egalitarian. By 1920, only lack of the franchise held together the conflicted suffrage alliance. Once the 19th amendment was ratified in the winter of 1920, divisions opened up quickly.[3]

In the last years of the suffrage struggle, the most militant wing of the movement had emulated British civil disobedience tactics, chaining themselves to the White House fence, enduring imprisonment and conducting hunger strikes to protest their treatment in prison. Once American women attained the vote, this faction of the suffrage alliance formed a new political association – the National Woman's Party (NWP). Their purpose in doing so was to foreground issues of women's rights in state and federal politics as well as in the courts. At first the NWP leadership drew support from African-American suffragists, who respected their militancy and embrace of civil disobedience. That embrace would soon grow cold.[4]

In winter 1921, a delegation representing five black women's organizations attended the NWP national convention to ask for the organization's aid in protesting the denial of voting rights to black people in the American South. The group came with evidence documenting "verified cases of the disfranchisement of our women" and asked the NWP to appoint a special committee to investigate these violations of the 19th amendment: "Five million women in the United States can not be denied their rights without all the women of the United States feeling the effect of that denial," the black activists wrote. "No women are free until all are free."[5]

This request for action by the NWP was unceremoniously rejected. As one Southern delegate explained to a New Yorker who supported the request, the NWP had agreed to ignore the disfranchisement of black voters as a condition of Southern states ratifying the 19th amendment. They could not now abrogate that deal. Instead they chose to abandon their African-American allies. It was a bitter moment – in many ways as painful as the splits that followed the passage of the 15th amendment.

Alice Paul, founder and leader of the National Woman's Party, was respected by the black activists who came to petition that day. They admired her Quaker convictions, her pacifism, her willingness to go to jail for the cause of women's rights. It was disillusioning and emotionally unsettling when Paul dismissed race discrimination as tangential to the cause of women's equality. Like Elizabeth Cady Stanton and Susan B. Anthony before her, Alice Paul knew better. But those in the NWP who supported that stance believed that it was too costly to adopt the position that "no women are free until all are free." Paul's belief that a laser-like focus on sex discrimination was the only way forward for the NWP would soon also alienate her from most working-class suffragists.[6]

Weary from the seemingly endless struggle for woman suffrage, NWP leaders had come to feel that the quickest route to systemic change was to promote a constitutional amendment that would ban any form of discrimination on the basis of sex. In 1921, the NWP announced that it would be pursuing an Equal Rights Amendment to the Constitution. The idea was to eradicate, with one stroke of the pen, any remaining legal distinctions between men and women. NWP allies in Congress introduced the amendment into the 1921 session of Congress. It was a staggeringly simple prescription for change. Written by Paul, it said: "Men and women shall have equal rights throughout the United States and every place subject to its jurisdiction," and "Congress shall have power to enforce this article by appropriate legislation." Paul was the primary driver of the amendment and also the main force behind the decision not to commit the party to investigating violations of black women's voting rights.[7]

The ERA seemed to many women's rights activists at the time a simple and effective tool for enhancing women's rights. But its introduction further splintered the old suffrage alliance, creating deep new divisions along lines of class. The problem was that the law threatened to nullify state labor laws protecting women workers from long hours, low wages and hazardous conditions in the workplace. Women labor activists and their allies had worked for decades to pass such laws. And, in the first years of the 20th century, they had been able to do so in states across the U.S. Working-class women activists and their middle-class allies in the Women's Trade Union League (WTUL) and the National Consumer's League fervently believed that such laws saved the lives of untold numbers of women workers and improved the lives of millions more.[8]

Rose Schneiderman, former cap maker and president of the WTUL, agreed that labor laws should eventually protect men as well as women. But, most trade unions resisted laws for men, arguing that men could regulate their own labor conditions through organizing and striking. The courts, too, proscribed states' ability to regulate men's hours, wages and work conditions. In 1905, a New York court had struck down the state's attempts to limit working hours for male workers. But, in 1908 in *Muller v. Oregon*, the U.S. Supreme Court affirmed protective laws for women workers, ruling that governments had a vested interest in protecting future mothers from physical harm. Chief Justice Josiah David Brewer wrote the unanimous decision. It did not over-rule the New York court. Instead it cited "differences between the sexes" and argued that, since "healthy mothers are essential to vigorous offspring, the physical well-being of woman becomes an object of public interest and care." The state had a right to "preserve the strength and vigor of the race."[9]

So, when the ERA was first introduced, laws protecting women workers were all they had. Schneiderman was not ready to give them up. Nor were millions of women workers. In the aftermath of the Triangle disaster, this was not an abstract discussion. People felt it keenly and they feared the consequences of undoing protective labor laws.

The basis on which *Muller* was decided exacerbated divisions among former suffrage allies. NWP activists believed that feminists, as they had now started calling themselves, should pursue a strategy that focused on sex equality alone. They saw in the ERA the potential for radical legal change. Members of the Women's Trade Union League and the National Association of Colored Women insisted that class and race were equally important considerations, sometimes more important. They sought a piecemeal approach to the struggle for equality – one that would acknowledge and target the multiple oppressions that working-class women and women of color (of all classes) experienced.[10]

Florence Kelley, leader of the middle-class National Consumer League, and Rose Schneiderman, leading the mixed-class Women's Trade Union League, saw *Muller v. Oregon* as a wedge decision. In their view, it opened up the legal possibility for government regulation of private workplaces for all workers. They believed that it would ultimately pave the way for state and federal governments to regulate working conditions, wages and hours for men as well as women. But for those like Paul who sought the eradication of all legal distinctions based on sex, Muller was a step backward, a hindrance to full equality.[11]

When the National Woman's Party first unveiled the Equal Rights Amendment in 1921, Women's Trade Union League and Consumer's League activists asked future Supreme Court justice Louis Brandeis, who had filed a crucial brief in the Muller case, to assess the impact such a law would have. Brandeis' unequivocal conclusion was that the ERA – as it was worded – would devastate the state laws protecting women workers.

Hoping to avoid a divisive battle, the WTUL, Consumer's League and the National League of Women Voters held a summit with leaders of the NWP to try to formulate wording for an Equal Rights Amendment that would not endanger existing labor legislation. They were encouraged by a compromise that had been struck in Wisconsin. The state ERA passed there explicitly exempted labor laws protecting women workers. But hope of compromise on the national level quickly evaporated when the NWP leadership announced that it would fight any "restrictions upon the hours, conditions and remuneration of labor" that did not "apply equally to both sexes." Former telephone worker and WTUL activist Mabel Leslie retorted: "We who have worked in industry know it is conditions we face, not theories, and we know that our hours will not be shortened nor our wages increased by wiping out what little support we now have on the statute books."[12]

The NWP forged ahead anyway. On December 10, 1923, the "Lucretia Mott Amendment" was introduced in Congress by two Republican legislators. One of them was Susan B. Anthony's nephew. The proposed amendment came on the heels of a Supreme Court decision earlier that year that devastated supporters of labor legislation. On April 9, 1923 the U.S. Supreme Court struck down minimum wage laws for women workers in *Adkins v. Children's Hospital of Washington, D.C.* Noting that women now had the right to vote, Chief Justice Sutherland argued that "contractual, political and civil" gender differences in the United States had "come almost, if not quite, to the vanishing point." Therefore, the court ruled, women workers – like men – could freely choose whether or not to work for a particular employer.

NWP supporters rejoiced but, for working-class women, *Adkins* was a terrible blow. State minimum wages boards vowed to continue enforcing their state laws. But they knew they were on shaky ground. Women's wages dropped in many parts of the country. The battle raged on but it was not until 1937 that the court overturned *Adkins*, ruling a minimum wage constitutional. One year later, the Fair Labor Standards Act created a federal minimum wage for all workers.[13]

In the end, ironically, the only hope for passing an ERA would have been to forge a compromise that would win the support of labor activists and their allies. Though the ERA was introduced into every session of Congress between 1923 and 1970, it did not even make it out of committee for a full vote more than twice in that time. The primary result of the ERA campaign over the long haul was to deepen divisions and heighten animosity among women's rights advocates. ERA supporters were frustrated by what they saw as the retrograde and reactionary sensibilities of opponents to the amendment. For those who saw the ERA as potentially damaging to the interests of poor and working-class women, its supporters appeared arrogant and selfish. The ERA struggle became, in Rose Schneiderman's words "a perennial headache, consuming time, energy, paper, postage and much language."[14]

The ERA battle, combined with the resistance of National Women's Party leadership to joining the fight against disfranchisement of African-Americans, left a large segment of the old suffrage alliance suspicious of anyone who called themselves "feminist" – an identity proudly claimed by NWP members. Like the splits in the old abolitionist alliance opened up by the passage of the 14th and 15th Amendments, the battles that followed ratification of the Susan B. Anthony Amendment in 1920 would haunt American women's rights activism for decades afterwards. Still, women's rights activism did not disappear in the inter-war years – far from it. Instead, the broad alliance became myriad movements – each in pursuit of distinct visions of legal, economic and political equality between the sexes.

The High Water Mark of Labor Feminism in the 1930s and 1940s[15]

As the 1920s wore on, it became clear that the momentum of government change – at least for a while – was on the side of the advocates for labor legislation. This was due in large measure to structural changes in state and federal governments sparked by the women's labor uprisings of the 1910s, the Triangle Fire and the alliance between women labor activists and progressive women reformers, especially National Consumer's League leaders Frances Perkins and Florence Kelley.

An eye-witness to the Triangle factory fire, Perkins had vowed in March 1911 to devote the rest of her life to transforming government so that it could prevent workplace tragedies in the future. In the aftermath of the fire, Perkins began to work closely with New York State Assemblyman Alfred E. Smith. He represented the Lower East Side and had personally visited the family of each fire victim. Perkins also came to know and work closely with State Senator Robert Wagner. The three served together on the New York State Factory Investigating Commission, created as a result of public outcry over the 146 young workers who died at Triangle.

Perkins engineered the appointment of Triangle Worker and International Ladies Garment Workers' Union (ILGWU) organizer Pauline Newman as investigator for the commission. She would later recall Newman leading Smith and Wagner through ice covered holes in the walls of upstate New York canneries that were the only exits in case of fire. Through such experiences, Perkins would later argue, the men developed a visceral understanding of the dangerous and exhausting conditions in which New York women labored. Both men were forever changed. When Smith became Governor of New York in 1918, he brought Perkins with him to Albany to help shape new regulatory agencies to improve workplace safety. She in turn brought women from the WTUL into state government. For the first time, state labor officials began to understand the working-class perspective.

Immigrant working women contributed mightily to the emergence of the idea that an important function of government was to regulate the workplace and protect workers. The gravelly voiced Newman, who had taken to wearing suits and ties and slicked back hair, and her WTUL comrade, 4 foot 9 inch red-haired firebrand Rose Schneiderman, became, by the 1920s, familiar figures in Albany and other state capitals. No longer strangers to the legislators and government officials they lobbied, these women came to be seen as the experts on needed labor reforms.

In the course of their legislative and suffrage work during the 1920s, women labor activists formed alliances with forward-looking and highly influential women reformers. Through Perkins, the working-class women of the WTUL came to befriend Eleanor Roosevelt, wife of New York State Senator and former Navy Department official Franklin D. Roosevelt. These educated and affluent women activists would help their friends in the labor movement carry the ideas and goals of working-class women to Washington, D.C. in the 1930s and 1940s.

Eleanor Roosevelt came into the world of New York City women reformers following World War I, when revelations of Franklin's affair with her social secretary Lucy Mercer changed the Roosevelts' marriage from a romantic to a political partnership. Worried that Franklin D. Roosevelt would never become president if

Eleanor sued for divorce, his mother Sara struck a deal with Eleanor. If Eleanor would stand by Franklin D. Roosevelt's side publicly, she would be free to pursue her own political life. Eleanor, who had taught in an immigrant school when she was young, had long been drawn to women's reform circles. During the 1920s, she immersed herself in the cross-class women's network that surrounded the Women's Trade Union League. Through "the League," as its members called it, Roosevelt became close with Rose Schneiderman. It was a friendship that would last nearly half a century.[16]

Eleanor Roosevelt had always made efforts to expose her husband – who had grown up the privileged prince of a secluded Hudson Valley estate – to the harsher realities of working-class life in New York. One famous Franklin Roosevelt story has him exclaiming in wonder at the living conditions of the immigrant poor in the neighborhood where Eleanor taught early in their marriage. "My God, I didn't know people lived like this," he is said to have exclaimed to his wife.

In the early 1920s, as Franklin Roosevelt recovered from polio, Eleanor Roosevelt and Frances Perkins brought Schneiderman, Newman and other immigrant workers to Hyde Park to visit and speak with him. It was a time, Perkins later wrote, when Franklin Roosevelt, because of his illness, was becoming conscious of "human frailty." It transformed his perspective in fundamental ways. Still, the two were amazed at how quickly Franklin D. Roosevelt bonded with Schneiderman and other immigrant women whose lives were so different from his. They were an unlikely match, the patrician, old-money Roosevelt family and these Jewish and Irish socialist women. But the exchange of ideas was charged and exciting, and the women became lifelong friends of both Roosevelts.[17]

The vision and political goals of the Women's Trade Union League circle were enshrined in Albany when Franklin D. Roosevelt became Governor of New York State in 1928 and ultimately carried to Washington, D.C. when Roosevelt was elected president in 1932. Frances Perkins became the first woman appointed to a federal cabinet post. Appointed Secretary of Labor in 1932, she served throughout Roosevelt's 12-year presidency. She, in turn, appointed WTUL President Rose Schneiderman to the National Labor Advisory Board that established federal wage, hour and safety standards in the early 1930s. Schneiderman was the only woman on the Board. She also worked with labor's most powerful leaders to shape Senator Robert Wagner's National Labor Relations Act, which Franklin Roosevelt signed into law in 1935. Still in force today, even if diminished in strength, the NLRA for the first time made it a violation of federal law to fire workers for joining a union; and it forced management to negotiate with labor in binding arbitration of worker grievances.[18]

The crowning achievement of this coalition's vision was the Social Security Act of 1935, creating pensions for retired workers. The WTUL and labor unions had sought such stipends for years. The Social Security Act also created unemployment insurance, payments to support the blind and the totally disabled, and Aid to Dependent Children. These protections for the nation's most vulnerable citizens grew out of women reformers' long campaigns for mothers' pensions. They remain the cornerstones of the modern American welfare state into the 21st century.

In 1936, Eleanor Roosevelt invited representatives to the WTUL national convention to sleep at the White House – a symbolic gesture that made visible to the nation the Roosevelts' respect for working women. New York City garment workers and Alabama textile workers appeared on the front page of the *New York Times* as guests of the President and First Lady. "Imagine me, Feigele Shapiro, sleeping in Lincoln's bed," one garment worker exclaimed. That access and influence was at the same time superficial and profoundly transformative. With the passage of the Fair Labor Standards Act of 1938, guaranteeing a 40-hour work week, a federal minimum wage, basic safety standards and time and a half for overtime work, Rose Schneiderman's prediction 30 years earlier that laws protecting women workers would lead to government protections for all workers was realized.[19]

Of course, the social safety net that became law in the first eight years of the New Deal was hardly complete – especially as far as women workers and workers of color were concerned. In their earliest incarnations, these legal protections embraced industrial workers (a majority of whom were still men) but excluded agricultural, and domestic workers – the fields in which the vast majority of women of color labored. Waitresses too fell outside the restrictions on wages, hours and working conditions. As Charles Houston of the National Association for the Advancement of Colored People (NAACP) put it: the Social Security Act created a safety net "with holes just big enough for the majority of Negroes to fall through."[20]

Frances Perkins, Rose Schneiderman and Works Progress Administration director Harry Hopkins all argued that agricultural and domestic workers should be covered by old age pensions and minimum wage laws. But a Congress dominated by Southern Democrats resisted. Treasury Secretary Henry Morgenthau testified before the House Ways and Means Committee that collecting payroll taxes from these groups would be impossible anyway because they worked in private homes and in far flung fields and valleys. And so the first social security legislation stopped short of covering vast numbers of women workers and workers of color. Labor feminists, farm workers and black civil rights groups did not give up, lobbying on a state-by state-basis during and after World War II. In 1950, they succeeded in expanding the social safety net. Social Security Act coverage was extended to agricultural and domestic workers, public employees and the self-employed.[21]

But campaigns for extended coverage were not the only battles waged by working women and their allies in this era. As Rose Schneiderman noted soon after the first federal protections for industrial workers were enacted, unless workers were organized into unions, they had no power to force employers to observe new federal wage, hour and safety standards. The 1930s and 1940s saw vast and intense organizing drives among unskilled industrial workers in coal, steel and automobiles (primarily male trades until the war years) and also in primarily female trades such as garment, textile, laundry and cannery work, retail store clerks and waitresses too. As many workers came to feel for the first time that the government was an ally, they organized and struck to bring private employers into line with new federal and state laws. Among these were workers who had never before been organized. African-American, Jewish and Puerto Rican laundry workers and hotel maids were brought into labor unions during the 1930s through their own energetic strikes and the determined help of WTUL organizers, particularly Rose Schneiderman.[22]

As hundreds of thousands of desperately poor African-Americans migrated from the South to northern and western cities in the 1930s and 1940s, a new women's labor problem emerged – the disturbing phenomenon of street-corner "slave markets." Immigrant housewives in New York, in Pittsburgh, St. Louis and Chicago, many of them former industrial workers or workers' wives, "whitened" and lifted themselves into middle-class status by bargaining for day labor with African-American migrant women. Every day, new arrivals from the South crowded onto street corners looking for work. White housewives seeking help with cleaning, cooking and laundry, would squeeze their arms, still muscled from field labor, to assess how much physical labor these migrants could perform in a day. It was a demeaning spectacle, spotlighting the desperation of those Depression years.

In the mid-1930s, NAACP investigator Ella Baker and journalist Marvel Cooke published searing articles exposing the conditions for household laborers. WTUL activists Pauline Newman and Rose Schneiderman sought to organize these domestic workers into some kind of union, while at the same time lobbying for state intervention to regulate street-corner markets. There were some limited victories. State employment bureaus were opened near where the slave markets had sprung up to regulate negotiations between employers and the women they proposed to hire. And in 1947, domestic workers were covered by federal as well as state labor protections. Still, these protections were difficult to enforce. So too were the victories of short-lived domestic workers' unions, which appeared, disappeared and reappeared through the remainder of the 20th century. Not until the 21st century were domestic workers' unions able to push through domestic workers' bills of rights in New York, California and other states.[23]

Though many of the goals of industrial feminists remained unachieved by the end of the 1930s, their ability to influence and in many ways transform government policy toward workers during the 1920s, 1930s and 1940s was remarkable. The labor and welfare state legislation of that era continues to affect all Americans into the 21st century. It is a history that often is told without description of the role of women, particularly poor, working class and immigrant women. But their vision and their activism was very much part of that history and of our world today.

World War II and Rosie the Riveter – Patriotism and American Women's Activism

In December 1941, the U.S. entered World War II, launching an era of total mobilization. A military draft eventually swept 10 million working-age men into the armed services. With American defense production ramped up to meet the needs of the war effort, women were recruited for defense production in vast numbers. By 1943, there were upwards of 19 million American women working for "Uncle Sam." Women defense workers built aircraft and ships, operated cranes, dug mines and manufactured munitions. And they riveted. Popularly known as "Rosie the Riveter", the woman war worker was depicted by *Saturday Evening Post* illustrator Norman Rockwell with muscled arms, a bandana on her head and wearing overalls. It was perhaps the butchest image of American women ever published in popular media.[24]

These were the famous women "behind the men behind the guns" – to paraphrase the popular propaganda song of the day. For good reasons, many activists predicted that war work would revolutionize women workers' position in American society. Women worked in mines and hoisted steel girders. Their exemplary performance in those jobs, many believed, would shatter notions of men's work and women's work. It would make clear that there were no good reasons for keeping women out of well-paid, skilled industrial trades that had previously been kept almost exclusively male terrain.

The need for women workers in defense industries during World War II did not automatically eliminate the obstacles that women had long faced in the job market however, particularly for women of color and recent immigrants. Many wartime manufacturers refused to hire women if they could find men to fill the jobs created by federal defense contracts. And among those who did hire women, many continued to pay female workers less than men, even for the same work. They fell back on old canards to justify pay inequities. Most popular of these was the myth that women did not work to support families but simply for "pin money" – a little extra to supplement husbands' salaries.[25]

Black workers faced even steeper obstacles. They were kept out of defense work so routinely early in the war that Brotherhood of Sleeping Car Porters' organizer A. Phillip Randolph and his aide, the openly gay pacifist Bayard Rustin, threatened a march on Washington to protest. To stave off a march that would have cast an international spotlight on American racism, President Roosevelt established the Fair Employment Practices Commission. The FEPC regulated hiring and promotion practices at defense plants working under federal contract. Explicit racism in such plants was outlawed. But, on a daily basis, black women workers continued to face resistance from white women who refused to work with them, shower with them, or share eating facilities. Still, some of that racism did break down over time, as black and white women worked together during long shifts over a the course of a long war. At a time when the military was still segregated, the integration of wartime defense labor for women was a marked change for millions of Americans.[26]

There were also significant victories in expanding federal protection for workers. The Women's Trade Union League, along with its allies in the Women's Bureau of the U.S. Department of Labor (which had been created after World War I in close cooperation with the WTUL) had long campaigned for federal equal pay legislation to bring women's salaries up to the level of men's. World War II helped get women a little closer to that goal. In 1942, worried that war production goals might be missed if women workers declared a strike, the National War Labor Board mandated that women in defense plants must receive the same pay as men for doing the same jobs. This was a major milestone: the very first time that the federal government had come out in support of equalizing status for male and female workers. Following the war, advocates of labor legislation successfully lobbied for equal pay laws in many states as thanks for women's wartime labor.[27]

And yet, significant as this all was, World War II brought incremental change, not revolutionary transformation. There were already 12 million women working when the war broke out. Seven million more were added to the labor force by the peak years of defense production. But only a little over 3 million worked in heavy industry. The rest continued to fill traditionally female niches in the labor force – domestic and agricultural work, canning, textiles, laundry and garment work.[28]

But, while the war did not transform the status of women workers, the labor demands of the war did enable working-class women to shift to better situations – at least temporarily. Millions of farm and domestic workers moved into typically female industrial jobs, often joining unions for the first time and now eligible to benefit from government labor protections and social insurance programs – wage and hour laws, social security, disability and unemployment insurance. Smaller numbers of women moved into the highly paid, skilled jobs that fueled the defense industry – airplane and ship production, tank and weapons production. They benefited from the 1930s organizing drives that had brought workers in these industries into unions. They reaped benefits from 1930s labor legislation as well.

Women migrated en masse from the rural South to cities like Detroit and Los Angeles, Las Vegas, San Francisco and Oakland – trading low-paid farm work for unionized defense jobs. Oftentimes they found themselves living in unusual circumstances during the war years. Especially in the regions where defense work was most plentiful, they lived in virtual "cities of women" where relatively few men of working age were to be found. Both performing heavy industrial labor and living in communities where women were in charge of all aspects of daily life reshaped their beliefs about women's capacities – for heavy labor, for financial management and earning, and for running their lives independent of husbands and fathers. Even as they missed their male loved ones and longed for their safe return from the battlefields of Europe and Asia, many women enjoyed a sense of freedom and accomplishment. These shifts in consciousness and identity would intensify a sense of disappointment when the war ended and millions of women were fired to open up jobs for returning soldiers.[29]

There were protests aplenty once the layoffs began. They were perhaps most intense among African-American women in Detroit who had become members of the United Auto Workers' Union through their wartime jobs. Male union leaders were ambivalent in their treatment of these new women members. When government contracts dried up after the war, and millions were faced with losing their jobs, many union men and most union leaders were happy to show women the door and wish them well. Some unions, however, handled matters a bit differently. The United Auto Workers created a women's division. Its leaders began to shift their view of the union's mission to incorporate such concerns as equal pay, child care, and confronting discrimination in hiring, promotion and retention.[30]

And there was a shift in many women's sense of themselves regarding work – especially when it came to jobs that had long been thought of as "men's work." As Lola Weixel of Brooklyn, New York explained, women found out that "it was possible to learn to weld and to learn it well" in just a short time. Men in industry, she said, had been sold a bill of goods about how long it took to train for skilled jobs. They were told that, she believed, to keep women workers and workers of color from challenging men in the trades.

Still, the work that women did during the war in steel and automobile plants, building ships and airplanes was marketed more as temporary women's work than as jobs they could hope to keep for a lifetime. Government-produced propaganda films compared wiring an airplane panel to embroidering, operating a drill press to operating a juice press in the kitchen. Women were still taking care of their men when they produced for the war effort – much as they would have if they had stayed in their own kitchens. Still there were important legacies of women's wartime union activity that fueled the expansion of the American welfare state and worker protections in the 1950s.[31]

In the years after World War II, trade union feminists and their educated middle-class allies were engines of progressive change in the labor movement and the Democratic Party. They elected women to leadership posts in local and national trade unions. They also pressed union leaders and liberal policymakers to extend legislated labor protections to women workers and people of color. Working-class feminists demanded "full industrial citizenship" in the 1940s and 1950s, both from reluctant male union leaders and from corporate employers seeking a return to pre-war gender norms. In so doing, they transformed the ideology and political vision of the labor movement. And they set the stage for the legal revolution in women's rights to come in the 1960s and 1970s.

In an era when many labor leaders were still promoting the idea of a family wage to enable the wives of working men to be stay-at-home mothers, labor feminists insisted that all women should have the right to adequately paid wage work. In addition, they wanted labor unions and government to provide greater support for working-class women in their roles as homemakers and mothers. They pressed union leaders to pay attention to workers' lives outside the paid workplace, successfully lobbying in many unions for contract provisions guaranteeing maternity leave. Subsidized day care, too, became part of labor/management negotiations. This was a significant departure for most major unions that reflected increasing labor activism by young wives and mothers.

By the end of the 1940s, historian Sue Cobble has shown, a great many working-class women were making arguments about the need for labor unions and government regulations to address problems specific to working women. These women insisted that paid labor was not a temporary experience of wartime but a permanent phenomenon that millions of women had to manage alongside child-bearing and child-rearing. To make that possible, they fought for maternity leave and benefits, child care, and flexible scheduling that enabled them to balance paid workplace and unpaid home responsibilities. Recognizing that the labor force was still largely sex-segregated, they moved beyond demands for equal pay and began talking about comparable pay for jobs of comparable worth to employers. These issues did not suddenly appear in 1960s and 1970s women's rights struggles. In the trough years of the 1940s and 1950s, these issues were on the front burner for tens of millions of American women.[32]

The United Auto Workers Women's Bureau was led from shortly after the war's end into the 1970s by firebrand Caroline Davis – the beautiful daughter of Kentucky coal miners who loved to read Sigmund Freud in her spare time and insisted that, had she not become a union organizer, she would have been a psychiatrist. Davis and other UAW women activists argued that discrimination against women and against African-Americans in the industrial workplace came from the same source. They saw it as the responsibility of good unionists to fight both together. Forty years before feminist and critical legal studies scholars would theorize about intersectionality, trade union feminists were arguing that the women workers of color faced intersecting and multiplying forms of discrimination. Their actions and their arguments helped lay the groundwork for the feminist theories and strategies of later decades.[33]

Black labor feminists also linked class, race and gender issues in those years. Laundry worker Dolly Robinson, packing house worker Addie Wyatt and Gloria Johnson of the electrical workers' union extended the integrated class, race, and gender vision of the early 20th-century women strikers into the post-World-War-II era and into the heavy manufacturing sector. Afro-Panamanian immigrant Maida Springer Kemp – a garment union organizer who was mentored by Jewish women trade unionists Pauline Newman and Rose Schneiderman – mobilized labor support for the burgeoning civil rights movement in the years after World War II. Kemp would later link her labor feminism and civil rights work to a more global struggle, mentoring labor activists in Africa during the anti-colonial struggles of the 1960s.[34]

The involvement and intercession of middle-class allies continued to be important to labor feminists through the 1940s and into the 1950s. Like their working- class colleagues, Frieda Miller and Esther Peterson had ties to the cross-class women's labor organizations of the early 20th century, especially the Women's Trade Union League. Miller, the long-time partner of former Triangle factory worker, ILGWU organizer and WTUL officer Pauline Newman, was appointed director of the Women's Bureau of the U.S. Department of Labor in 1943–1944. A former economics professor, Miller had been drawn into the trenches of the labor struggle by the charismatic Newman in the World War I years and was appointed New York State Industrial Commissioner in the late 1930s. After World War II, she served as a link between industrial feminists of the pre-war years and the labor feminists who came of age during the war.

Miller worked to guarantee unemployment insurance to workers laid off during the post-war economic contraction. After 25 years in the WTUL, she understood that most women workers could not simply return to being homemakers after the war. They needed jobs; their families needed their income. To help them find work, she surveyed tens of thousands of wartime workers to see what skills they thought they had to offer in peacetime. She then convened conferences of union leaders and women's groups to create a blueprint for re-employing and re-deploying women war workers. Testifying before Congress for equal pay legislation, she called for a shift in emphasis in the federal government's relationship to labor – from protection to equality in the workplace.[35]

Esther Peterson's work as a labor feminist in federal government mostly came later – in the 1960s and 1970s – but she too linked the vision of pre-war industrial feminism to post-war Democratic liberalism. The child of Danish immigrants, she was drawn into labor activism in the 1930s as a teacher at the Bryn Mawr Summer School for Women Workers and she later became a lobbyist for the Amalgamated Clothing Workers' Union. Like Maida Springer Kemp, she was mentored and taught by immigrant women trade unionists who had come of age in early 20th-century labor struggles – among them Schneiderman and Newman. Peterson would achieve positions of influence in the administrations of John Kennedy, Lyndon Johnson and Jimmy Carter – helping to persuade these Presidents to deploy the powers of the federal government to support gender equity in the workplace. Peterson can be seen as a living link between the so-called First Wave of feminism and the so-called Second Wave of the 1960s and 1970s. Her career is an illustration of how inaccurate it is to see these waves of feminist activity as separate or disconnected. Essential work was done in the trough years of the 1920s, 1930s and 1940s, and important victories were achieved. The waters of change never stopped moving because women activists never ceased their agitation.[36]

Mothers, Consumers and Women's Labor Auxiliaries in the 1930s and 1940s

Another stream of women's activism in the 1930s and 1940s fed and overlapped with labor feminism. It was a nationwide uprising by mothers against the high cost of living. From New York City to Seattle, from Richmond, Virginia to Los Angeles, and in hundreds of cities, small towns and farm villages in between, poor and working-class wives and mothers staged anti-eviction protests, consumer boycotts, rent strikes and protests for better education and affordable public housing. They created large-scale barter networks – trading labor for food, fresh caught fish and hand cut timber for potatoes, wheat and apples. And they lobbied for legislation to limit the cost of staple foods and housing. Militant and angry, they demanded a better quality of life for themselves and their families. Echoing the language of trade unionism, they asserted that housing and food, like wages and hours, could be regulated by organizing and applying economic pressure.[37]

Women's decision to politicize their position as consumers was one of the signal developments in early 20th-century American politics. In the 1910s, middle-class women consumers had marshaled support for women workers through the educational and union label campaigns of the National Consumer's League. The militant housewives' movement of the 1930s and 1940s, kick-started by the Depression that had left millions of mothers unable to adequately shelter, clothe or feed their children, was a bit different. It sought to bring government into the business of regulating "the high cost of living." Angry wives and mothers had come to believe that government could and should regulate prices as well as wages. That belief was deeply influenced by Franklin Roosevelt's New Deal, with its call for various constituencies – labor, youth, business, African-Americans – to organize "special interest groups" that could effectively appeal to government to get their needs met. This movement sought to address the most basic of needs.

The Depression era housewives' movement also built on a tradition of immigrant and working-class women protesting sudden rises in the costs of food and shelter. As early as 1902, tens of thousands of immigrant mothers in New York City had boycotted kosher meat to protest increasing prices. They were not quiet about it either, wrecking shops of butchers who refused to cooperate, smashing windows, tearing meat out of the hands of shoppers who violated the boycott and slapping police. There were repeated meat and milk boycotts in 1904, 1910 and 1917 – as World War I raised prices throughout the U.S. In 1907, 1910 and 1919, tens of thousands of New York wives and mothers had staged rent strikes to demand adequate housing at affordable prices.[38]

If the militancy of the movement in the 1930s and 1940s was no more intense than that of the earlier period, the scale and scope of organizing was unprecedented in U.S. history. This was a nationwide movement involving immigrant as well as native-born mothers, black and white, Jewish and Christian. During the early years of the Depression, they organized to stave off imminent disaster. During the first years after the 1929 crash, their focus was on self-help. They set up barter networks, community gardens and neighborhood housewives' councils to offset the high costs of rent and food. By the mid-1930s, poor and working-class housewives, like farmers and factory workers, had begun to see themselves as a group that could maximize their economic and political power by working together. By organizing and lobbying, as well as engaging in aggressive and sometimes violent protests, they tried to force local businesses, mid-level wholesalers and the New Deal state to respond to their concerns and address their needs.

Housewives' activism in the 1930s and 1940s was covered extensively both by left-wing and more mainstream media who could not resist poking fun at the very idea of a housewives' movement. In the summer of 1935, one *New York Times* headline blared: "Women Picket Butcher Shops . . . Slap, Scratch, Pull Hair: Men are the Chief Victims." When a housewives' delegation descended on the office of Secretary of Agriculture Henry Wallace to demand federal action to lower meat prices the headline read: "Secretary Wallace Beats Retreat From Five Housewives." Underlying this ridicule, however, was real tension. Politicized consumers had become a force to be reckoned with.[39]

The period saw three nationwide meat boycotts: one in 1935, another in 1948 and a final one in 1951. These boycotts reflected two key changes from the earlier protests. One was the increasing presence of the telephone as an organizing tool for women. The second was the transformation of the federal government into a regulatory state with an interest in, and infrastructure to, enforce limits on prices of basic goods.

The key organizers of the 1930s housewives movement had all been labor activists before the Depression. Seattle organizers Jean Stovel and Mary Farquharson were active in the American Federation of Labor before organizing the Washington barter movement. Mary Zuk was the daughter of a mining union activist and was a unionized auto worker herself before founding the Detroit Women's Committee Against the High Cost of Living. Rose Nelson, one of the leading New York City organizers, had worked for the International Ladies Garment Workers' Union (ILGWU) before she helped found the United Council of Working Class Housewives (UCWCH). And the woman she founded it with was the best known housewife organizer of that era, Clara Lemlich Shavelson – the same "sparkplug" who set off the 1909 shirtwaist "uprising."

Clara Lemlich came of age during the years of the Lower East Side food and rent boycotts. During World War I, after she married printer Arthur Shavelson, she and other community organizers helped to spread meat boycotts and rent strikes throughout the city, by soliciting and winning support from women's synagogue groups, trade unions and the community councils that had been organized to support soldiers. By 1926, Shavelson was working through the Communist Party USA, which supported women's subsistence organizing around food and hunger.

More mainstream trade unionists like Rose Schneiderman and Pauline Newman also sought ways to bring housewives into the working-class struggle. Three decades of organizing had left them painfully aware that working women lacked the economic power to achieve their social and political goals. But American working-class women spent billions of dollars annually on their families. Organized as consumers, even poor women could wield real economic power. By the Depression, women organizers were ready to try to link the home to labor unions and government in a dynamic partnership, with wage-earning women and housewives as full partners.

This organizing effort came to fruition first in the summer of 1935 when a strike that began in New York City spread throughout the United States. Jewish and African-American housewives were central to the strike in New York and beyond – organizing successful boycotts that summer in Los Angeles, Chicago, Cleveland and San Francisco. However, the movement drew other groups of women as well – Polish immigrant and native-born housewives in Detroit, Finnish and Scandinavian women in Washington State and in Minnesota, white Protestant farm women in Texas. There were differences between the groups. American-born Protestants were less confrontational in their tactics. They signed pledges not to buy meat at inflated prices rather than picketing butcher shops; they collected signatures on petitions for price regulation rather than marching on City Hall. All of the women were after the same thing however – regulation on how high the price of staple foods could go.

The movement spread very rapidly and lasted into the early 1950s. In Los Angeles, 10,000 housewives so completely shut down meat sales in certain parts of the city in 1935 that prices came down and stayed down. In Philadelphia, Chicago, Boston, Paterson, New Jersey and Kansas City, housewives' councils also had success at bringing prices down. On June 15, 1935 a delegation of housewives from across the country confronted Secretary of Agriculture Henry Wallace to urge him to rein in wholesale prices. They did not believe that farmers and drought were responsible for the high prices of meat. They saw price gouging by major meat companies as the problem. In August 1935, housewife activists returned to Washington to demand a 20% cut in meat prices, prosecution of meat profiteers and an end to meat processing taxes.

When they were not respectably lobbying, housewife protestors in Detroit, Chicago and smaller cities broke into warehouses, poured kerosene on stocks and set thousands of pounds of meat aflame to protest wholesalers' hoarding of supplies to artificially inflate prices. When several Detroit housewives were jailed for such activities, hundreds of their angry comrades marched on the city jail to demand their release – jeering loudly when one of the leaders told the crowd of her mistreatment at the hands of police. By early August 1935, retail butchers in Detroit were pleading with the governor to send in troops to protect their meat supplies.[40]

As the 1930s wore on, leaders of the housewives' consumer movement became increasingly focused on electoral politics. Clara Lemlich Shavelson ran for New York State Assembly several times. Mary Zuk, Detroit's "strong jawed 100 lb. mother of the meat strike" was elected to the Hamtramck, Michigan City Council. Although the local Hearst paper warned that she and her allies advocated "the break up of the family" a strong housewife voting bloc carried her to victory on a platform that called for the City Council to regulate food prices, rents and utility costs.

In Washington State, three housewife activists were elected to the state Senate. They campaigned for a Production For Use initiative that would outlaw destruction of food to prop up retail prices. The initiative also called for a public distribution system that would allow workers to buy food directly from farmers. Although the initiative failed by a narrow margin, Washington voters approved state ownership of public utilities. Housewife activists and their husbands were able to pass similar measures in cities and municipalities across the country. At war's end they also traveled to Washington, D.C. to demand the continuation of the wartime Office of Price Administration and more federal funds for construction of public housing in overcrowded neighborhoods.[41]

The coalition of housewives' consumer groups and union auxiliaries continued to grow. Housewife activists' delegations to Washington became annual events through the 1940s (with a brief break during the war). In the summer of 1948, housewives in Texas, Ohio, Colorado, Michigan, Florida and New York boycotted meat again. This strike showed the power of the telephone as a housewife's organizing tool. "We have assigned fifty-eight women ten pages each of the telephone directory," explained one Cincinnati strike leader when asked how the women could have organized so quickly across so much space. In 1951, a housewives' meat boycott, also organized via telephone, forced wholesale distributors in New York, Philadelphia and Chicago to lower their prices. In New York City alone, a million pounds of meat a week went begging during the boycott. Fearing for their jobs, unionized butchers, then retailers and ultimately even wholesalers called on the federal government to institute price controls on meat.[42]

The movement was ultimately undone by the rising power of anti-Communist politicians. As early as 1939, Hearst newspapers were charging that the housewives' consumer movement was nothing more than a Communist plot to sow seeds of discord in the American home. The Dies Committee in Congress began investigating housewife activists for subversion. The investigations were stopped during World War II but resumed shortly after the war as anti-Communism began to build to a fever pitch. In 1949, the House Committee on un-American activities held hearings on Communist infiltration of housewife lobbying groups. In 1950, leading housewife activists were ordered to register as "foreign agents." By the mid-1950s, there was little left of the movement. Fear of government harassment and blacklisting by employers fueled discord and suspicion among the activists.

The unique alliance that created a nationwide housewives' movement from the early part of the 20th century through the 1940s would not re-emerge but it did lay the groundwork for later tenant and consumer organizing in the 1970s. And it permanently politicized consumer issues. The nation had developed a "consumer consciousness" as a result of the housewives' uprisings, *The Nation* magazine noted in 1937, forcing male union leaders to acknowledge that the "roles of producer and consumer are intimately related."[43]

Housewives' struggles alleviated the worst effects of the Depression in many working-class communities – bringing rents and food prices down, preventing evictions, and spurring the construction of more public schools, housing and parks. During and after World War II, housewife consumer activists forced the government to play an active role in regulating the costs of food and shelter. The three national meat strikes led to Congressional investigations into the structure of the meat industry and subsequent price reductions nationwide.

Finally housewives' consumer struggles left a lasting impact on the women who participated in them. As Brooklyn activist Dorothy Moser recalled, "It was an education for the women that they could not have gotten any other way." Immigrant women, poor native-born women, black and white women, learned to speak effectively in public, to lobby in city, state and federal government offices, to challenge men in positions of power and sometimes to upend and reconfigure the power relations in their own families.[44]

In all of these ways, the housewives' uprisings of the first half of the 20th century were as important and transformative politically, economically and socially as more conventionally "feminist" movements. Though the women involved in these movements were driven to activism initially by their responsibilities to husbands and children rather than by a desire to advance their own agendas, becoming politically active did ultimately empower them in all sorts of ways. In rethinking the narrative of American women's activism, and in writing the history of varied feminisms, it is crucial to include the sustained and militant action of wives and mothers and to understand the ways that such movements both altered the political landscape and fueled later activism of more explicitly "feminist" kinds.

Notes

1 Nancy Cott, *The Grounding of Modern Feminism* (New Haven: Yale University Press, 1989).
2 Harriet Stanton Blatch to Rose Schneiderman, May 2, 1910. Cited in Annelise Orleck, *Common Sense and a Little Fire: Women and Working Class Politics in the United States* (Chapel Hill, NC: University of North Carolina Press, 1995), p. 95.

3 Kathleen Blee, *Women of the Klan: Racism and Gender in the 1920s* (Berkeley: University of California Press, 1992).

4 Cott, op. cit.

5 Freda Kirchwey, "Alice Paul Pulls the Strings," *The Nation*, 2 March 1921; see too Roslyn Terborg-Penn, *African-American Women in the Struggle for the Vote* (Bloomington: Indiana University Press, 1998); Christine Bolt, *Sisterhood Questioned: Race, Class and Internationalism in the American and British Suffrage Movements* (New York: Routledge, 2004).

6 Katherine Adams and Michael Keene, *Alice Paul and the American Suffrage Campaign* (Champaign-Urbana: University of Illinois Press, 2007); Mary Walton, *A Woman's Crusade: Alice Paul and the Battle for the Ballot* (New York: Palgrave, 2010).

7 Sibyl Lipschultz, *Social Feminism, Labor Politics and the Supreme Court of the 1920s* (New York: Routledge, 2003).

8 Landon Storrs, *Civilizing Capitalism: The National Consumer's League, Women's Activism and Labor Standards in the New Deal Era* (Chapel Hill, NC: University of North Carolina Press, 2000).

9 *Muller v. Oregon*, 208 U.S., 412, (1908).

10 Orleck, *Common Sense*, Ch. 3.

11 Katherine Kish Sklar, *Florence Kelley and the Nation's Work: The Rise of Women's Political Culture, 1830–1900* (New Haven, CT: Yale University Press, 1998); and Katherine Kish Sklar and Beverly Palmer, eds., *The Selected Letters of Florence Kelley, 1869–1931* (Urbana-Champaign: University of Illinois Press, 2009).

12 See Orleck, *Common Sense*, pp. 140–141. See too Third, Fifth and Eighth Annual Reports of the U.S. Women's Bureau, cited on those pages.

13 Adkins cited in Alice Kessler-Harris, *A Woman's Wage: Historical Meanings and Social Consequences* (Lexington: University Press of Kentucky, 1990), p. 52.

14 Orleck, *Common Sense*, p. 141.

15 The term "labor feminism" comes from the very fine study of the evolution of industrial feminism after World War II, Dorothy Sue Cobble, *The Other Women's Movement: Workplace Justice and Social Rights in Modern America*. (Princeton: Princeton University Press, 2004).

16 For biographical information on Eleanor Roosevelt, the best source remains Blanche Wiesen Cook's two volume biography. *Eleanor Roosevelt, Vol. 1 1884–1933* (New York: Viking, 1992) and *Eleanor Roosevelt, Vol. II, 1933–1938 The Defining Years* (New York: Viking, 1999). Vol III is still in process. For a close discussion of Roosevelt's involvement in labor causes see Brigid O'Farrell, *She Was One of Us: Eleanor Roosevelt and the American Worker* (Ithaca: Cornell University Press, 2011).

17 Jean Edward Smith, *FDR* (New York: Random House, 2007), p. 47; Frances Perkins, *The Roosevelt I Knew* (New York: Viking Press, 1945). See description of these conversations in Orleck, *Common Sense*, pp. 147–160.

18 Orleck, *Common Sense*, pp. 146–154.

19 *New York Times*, May 1, 5, 6, 7, 1936; cited in Orleck, *Common Sense*, p. 158.

20 Alice Kessler-Harris, *In Pursuit of Equity: Women, Men, and the Quest for Economic Citizenship in 20th-Century America* (New York: Oxford University Press, 2001), p. 96.

21 Larry Dewitt, "The Decision to Exclude Agricultural and Domestic Workers from the 1935 Social Security Act," *Social Security Bulletin*, Vol. 70, No. 4, 2010 (Washington, D.C.: Government Printing Office).

22 New York Women's Trade Union League Annual Report, 1934. *Papers of the NYWTUL and Its Principal Leaders (UMI Microfilm); New York Times* January 22, 24, February 2, 11, 12, 13, 1934. January 22, March 6, 8, July 5, 1938. Rose Schneiderman, *All For One* (New York: Eriksson Press, 1967), pp. 116–117.

23 Marvel Cooke and Ella Baker, "In a Bronx Slave Market," *The Crisis*, June 1935. NYWTUL Annual Reports, 1939–1940; 1941–1942. Reel 4, NYWTUL Papers.

24 Maureen Honey, *Creating Rosie: Class, Gender and Propaganda During World War II* (Amherst: University of Massachusetts Press, 1984); Maureen Honey, ed., *Bitter Fruit: African-American Women in World War II* (Columbia: University of Missouri Press, 1999).

25 Connie Field, director, *The Life and Times of Rosie the Riveter* (1980); see too Sherna Gluck, ed., *Rosie the Riveter Revisited: Women, the War and Social Change* (New York: Penguin, 1988).

26 Karen Tucker Anderson, "Last Hired, First Fired: Black Women Workers During World War II," *Journal of American History*, 69, 1982: 82–97; Sherrie A. Kossoudji and Laura J. Dresser, "Working Class Rosies: Women Industrial Workers during World War II," *Journal of Economic History*, Vol. 51, 1992, pp. 431–446.

27 General Order No. 16; Adopted 24 November 1942. published in National War Labor Board Press Release, No. B 693, June 4, 1943, in "Chapter 24: Equal Pay for Women," *The Termination Report of the National War Labor Board: Industrial Disputes and Wage Stabilization in Wartime*, January 12, 1942–December 31, 1945, Vol. I, 290–291.

28 Alice Kessler-Harris, *Out to Work: A History of Wage Earning Women in the United States 20th Anniversary Edition* (New York: Oxford University Press, 2003).

29 Marilynn Johnson, *The Second Gold Rush: Oakland and the East Bay in World War II* (Berkeley: University of California Press, 1996).

30 See Anderson, op. cit.

31 See Connie Field, director, *The Life and Times of Rosie the Riveter* (1980), for telling interviews with Wanita Allen, Gladys Belcher, Lynn Childs, Lola Weixel and Margaret Wright – WW II industrial workers and excerpts from U.S. propaganda films.

32 Dorothy Sue Cobble, *The Other Women's Movement: Workplace Justice and Social Rights in Modern America* (Princeton: Princeton University Press, 2004), pp. 12–15.

33 ibid.

34 Yvette Richards, *Maida Springer Kemp: Pan Africanist and International Labor Leader* (Pittsburgh: University of Pittsburgh Press, 2000).

35 Author's interview with Miller's daughter Elisabeth Burger, March 25, 1985; see too Frieda Miller, "What's Become of Rosie the Riveter?" *New York Times Magazine*, May 5, 1946.

36 The fullest account of Peterson's government career can be found in Cynthia Harrison, *On Account of Sex: The Politics of Women's Issues, 1945–1968* (Berkeley: University of California Press, 1989).

37 For a full treatment of this movement, see Annelise Orleck, "We Are That Mythical Thing Called the Public: Militant Housewives During the Great Depression," *Feminist Studies*, Vol. 19. No 1. Spring 1993.

38 *New York Times*, May 23, 24, 26, 1902; July 13–September 2, 1904; November 30–December 9, 1906; December 26, 1907–January 27, 1908. See too Orleck, "Mythical," op. cit.; Orleck, *Common Sense*, Chapter 6; Paula Hyman, "Immigrant Women and Consumer Protest: The New York City Kosher Meat Boycott of 1902," *American Jewish History*, (1980) Vol. 70, No. 1. pp. 91–105.

39 *New York Times*, July 28, 1935; *Chicago Daily Tribune*, August 20, 1935. Coverage of housewives' consumer actions in the summer of 1935 can be found in the above-mentioned newspapers as well as *Newsweek, The Nation, The New Republic, The Saturday Evening Post, Harper, Christian Century, Business Week* and *American Mercury* among others. See Orleck, "Mythical," op. cit., for more.

40 Orleck, "Mythical," op. cit.

41 *The Nation*, August 19, 1939; "A Few Honest Questions and Answers," Leaflet of the Washington Commonwealth Federation, Burke Collection, University of Washington libraries.

42 *New York Times*, February 24, 26, 27, 28, 1951. June 14, 1951.

43 *The Nation*, June 5, 12, 1937.

44 Author's interview with Dorothy Moser, March 27, 1986, New York.

3

VARIETIES OF FEMINISM IN A CONSERVATIVE AGE

Rethinking Women in the 1950s

American popular culture has often portrayed the 1950s as a golden era of old-fashioned gender norms when women were real women and father knew best. In this nostalgic vision, women willingly gave up wartime defense jobs after World War II to return home to suburban cul-de-sacs where they lived contentedly ever after – raising well-fed babies and enjoying comfortable lives. This was the 1950s evoked in such popular television family sit-coms as "Father Knows Best" and "Leave it to Beaver." It was a white, middle-class 1950s, an untroubled "Happy Days," as one 1980s television evocation of that time dubbed the era. But, as historian Stephanie Coontz has shown us, these images are part of a carefully constructed and highly politicized fantasy. It is nothing more or less than "the way we never were."[1]

There was some truth to the fantasy. Americans after World War II married younger, at higher rates, and were more likely to stay together than in later decades. Soldiers returned home to wives who were usually very happy to see them, and young families migrated en masse to the new suburbs springing up on the outskirts of cities across the country. Still, most American women, whether they were married mothers or single working women, were not June Cleaver – the television mother of suburban imp Beaver Cleaver. June never appeared in a wrinkled dress or did kitchen work without donning a string of pearls. She was unflappable in the face of daily domestic dramas as was her soft-spoken and always wise husband Ward. There was no tension, no jockeying for position in these homes. Men and women walked easily in their roles.[2]

And yet, one need only turn to the equally, if not more, popular television family shows of the time – "I Love Lucy" and "The Honeymooners" – for a sense that gender roles were not nearly as stable as they appeared in the television sub-urbs. If these shows are any reflection, jockeying for position between husbands and wives was a regular part of married life in those years – at least in the city, where these shows were set. In these urban television families men spoke Spanish, drove buses and dug sewer tunnels beneath the city streets. Their wives were sarcastic and edgy; they gently deflated their husbands' masculinity and they con-stantly inverted gender norms for laughs. Indeed the entire comedic structure of these shows revolved around up-ending men's and women's appointed roles. If we are most ticklish where we are most tense, then the popularity of these shows suggests that gender in the 1950s was fraught and contested terrain.[3]

Perhaps that is not so surprising after all. There is another well-known narrative of the post-World War II era that highlights women's deepening discontent. Millions of American women did indeed return from war work, the military or college to raise children at home between 1945 and the 1960s. But they did not do so happily, according to this historical recounting. They found home life con-straining; and they chafed against it, longing for a kind of life and work that would be more meaningful and fulfilling.

This view of the 1950s was most famously and powerfully chronicled in Betty Friedan's *The Feminine Mystique*, an exploration of middle-class women's gnawing unhappiness – what *Time* magazine in 1962 called the "problem that has no name." First published in 1963, *Mystique* sought to answer a question that Friedan argued was on the minds of many Americans, even if only a few dared utter it. Why, if middle-class American women lived in greater material comfort than ever before, did they seem to be so lost and so unsatisfied? Friedan blamed isolation in the home, thwarted career ambitions and intellectual stagnation. She pointed to a culture in which women were seen not as individuals but only as wives and moth-ers, not as autonomous adults but only in relationship to their parents, husbands and children.[4]

Three years before *Mystique* came out, Friedan published an article in *Good Housekeeping* magazine entitled "Women are People Too." This 1960 article described a feeling that women were reluctant to name publicly: "a strange stir-ring, a dissatisfied groping, a yearning, a search . . . They tell us . . . that all our frustrations were caused by education and emancipation," Friedan wrote. "They tell us to pity the 'unfeminine,' 'unhappy' women who once wanted to be poets or physicists or Presidents . . ." Women believed that they were supposed to be complete and content if they had a husband and children, Friedan admitted. But "sometimes a woman says, 'I feel empty, somehow,' or 'useless,' or 'incomplete,' or she says it is 'as if I do not exist.'" Friedan's article sparked an immediate and powerful response. "I actually wept when I read it," one reader wrote to the maga-zine. "It struck at the very heart of something that has caused me many hours of discontented soul searching," wrote another. These letters came from all kinds of women, rural and urban, middle- and working-class. Setting out to write a larger treatment of this issue, Friedan knew that she had touched an aching social nerve.[5]

When Friedan's book *The Feminine Mystique* was published in 1963, it exploded like a bombshell in well-heeled suburban neighborhoods across America – literally changing lives. One of the most successful polemics ever published in English, *Mystique* is widely seen as the book that set off a revolution, kick-starting a new explosion of American feminist activism that lasted through the 1970s and left American society permanently changed. That is both true and not true.

In some ways, the book was quite narrow in scope, drawn on interviews with and data from a highly privileged group of women – the Smith College class of 1942. In that sense, *The Feminine Mystique* was not really the portrait of a generation. It was a window onto a rather rarified subculture. And yet, the book sent out ripples that traveled far beyond that small, comfortable world because it so powerfully evoked a moment when expectations were raised and then suddenly deflated. Its evocation of women's disappointment struck a chord even among those whose lives were starkly different from the well-educated suburban wives and mothers interviewed by Friedan. The book certainly rocked the worlds of many affluent stay-at-home suburban moms. But it also touched urban working-class women, immigrant and African-American women who had always worked for wages in addition to raising families.[6]

These women were frustrated too, but their discontents were rooted in different cultural and economic circumstances. These were the 12 million women who had worked for wages before the war and who had no choice but to continue working afterwards. These were women who had to work, as Lola Weixel said about herself in the 1980 documentary *The Life and Times of Rosie the Riveter*, because "we were working people." Like Weixel many of them had enjoyed their wartime experiences doing well-paid work in unionized jobs. They were excited to have learned skills they hoped to continue using after the war. And, like Weixel, many working-class women were angry that these newly acquired skills were never tapped.

For many women, the war had provided the first decent jobs they had ever had. After lifetimes of laboring at underpaid, non-unionized jobs, millions of working-class women were proud to be earning enough to support their children. They bitterly resented being forced, at war's end, to return to less satisfying, lower-paid work in garment factories, kitchens, laundries and in domestic service.

Still they had to work, and so they did, suppressing simmering frustrations that would burst forth in the coming years. The numbers of wage-earning women in the U.S. continued to rise through the 1950s. By 1960, women made up more than one-third of the paid labor force in the U.S. And nearly two-thirds of employed women were married. Among them were millions who chafed against the idea that women were nothing more than wives and mothers. But, for them, the solution that Friedan offered – going out to work – was not enough. They knew that getting out of the home to work for wages was not inherently liberating. For them, the answer had to include a fair shot at jobs that brought respect and decent pay, access to government benefits, affordable child care and higher education.[7]

For women of color, the war had brought improvements but also bitter disappointments. Many African-American women had migrated from the rural South to trade jobs picking cotton or cutting cane for union jobs making tanks or ships in Detroit and Los Angeles. At war's end, they experienced a fall that was long and hard. They returned to jobs that were neither unionized nor covered by Social Security. They could no longer claim workmen's compensation if they were hurt on the job. Employed in private homes, or in restaurant kitchens, they could not be assured of old age pensions.

Though every movie theater in the country showed government-produced newsreels that depicted women war workers happily hanging up their factory tools and returning home, women did not accept either wartime exploitation or post-war layoffs without a fight. During the war, black women workers in defense plants from Seattle to New York protested discriminatory treatment, segregated restrooms and changing facilities, union locals closed to black workers and no access to decent housing for their families. These protests continued as black women workers – last hired – became first fired. Though it is not often discussed in histories of civil rights struggle, the frustration and disappointment of being unceremoniously fired from their hard won factory jobs certainly paved the way for women's civil rights activism in the 1950s and 1960s.[8]

For Japanese-American women, the war years and the aftermath were a twisted mixture of wrenching losses and expanding horizons. Of the more than 112,000 Japanese-Americans deported to internment camps during the war, two-thirds were citizens. As an experiment to get Japanese-American youth to assimilate to American language and culture, administrators of the internment camps offered young women internees a chance to enroll in colleges in the mid-West, far from historic centers of Japanese immigrant settlement on the West Coast. Many young women jumped at the opportunity to get an education. For those who came from traditional families, this was a chance they might not otherwise have had. In some cases, their families joined them at the war's end in Chicago, Minneapolis, Kansas City and other mid-Western towns. Others returned to the West Coast, swallowing bitter memories of how neighbors and schoolmates had treated them before the deportation.[9]

No one was allowed to leave the camps, even at war's end, without proving they had jobs and homes – exactly the pieces of their lives that had been torn away from them at the time of internment. The greatest number of job offers flowing into the camps after 1945 were for domestic service positions, the only kind of paid labor that was available for most Japanese-American women through the 1930s. Looking for other kinds of work, Japanese-American women and men faced severe discrimination when they returned to the West Coast. They scattered in hopes of finding opportunity. By 1967, only 4% of Japanese-Americans lived in primarily Japanese communities. The interment process had broken up long-established ethnic enclaves in California and Washington, leaving former fishermen stranded on the prairies.

But, Japanese-American women fought discrimination energetically in the years after the war, and slowly job opportunities multiplied. By 1950, far more Nisei (second generation) Japanese-American women were working in clerical and sales jobs, as factory workers and beauticians than as domestics. Although a gap remained between pay and educational achievement, the fierce hostility of the war years began to abate.[10]

The post-war years brought improvements too for Chinese-American women who had enthusiastically joined in the war effort as defense workers, volunteers and members of women's Army, Navy and Air Force battalions. Chinese-Americans had energetically campaigned to differentiate themselves from the Japanese enemy during the war. The U.S. alliance with China during World War II softened popular opinion of Chinese-Americans considerably. Congress repealed the Chinese Exclusion Acts that had severely limited Chinese women's immigration to the U.S. since the late 19th century. It also passed new legislation that opened up the doors to mass immigration from China.

Most of those who came were women. Between 1946 and 1952, 90% of Chinese immigrants to the U.S. were women. Throughout the 1960s, women immigrants from China far outnumbered men. Since the 19th century, Chinese America had been largely a "bachelor society" – a sex ratio of nearly three men to every one woman as late as 1940. With the mass immigration of women after World War II, Chinese America had equal numbers of women and men by the late 1960s.[11]

Many of the Chinese women entering the U.S. after World War II came from households where male breadwinners had been absent for many years. They or their mothers had assumed both male and female responsibilities and earned a greater share of power and respect than was traditional in Chinese families. They expected to continue in these roles once living in the U.S. In America's China-towns, they became full partners either in small producer households, where families lived over laundries, restaurants and shops, or they found themselves entering local factories where they quickly absorbed and adopted the ideology of trade union solidarity. Drawing on labor union ideology and their newfound solidarity with other women workers, newly-arrived immigrant women made claims to political, social and economic power in Chinese enclaves across the U.S. during the 1950s and early 1960s.[12]

Just as Chinese immigrant women became a significant presence in the U.S. for the first time, competition was heating up between the U.S., the Soviets and Communist China for hearts and markets in Asia and Africa. Seeing racial liberalism as a potential weapon in the Cold War, many American politicians began to tout multi-culturalism as a strength of American democracy. In that spirit, Chinese immigrant women suddenly found themselves lionized both for choosing the U.S. and for their displays of self-sacrifice and hard work.

In the Spring of 1952, Toy Len Goon, a widowed Chinese immigrant mother of eight who ran a hand laundry in Portland, Maine, was chosen as American Mother of the Year by the American Mothers Committee. Created during the Depression to call attention to rising mother and child poverty in the U.S., the AMC highlighted a telling mixture of qualities in its earlier honorees. In the previous six years, the AMC had honored an African-American and a Chippewa mother as well as four white mothers of various ethnic backgrounds. And, though it valorized devotion to children, the organization had also shown an interest in civic activism and professional accomplishment. A teacher, a businesswoman, a nurse and a doctor were among those honored. Mrs. Goon was the first mother of the year who did not have a college degree, and the first working-class woman to receive the award.

Goon soon became a national and an international symbol. On Mother's Day 1952, she was invited to Washington, D.C. to pose with her children on the steps of the Capitol, along with members of the Maine congressional delegation and the Chinese ambassador to the U.S. Both the Chinese press and American media gushed over her old-fashioned values and her success at raising children who had attended college and pursued professional careers. Chinese immigrant media in the U.S. saw her award as recognizing the contributions of Chinese-Americans. News agencies in Taiwan touted the award as a legitimation of traditional Chinese maternal values. That a working-class Chinese single mother was heralded as a "model for all American mothers" in 1952 reminds us that popular understandings of motherhood in those years extended beyond the borders of white suburban housing tracts. That Mrs. Goon's story was used by Washington, Taiwan, and the Chinese immigrant media, illustrates how valuable maternal imagery was as political currency. Motherhood and its representations became weapons in the intensifying Cold War. And the repercussions played out both in intimate and highly public ways.[13]

Gender, the Family, Sex and the Cold War

The years after World War II were a time of war-weariness and deep-seated societal fear. The creation of atomic weapons, the "fall" of China to Communism and Soviet expansion into Eastern Europe had all intensified American anxieties. Seeking retreat into a comfortable zone of privacy, many Americans began to see the traditional family – "built on the idea of father as breadwinner and the mother as nurturer of children,"[14] as one post-war U.S. government propaganda film put it – as the best bulwark against uncertainty abroad, and the triumph of godless Communism at home.

To strengthen that fortress family, the federal government enacted policies that supported suburban sprawl. New tract developments were built across the U.S. with help from taxpayer dollars. The federal highway system was dramatically expanded. The Federal Housing Authority awarded low-interest home loans to returning veterans so that they could move their families from densely populated cities to suburbs where they could afford homes. These developments and the federal loans that made them possible subsidized the transformation of urban ethnics, children of immigrants from Eastern and Southern Europe, into "white" property owners, suburbanites, and members of idealized middle-class nuclear families.

When African-American, Mexican-American and Chinese-American veterans attempted to move their families to some of these same suburbs – they faced fierce opposition from unfriendly mobs, often led by white housewives. Freshly migrated from immigrant-dominated inner-city neighborhoods, many of these women were anxious to stake their claim to the white feminine mystique that more affluent women were already tired of.[15]

These new suburban housewives began to see themselves as America's salvation in a dangerous world. Historian Elaine Tyler May coined the term "domestic containment" to describe the deployment of traditional family ideology as a weapon to contain the spread of Communism. For many housewives on the suburban barricades in the 1950s, they were more concerned with containing the spread of black, brown and yellow families from the cities to the suburbs. In their view, it amounted to much the same thing anyway. Civil rights activism and Communism were indistinguishable.[16]

American democracy was represented in the battle against Communism by the gleaming new suburban kitchen. When Vice-President Richard Nixon traveled to Moscow to debate Soviet Premier Nikita Khruschev on the relative merits of capitalism and Communism, the U.S government actually built a model suburban home in the middle of a Moscow park. Under TV lights and against the backdrop of gleaming modern appliances, Nixon set out to show the world a standard of living possible only under American-style capitalism.

Shortly thereafter, when President Dwight Eisenhower invited Khruschev to visit the U.S. he planned to fly the Russian premier over the Maryland suburbs ringing Washington, so that Khrushchev could see the houses and swimming pools. He also wanted Khrushchev to look down and see some of the 60 million automobiles that Americans then owned. Suburban homes, along with the highways and cars that connected them to men's workplaces were Eisenhower's wager for supremacy in the post-war competition with Soviet Russia.[17]

But, beneath the gleaming facades of the new suburban American revolution, and especially back in the cities from which so many had fled after World War II, lay a sense that all this new wealth was potentially at risk. Americans feared deviance on the part of their neighbors. They equated difference with subversion. Polls showed that a majority of Americans believed that inter-racial marriage and homosexuality should remain illegal. One in three Americans believed that members of the U.S. Communist Party should be imprisoned. A smaller group supported executing unrepentant Communists. In that climate of mistrust and recrimination, Congressional, state and city investigating committees were convened to ferret out subversives. Film stars, office workers and teachers, postal workers and firemen were called to testify about Communist infiltration of American homes, schools, media, workplaces and halls of government. Gender normativity came to be seen as a mark of trustworthiness. Those who chafed against conventional gender roles were seen as weird or "queer," or even worse – traitors.

The case of one such mother riveted attention around the world. In the Spring of 1950, two Jewish New York Communist Party activists – Julius and Ethel Rosenberg – were arrested and charged with treason – for allegedly stealing the secret of the atom bomb and passing it to the Soviets. The crime was supposed to have been committed during World War II, when the U.S. and the U.S.S.R. were allies. No civilian had ever been executed for treason in peacetime. Still the two were put on trial for their lives.

The trial made a mockery of due process. Prosecutors interrogated key witnesses together and then used them to corroborate each other's testimony in court. In lieu of hard evidence, witnesses were allowed to manufacture replicas to show the jury. It seemed implausible that a mechanical engineer could possibly have made off with anything substantive about nuclear weapons production when even highly placed nuclear physicists at the Los Alamos laboratories were allowed only the most fragmentary information. But the case was almost literally radioactive. No one wanted to look too closely. Prosecutors stirred a simmering pot of cultural anxieties and the media stoked the flames – creating an upwelling of support for the death penalty.

Debate rages to this day over the guilt or innocence of Julius Rosenberg, but no one has ever thought that Ethel was guilty of anything. There was no evidence that Ethel had committed a crime and none of the prosecutors believed she had. They leveled charges against her in the hope of convincing her husband to confess. In court and in the press, Ethel was tried for being a traitor to her sex. Federal prosecutors and the press portrayed Ethel as cold, calculating, the driving force behind a weak man – a sinister version of the overbearing mother and wife so vilified in 1950s popular culture. News articles described her as steely and, apparently equally damning, as plain and plump. Without hard evidence of anything Ethel had typed, prosecutors portrayed her as a frightening perversion of the good secretary, dutifully taking notes for her husband the spy. Ethel, they argued, in opening statements "sat at that typewriter and struck the keys, blow by blow, against her own country." It was for that crime that she was sentenced to die in the electric chair alongside her husband.[18]

Ethel Rosenberg's quiet dignity in the face of her impending execution was described by reporters and political leaders alike as unwomanly and unnatural. President Dwight Eisenhower wrote that he would normally balk at executing a woman but that Ethel was, in his view, the stronger of the couple, the ring leader who had dragged her husband into wrongdoing.

When she wrote the President to plead that he spare her for the sake of the couple's two children, Eisenhower demurred. He told his son that he thought she had tried to manipulate Americans' natural affection for mothers to aid the Communist cause. If he spared Ethel Rosenberg, Ike worried, the Soviets would use more women as spies in the future. Ethel's strength became a mark of her guilt. The tabloid press made much of the fact that – even in the death chamber – it took more electricity to kill Ethel than to kill Julius.[19]

Ethel Rosenberg herself summoned the ideology of sacred motherhood in a letter she wrote shortly before the execution. Though she had been a factory worker and a union organizer, a singer and an actress, in the end – as she faced leaving her two small sons alone – she was most caught up in her identity as a mother. In a letter addressed to American mothers, Rosenberg accused her executioners of laying "unclean hands on our sacred family." And she issued a challenge to her fellow mothers to speak out on her behalf: "Tell me, oh my sister Americans, how long shall any of your husbands and children be safe if you permit by your silence this deed to go unchallenged."[20]

Around the world many protested the couple's electrocution, but in the U.S. there were few who did. Garment strike leader and Depression-era housewife organizer, Clara Lemlich Shavelson, was among the few, even in the Communist Party, who descended on the White House to protest. Even on the Left no one wanted to be associated with the Rosenbergs, Shavelson's daughter Martha Schaffer later recalled. "We were all afraid. People were burning books from their own shelves." Schaffer continued: "I think it was, for any activist woman with children, a horrifying thing."[21]

The Rosenberg executions cast a long shadow in the summer of 1953. The young poet Sylvia Plath was not a political activist. Still she did not fit easily into the gender norms of the moment and the Rosenberg executions haunted her. "That's all there was to read about in the papers," a horrified Plath wrote in the opening paragraph of her autobiographical novel *The Bell Jar*, "goggle-eyed headlines staring up at me from every street corner . . . It had nothing to do with me but I couldn't help wondering what it would be like, being burned alive all along your nerves."[22]

It was difficult to protest in Cold War America without being labeled both deviant and subversive. Being so labeled came at a cost. The 1950s are widely thought of as an era of political intolerance. But it was also a time of crack-downs on sexual dissidence. "Perversion" came to be seen as synonymous with subversion. Anyone who expressed sexuality that was not hetero-normative came in for scrutiny and suspicion, investigation and even blacklist. There was a lavender scare along with a red scare.

Just as the obsessive Communist-hunting in the 1950s was a backlash against the political radicalism of the 1930s and 1940s, the lavender scare of the 1950s was an attempt to shut the door on an era of sexual experimentation during World War II. Gay men and lesbians had been able to live relatively open lives in the military forces during the war, especially in combat zones. And a new gay and lesbian public culture began to emerge in many American cities, including Washington, D.C. Young gay men and women flocked to the capital during the 1930s and 1940s to find jobs in the federal workforce. Far from families and the churches of their upbringing, they created a flourishing subculture.[23]

Conservatives in both political parties pointed to D.C.'s gay underground as emblematic of the corruption and moral decline of the Roosevelt-Truman years. Alfred Kinsey's 1948 report, proving that large numbers of Americans had engaged in same-sex eroticism during the 1930s and 1940s, fueled those who argued for a crackdown. The fortress family was under threat. Clearly something had to be done.[24]

Conservatives in Congress passed the Miller Sexual Psychopath bill, criminalizing homosexual activity between consenting adults in the District of Columbia. They pressured Truman to sign it and he did. In 1950, Republican Senator John Wherry of Nebraska and Democrat Clyde Hoey of North Carolina pushed for a full investigation of homosexuality in the federal government workforce. Though Truman was able to press the Hoey Committee to hear testimony from physicians who argued that the morality and intelligence of homosexual women and men was identical to that of the general population, the Committee concluded that homosexuals were "unsuitable" employees anywhere in the federal government.

Not a single case was found of gay men or lesbian women passing on sensitive documents to foreign powers. Still, the Committee concluded that, because homosexuality was societally stigmatized, lesbians and gay men were vulnerable to blackmail by foreign agents who could threaten to expose their secret sexual lives. "One homosexual can pollute a government office," the committee noted in its final report. The Truman administration was somewhat reluctant to persecute gay and lesbian federal employees. But he did. Scores were fired during his presidency.[25]

The investigations heated up after Dwight Eisenhower took office. In 1954, Ike issued an executive order replacing Truman's requirement that federal employees be politically loyal with a mandate that federal employees be men and women of good "character." This executive order explicitly banned employment of homosexual men and women. More people lost their jobs over the next few years for being gay or lesbian than for being suspected of Communist ties. By the end of the 1950s, thousands of gay men and lesbians in the federal workforce – from the post office to the state department – had lost their jobs. Many others resigned for fear of being targeted. This campaign had a ripple effect in the private sector. Corporations and universities began to purge lesbians and gay men. One lesbian reflected: "It has never been easy being a lesbian in this country, but the 1950s was surely the worst decade in which to love your own sex."[26]

Like women of color forced out of their wartime jobs, like Japanese-Americans robbed of their homes and businesses, lesbians and gay men began to organize and to sue in court for protection against discrimination. Protests and court cases slowly picked up steam in the 1950s. By the early 1960s, "homophile" groups staged regular protests at the White House and some signal court victories were won. But it would take another decade and a half of struggle, and the rise of global women's and gay "liberation" movements before federal policies banning the employment of lesbians and gay men were fully lifted.

In spite of the repression, the investigations, the ruined careers and reputations, the fear and self-censorship, the mystique of hearth and home, the 1950s was also an era of wide-spread and courageous protest by women, especially women of color. These women did not – at least at first – pick up protest signs, march, sit-in, commit acts of civil disobedience and go to jail in the name of women's rights. They did so in the name of their class, their race, and most often their children. This latter role protected them somewhat from the violence of their times, but by no means completely. In time, protesting led many of these women to rethink their roles as wives, as mothers, and as women in the mid-20th-century U.S.

Class, Race and Motherhood: Women's Protest in the 1950s: New Mexico

In the early summer of 1951, as a strike by Mexican-American mine workers in Hanover, New Mexico dragged on into its 8th month, owners of the Empire Zinc mine won a court injunction banning miners from walking picket lines outside the mine. The men were protesting payment of lower wages to Mexican-American miners, who did the same jobs as white men. They were also upset about a job classification system that reserved the lowest paid mine jobs for Mexican workers. With their backs against the wall, and the strike on the line, the men agreed to a controversial suggestion by Virginia Chacón, wife of miner's local union President Juan Chacón. The women had been talking, she said, and they wanted to picket in place of the men. They even suggested bringing their children to the line. Since they were not technically on strike, it would not be a violation of the court order for them to picket. Chacón and many other male strikers voted against the idea but, in the end, the women prevailed.

Wives and children of the zinc miners – members of the Mine-Mill Ladies Auxiliary 209 – walked the picket line for the next seven months, almost as long as the men had. They were harassed and threatened by company guards and strike-breakers brought in by Empire. The women were arrested and jailed by the local sheriff. And, in addition, they had to deal with increasingly restive and cranky husbands – who were left to take care of dishes, laundry and babies while their wives did the work of the union.

As had happened during the Great Depression of the 1930s when wives of miners, mill workers and automobile makers protested in support of their husbands, joining the strike made the women of Hanover, New Mexico increasingly aware of the politics of gender in their community. Some of this was sparked by their own sense of relief at getting out of the house. They enjoyed doing work that was widely considered worthwhile. The women laughed and joked on the picket line. They sang, they walked, they bantered with deputies and mine guards. They made speeches and talked to reporters and amazed themselves at their ability to do so with style and considerable persuasive power. They got angry and felt a sense of their well-deserved rage.

And when they were threatened, harassed and jailed, they fought back. They surrounded cars bringing strikebreakers to the mines and pushed them out of the way – refusing to break their picket circles. They wielded knitting needles and pins as weapons to defend themselves. They threw rotten eggs and hot peppers at strikebreakers and mine police. They women showed courage and spirit on the line and in prison. And they received national attention and admiration. When 58 of them were arrested and jailed, 300 more women came from other parts of New Mexico to take their places. The strike became a rallying cause among Mexican-Americans across the Southwest.[27]

Something else happened as well. The strike awoke Mexican-American working-class women to the particular dimensions of their oppression. They began to articulate a connection between their own workplaces – the homes where they labored day and night – and the struggle of their husbands against racial discrimination and for improved wages, hours and conditions. In the middle of the 20th century, when post-war prosperity and gleaming kitchens were touted by Vice-President Nixon in Moscow, these women had to cook, raise children, clean their homes, do dishes and laundry without the benefit of hot running water. By strike's end, these women, previously seen both by their husbands and the outside world as silent and docile, were loudly explaining both to their husbands and to mine owners that they wanted respect for the work that they did in the home. And they wanted more: they wanted a share of the modern conveniences enjoyed by middle-class housewives throughout the U.S. They wanted hot running water.[28]

The struggles of a group of poor, disfranchised Mexican-American wives and mothers, in a strike that might have gone little noticed outside the Southwest and outside Mexican America, soon became world famous. In 1954, a group of Hollywood veterans, under blacklist by the major film studios for alleged Communist Party affiliations, released a remarkable film about them called *Salt of the Earth*. *Salt* starred Juan Chacón as a striking zinc miner, Mexican actress Rosaura Revueltas as his wife, and men and women who had actually been involved in the Empire strike. It also foregrounded the struggle of the women of "Zinctown" in ways that were quite remarkable nearly a decade before the publication of *The Feminine Mystique*.

The film applauds Mexican-American wives and mothers demanding political equality by putting their bodies on the picket line. The women in the film insist that they should be voting members of the union. When sheriffs tear-gas the picketing women, they hand babies to their nervous husbands and use shoes and other weapons to knock guns out of the hands of police.

In perhaps the most famous scene in the film, Esperanza's husband Ramón is hanging laundry while his wife sits in jail. When a friend comes by to ask him how he is, he says disgustedly, "¡Este no tiene fin!" (This has no end.)

> Three hours just to get enough water to wash this stuff . . . If this strike is ever settled, which I doubt, I'll never go back to work for that company, unless they install hot running water for us. It should have been a union demand from the beginning.[29]

Taking their lead from the women of New Mexico, the film's writers, actors and directors pushed American unions to incorporate the needs and goals of housewives as well as women workers into the working-class struggle. This was a pointed critique at a time when women in the auto unions and other industrial sectors that had employed women war workers were pressing male leadership to address such women's issues as child care and maternity leave, to see these issues as integral to the labor struggle.[30]

Both for its race and gender politics, and because the actors, writer, director and producer of "Salt" had once had Communist Party ties, the film was attacked literally and figuratively. California Republican Donald Jackson, a member of the House Committee on Un-American Activities, argued on the floor of the U.S. Congress while the film was still being shot, that it was "deliberately designed to inflame racial hatreds and to depict the United States as an enemy of all colored peoples." His speech also called the film, "a new weapon for Russia."[31]

These attacks spurred vigilantes to assault the film's cast and crew and sparked the arrest of the film's star, Rosaura Revueltas, on immigration charges. In an effort to stop the filming, Revueltas was deported. The film's final scenes were shot in Mexico and smuggled back over the border. Few movie theaters in the U.S. would show the film in 1954, when it came out. But its influence rippled slowly through the U.S. and the world. Depicting gender and race dynamics of the pre-civil rights movement 1950s in ways that dramatically recast the dominant images of the time, *Salt of the Earth* continues to be shown and taught into the 21st century.[32]

The Communist Party USA and some of the progressive unions with ties to the Party grappled with issues of gender equality and "male chauvinism" long before the 1960s. Though Mexican, African-American and Jewish women often sought in vain to hold Party leaders to their promises of supporting sex equality, the CP and progressive unions were among the few social networks of the time where concerns of race, class and gender came together. Betty Friedan was an activist in the CP-affiliated United Electrical Workers Union before she became a journalist for more mainstream women's publications in the 1950s. That experience shaped her view of how gender and class worked in tandem. Historian Erik McDuffie has argued that "for black Communist women and their male comrades, making new women and men was just as important to black liberation and socialism as dismantling Jim Crow and colonialism." The CP social milieu was far more open to inter-racial couples, egalitarian heterosexual partnerships and homosexual relationships than American culture at large in those years.[33]

That said, neither the CP nor the CP-affiliated unions were feminist paradises – far from it. Blynn Garnett, who was raised by a lesbian couple who were members of the Communist Party in Manhattan in the 1940s, recalled that the Party frowned on same-sex relations as "bourgeois deviationism." Her mothers were able to be open about their relationship in Party circles, but felt pressure to follow what Garnett described as "pretty traditional gender norms in the way they dressed and behaved."[34]

Many women from New Mexico mine country reported profound changes for the better in their lives and relationships after the strike and the making of "Salt." But, for others, troubled relations with men continued. Chana Montoya, whose husband was once President of mine union local 890, was finally driven out of her marriage after years of physical abuse. When she took her seven children to California to get away from her abusive husband, he followed her. Unable to convince her to return, he shot and killed her. At his trial he defended himself by saying that he was only trying to save his children from being brainwashed by a Communist. As much as the 1950s were more textured and complicated than popular imagery has suggested, ideologies of motherhood and the chilling shadows of the Cold War nevertheless hung over everything and everyone.[35]

The Civil Rights Movement as a Women's Movement

Still women continued to protest throughout those years. Among the most famous, the most iconic, images of women's protest in the 1950s, is that of Rosa Parks, sitting alone, in the white section of a Montgomery, Alabama bus. Her act of defiance, refusing to give up her seat to a white man, is one of the only moments in the history of American civil rights activism that almost every American school child is taught. She sits alone and upright, a woman of indeterminate age, tired after a long day of work, bucking the tide of segregation. Parks' act is usually taught to young schoolchildren as a spontaneous decision made by a previously apolitical woman – the rebellious act that sparked a movement that changed America.[36]

Parks' act is most often seen as a cameo performance, a relatively minor lead-in to the main drama whose star was of course Martin Luther King Jr., the respectable minister and golden-tongued orator who has become for most Americans the only identifiable face of civil rights activism. To the extent that the average American imagines other leaders in the movement, they tend to see other educated men – the Reverend Ralph David Abernathy, the Reverend Jesse Jackson, the Reverend James Lawson and a few, like Congressman John Lewis, who were not ministers. Women's activism in the civil rights movement receded from view so quickly and so completely that it is a shock to most people when it is pointed out that the civil rights movement that brought down Jim Crow segregation in the American South, finally fulfilling the promises of the 14th and 15th amendments, was in many ways a women's movement. Though it was a movement that mobilized women and men, old and young, black and white, numerically there were more women than men. In some parts of the South the disparity was overwhelming.

This was so from the first organized resistance galvanized by Rosa Parks' act of defiance – the Montgomery Bus Boycott of 1955. After the 1954 *Brown v. Board of Education* decision, in which the U.S. Supreme Court ruled that separate was inherently unequal, many African-Americans in various parts of the South began to think of ways to test and challenge segregation in its varied forms. The buses of Montgomery, Alabama were a painful manifestation of the damages wrought by Jim Crow – particularly for the working-class black women who rode them across town to and from the affluent neighborhoods where they worked as domestics in white women's kitchens.

African-American men in Montgomery often worked together in factories or other job sites to which they could carpool. Black middle-class women, of whom there was a sizeable population in Montgomery – teachers and nurses and social workers – tended to work downtown or in majority black neighborhoods. It was domestic workers who had to travel clear across a sprawling new South city to earn their keep, from the black neighborhoods to the most comfortable white areas of town. It was black working-class women who rode the bus every day and who had to give up their seats to any white person who boarded if there were no more seats available in the white section. And they were tired and frustrated long before Rosa Parks refused to give up her seat.

As is so often the case in the history of women's activism, the most commonly taught version of the Montgomery Bus Boycott explains it as the result of one woman's sudden emotional reaction. A tired Rosa Parks spontaneously refused to give up her seat. The next morning, 50,000 leaflets supporting boycott magically appeared in the doorways and mailboxes of Montgomery's black neighborhoods. By the time people were set to commute to work, between 40,000 and 50,000 African-Americans had decided to boycott the city's segregated buses. A spontaneous protest picked up steam and the community boycotted for a year until the Supreme Court struck down segregation on public buses. The truth is, of course, more nuanced.

While it was undoubtedly a very busy night in black Montgomery, this widely taught boycott fairy tale reinforces ingrained notions of women's political behavior. They don't plan carefully. Rather they rise up emotionally, like a flood tide, without warning. In fact, the Montgomery Bus Boycott had been planned for a long time. The idea had been percolating at least since an eight-day boycott by black bus riders in Baton Rouge, Louisiana in 1953. For women who had to ride the bus to their jobs cleaning houses, daily humiliations at the hands of white people were wearing them down, like sand rubbing against already inflamed skin.

Three other African-American women had expressed their frustration with the segregation of public buses in Montgomery before Parks became a legend for doing so. Nine months before Rosa Parks refused to give up her seat, a 15-year-old African-American girl named Claudette Colvin was dragged kicking and screaming from a bus after refusing to move from the whites only section. She had been inspired by high school history teachers who taught her about Jim Crow laws in the South and about the injustices that black people had long suffered. Eight months before Parks' act of protest, college educated Aurelia Browder refused to give up her seat. And one month after that an 18-year-old named Mary Louise Smith was arrested for refusing to vacate her seat.

Browder, the oldest and the best educated, was chosen to be the lead plaintiff in the court challenge to bus segregation that eventually resulted in the Supreme Court's Browder decision ending segregation on public buses.[37]

Sentiment in support of a boycott had been building for some time in the city. The Montgomery Women's Political Council, an organization of black women teachers, professors, social workers, nurses and college students, had been planning the boycott for some time before it actually began. These women have largely disappeared from the history of the civil rights movement but they have not disappeared from the consciousness of black Montgomery.[38]

The leaflets that followed Parks' arrest noted the others who preceded her:

> Another Negro woman has been arrested and thrown into jail because she refused to get up out of her seat on the bus and give it to a white person . . . Until we do something to stop these arrests they will continue. The next time it could be you or you or you.

These words spoke to a long-simmering discontent among black women in Montgomery and across the South. Written and distributed by middle-class black women, these leaflets were intended to affirm the dignity and citizenship rights of black elites while also speaking to the aggrieved sensibilities of working-class black women in the city.[39]

Coverage in the white-owned *Montgomery Advertiser* spoke to another set of relationships between women that would be important in this strike. The paper reported that it had first learned that black bus riders were protesting when white housewives called to say that their black maids had asked for Monday off to enable them to support the boycott. As the boycott dragged on, it picked up support among white housewives. They told their black employees not to worry about being late for work. It was "understandable," if they had to walk or find other transportation. Sometimes white women employers drove domestic workers to their jobs. Middle-class black women activists also helped boycotters by driving them to work in car pools, as did men.

In all of these ways, the Montgomery Bus Boycott was a woman-led movement. It was not explicitly feminist, though it was sustained for a year before the Supreme Court ruled in their favor by a group of women workers who were making claims for their dignity and their rights. It was not exclusively an uprising of women, but women were its main organizers and foot soldiers. These women asked the young Martin Luther King Jr., fresh from graduate school in Boston, to speak for the movement. He became the spokesperson but they were the movement's blood and bone.

Civil rights historian Charles Payne once said of the civil rights movement that "men led but the women organized." Since he made that claim in the late 1980s, an important new literature on women in the civil rights movement has emerged, making clear that women led too. But their leadership has only recently been recognized because it looked a little different from that of the male ministers who became the recognizable faces and voices of the movement. From the visionary bottom-up organizing of Ella Baker and Septima Clark in the 1940s and 1950s, to the stamina of the domestic workers, teachers and social workers of Montgomery, from the courageous students who integrated Little Rock Central High in 1957 to the college students of the Student Non-Violent Coordinating Committee who led sit-ins and voter registration drives in the early 1960s, from six-year-old Ruby Bridges walking alone every day into William Frantz Elementary School in New Orleans to the electrifying leadership of middle-aged former sharecroppers Fannie Lou Hamer and Unita Blackwell in Mississippi in 1964, the Southern black freedom struggle was a revolution which women organized and led, and for which they put their bodies, voices, hearts and minds on the line. It was one of the high water marks in the history of American women's activism and in the history of American politics writ large. So why don't we think of it that way?

One reason is that the movement has become synonymous with a very masculinist definition of leadership in the person of Martin Luther King Jr. and other ministers who were eloquent movement spokesmen. They saw revolution, in King's words, as emanating "from the pulpit down to the pews." That vision of how change is made excluded most women from official leadership posts in civil rights organizations through the 1960s. When journalists and scholars looked at the movement, they saw the organizations that represented it: the Southern Christian Leadership Conference (SCLC), the Congress of Racial Equality (CORE) and the National Association for the Advancement of Colored People (NAACP). These all had men at the helm and men as spokespeople, hiding the crucial work performed by movement women.

And many of those male leaders believed that was how it should be. Dorothy Height of the National Council of Negro Women recalled planning for the 1963

March on Washington. Women activists were stunned that the organizers did not include a single woman speaker:

> There was an all-consuming focus on race. We women were expected to put all our energies into it . . . there was a low tolerance level for . . . questions about women's participation . . . It was thought that we were making a lot of fuss about an insignificant issue.

Women activists found this galling, she recalled, because "we knew most [civil rights] organizations were largely made up of women, children and youth."[40]

Women were also the primary organizers of the main civil rights groups. Ella Baker became a field secretary for the NAACP in 1940 and traveled throughout the South as well as the North organizing. After the Montgomery Bus Boycott, she was one of the seasoned activists who were sent by national civil rights leaders to help the young Martin Luther King Jr. Baker's bottom-up style was much more successful at building membership than the top-down approach used by most male NAACP organizers. People related to her, felt listened to by her. She set up the Southern Christian Leadership Conference for Dr. King in 1957. Frustrated by increasingly entrenched hierarchy in that organization, she "midwifed" the birth of the Student Non-Violent Coordinating Committee in 1960. Yet few people know her name. Part of the reason for that was because she was more interested in lighting the flame of leadership in others than claiming the spotlight for herself.[41]

It can be argued that it was grassroots organizing that ultimately cracked and brought down the system of racial apartheid in the American South. Litigation made a difference. Lawsuits by people on the ground led to Supreme Court decisions desegregating schools, buses, and other public facilities. But neither the edifice of legal segregation, nor segregationist social relations would have been overturned without an upwelling of resistance from the ground up, an activist wave of epic proportions. Ella Baker argued that true revolution rose "from the pews up." She believed that congregations led and educated ministers followed, that the poor and disfranchised broke ground for the more affluent and comfortable, not the other way around. Much of the kind of activism that Baker was talking about came from black women, who made up the majority of those who joined in civil rights agitation between 1954 and 1965.

Anthropologist Karen Sacks, trying to understand the role of women in the civil rights and labor movements, argued that traditional definitions of leadership were inadequate. She coined the term "center women" to describe a horizontal form of leadership quite distinct from the vertical notion of leadership from the top-down. Building on her work, sociologist Belinda Robnett added the concept of "bridge leadership" to explain a kind of activist who built bridges between movements and communities. Mississippi Freedom Democratic Party activist Victoria Gray told Robnett that leadership among women civil rights activists had "a lot to do with a kind of loyalty and influence that you are able to elicit from the people around you." Bridge leaders and center women did not need titles or clerical collars. They were not spokespeople who stood in front of a crowd. Rather they were sufficiently respected by, and enmeshed in, their communities that other women willingly marched alongside them.[42]

People did not make the decision to become involved in civil rights activism lightly. Most often they were exposed to the civil rights movement through already existing women's networks in local churches, community groups and schools. They knew that becoming active in the movement meant putting their own lives on the line. Many black Southerners also, rightly, feared that becoming active in the movement might put families in danger as well. Popular civil rights history, the only kind that most people learn in school, has left us to imagine that the golden tongue and courage of Martin Luther King Jr. was all it took to move a generation to rise up. This is partly true. Millions were moved by his eloquence. But it was not enough to get most people to put their bodies on the line in freedom rides and voter registration drives. They were moved to action by the example of people whom they already knew and respected. Often, these were older women.

A culture of respecting elders – male and female – was central to the movement from its inception. And one of the people most responsible for creating that culture of respect was educator Septima Clark. Born in South Carolina at the end of the 19th century, the daughter of a former slave and a Haitian immigrant laundry woman, Clark benefited from her parents' insistence that each of their eight children would be educated. Clark earned credentials to become a teacher and found work on St. John's Island, in a school of 132 students that spanned 1st to 8th grade. There she learned to communicate in Gullah – a dialect spoken by people of the Georgia and Carolina sea islands that combined English with West and Central African languages.

When adults in the community came to Clark for help learning to read and write, she knew she had found a calling. Her years on St. John's Island began a lifetime of work creating adult education programs for the black freedom struggle. Clark saw education as a tool that people could use to solve the problems they faced in their daily lives. She also believed that the wisdom and skills they acquired over the course of those lives were worth sharing with the next generation. Clark endeavored not only to teach adults but to create schools where African-American adults could also offer their life-learning to younger students. Treating them with respect, she argued, was crucial to their liberation and to the ability of their children to form healthy identities as they were growing up.[43]

When South Carolina fired her from her teaching post for refusing to give up her NAACP membership, Clark took a post at the Highlander Folk School in Tennessee, a retreat center for radical activists since the 1930s. There she worked on her idea for Citizenship Schools for adults, partnering with Esau Jenkins, a farmer and bus driver from St. John's whose formal education had ended at the age of nine. The two developed an idea for schools where adults would be taught to read with an eye toward enrolling black citizens to vote and where math would be taught in ways that helped prevent black adults from being cheated by employers and banks.

South Carolina public school officials refused to fund the project, so Clark and Jenkins raised money through Highlander. The first citizenship school – taught by Clark's cousin, hairdresser Bernice Robinson – opened on St. John's Island in 1957, teaching adults how to sign their names and how to read and interpret South Carolina's election laws. In 1958, Clark, Robinson and SCLC developed a program to train citizenship-school teachers across the South. The schools were wildly successful in rural areas, drawing both women and men as students. Between 1962 and 1966, SCLC and other civil rights groups trained 10,000 citizenship-school teachers. They in turn taught and registered 700,000 African-American adults to vote. By 1970, the schools had touched more than a million people's lives, spreading literacy across the black South.[44]

The Citizenship Schools and the Septima Clark model for enabling black Southern adults to achieve political and financial literacy became an integral part of the civil rights movement. Clark and her Citizenship Education program directly paved the way for the Freedom Schools developed by the Student Non-Violent Coordinating Committee in the 1960s. Clark's ideas also were used in creating the Head Start nursery program, a signal part of Lyndon Johnson's War on Poverty that continues to provide pre-kindergarten education in poor neighborhoods across the U.S. Clark's pedagogical philosophies also influenced SNCC-leader Bob Moses's Algebra Project. In the 1990s, Algebra Project staff began training math teachers in new pedagogical strategies designed to make math legible to poor children in the context of their daily lives. Clark's significance to the black freedom struggle cannot be overstated, yet few 21st century students know her name.

One reason for this is that Clark's intellect and organizing skill were denigrated not only by white South Carolina elites but even by her male allies in the movement. They saw her as visionary but unprofessional, energetic but incapable of strategic planning or management. It was typical of the way women activists have been dismissed in every era. In 1961, when Tennessee authorities threatened to close Highlander, its director Miles Horton sought a new position doing voter registration oversight for the U.S. Justice Department. Recommending him for the job, key Highlander staff elevated Horton's role in the adult education movement by diminishing Clark's.

Although Highlander leaders acknowledged that the original vision for the Citizenship Schools came from Clark, they argued that the program only became what it did through Miles Horton's "constant . . . guidance . . . Mrs. Clark apparently could not grasp principles or conceptualize a systematic methodology. She is not aware even that she lacks this capacity." Clark, who had an M.A. in education and decades of teaching and organizing experience, felt that this flagrant disrespect of her capacities was clearly gendered. She angrily rejected such treatment from both white and black men.

"I was on the Executive Staff of SCLC, but the men on it didn't listen to me too well," she told an interviewer for the Martin Luther King Center.

> They liked to send me into many places because I could always make a path in to get people to listen to what I have to say. But those men didn't have any faith in women, none whatsoever. They just thought that women were sex symbols and had no contribution to make. That's why Rev. (Ralph) Abernathy would say continuously, "Why is Mrs. Clark on this staff?"

The refusal even of their allies to see black women's contributions to the civil rights movement effectively erased them from its histories for years. Few people in the 21st century have heard of Clark or Ella Baker. Fewer still understand that they were at least as important as the movement's famous men.[45]

Looking at the role that older women played in the movement makes clear that mass protest didn't spring out of nowhere. Baker grew up in the first decade of the 20th century listening to her once-enslaved Virginia grandmother tell of how she resisted her masters. When Baker migrated to Harlem in the 1920s, she became an organizer of housewives' protests against high rent and food prices. She later became an advocate for African-American migrant women who sold their labor as domestic workers on the street-corners of New York, and an activist for school desegregation in New York City. Baker's career illustrates the links between the civil rights struggle of the 1950s and earlier peaks of women's activism. And it illustrates how, for these women activists, struggles for educational, political and economic justice had always been intertwined.[46]

Like Clark, Ella Baker chafed at the way that male ministers treated seasoned women activists in SCLC. "The combination of being a woman, and an older woman, presented some problems," she recalled. She found that the "basic attitude of men, and especially ministers" was that women were meant for "taking orders, not providing leadership." She knew that attitude "would never have lent itself to my being a leader in the movement there." And so, when black college students, male and female, began sitting in at lunch counters across the South in 1960, Baker called them together to create a democratic, consensus-based civil rights organization. Out of that meeting, the Student Non-Violent Coordinating Committee was born. Baker would never say that she founded SNCC. Instead, she called herself SNCC's "midwife." The students gave her the Swahili nickname "Fundi" – which means one who teaches the next generation.[47]

Baker argued that "strong people do not need strong leaders." Like Clark, she believed that the most important role of an organizer, "the major job, was getting people to understand that they had something within their power that they could use, and it only could be used if they understood what was happening and how group action could counter violence." She sought to nurture the spark of activism and leadership in everyone. For her, struggling for freedom meant more than overturning unjust laws. It meant combating the internalized racism, sexism and classism that made poor black men and women feel that they were lesser human beings.[48]

No one better illustrated the power of Clark and Baker's vision than Mississippi sharecropper Fannie Lou Hamer. Raised in poverty as one of 20 children, Hamer did not even learn she had the right to vote until she was 45. Outraged that a physician had sterilized her without her consent, she attended her first SNCC meeting to find out how she could best seek justice. Hamer soon risked life and limb to register herself and others to vote. She endured shootings, beatings and derision, growing in confidence and voice. At the Democratic National Convention in 1964, she challenged President Lyndon B. Johnson on national television to seat an integrated Mississippi delegation (the Mississippi Freedom Democratic Party). Her description that day of the terrors that black citizens endured at the hands of segregationist Democrats in the South was so powerful that Johnson broke into her testimony to make a speech of his own.[49]

Though Hamer famously said that day in 1964 that she was "sick and tired of being sick and tired," she continued to organize furiously until cancer ended her life in 1977. Like Clark and Baker she focused on education, working to establish Head Start nurseries in Mississippi, where local adults helped to teach pre-school children. After the passage of the Economic Opportunity Act in 1964 she fought to bring federal War on Poverty monies into the Delta to construct affordable housing. And in 1971 she became one of the founders of the National Women's Political Caucus, which helped women candidates run for elected office.[50]

Though most people think of 1960s and 1970s feminists, when they hear the phrase "consciousness raising," it was Clark, Baker and Hamer who first developed this as a powerful weapon of political and personal liberation. A generation of young black and white women who participated in the freedom struggle were inspired and educated by these remarkable activists. When they dispersed after 1964, some staying south, others moving back to cities and college campuses throughout the U.S., they brought with them the idea that political and personal empowerment were linked. It was a philosophy and a practice they had learned through their exposure to Baker, Clark and Hamer. Like Hamer herself, they also carried the ideals of equality under the law to Washington, D.C. where they began to turn it toward improving the status of women.[51]

Notes

1 Stephanie Coontz, *The Way We Never Were: American Families and the Nostalgia Trap* (New York: Basic Books, 1992).
2 Joanne Meyerowitz, ed., *Not June Cleaver: Women and Gender in Post-war America, 1945–1960* (Philadelphia: Temple University Press, 1994).

3 Elaine Tyler May, *Homeward Bound: American Families in the Cold War Era* (New York: Basic Books, 20th Anniversary Edition, 2008).

4 Betty Friedan, *The Feminine Mystique* (New York: Vintage, 1963).

5 Betty Friedan, "Women are People Too," *Good Housekeeping*, September 1960. See too, "How Readers Reacted," http://www.goodhousekeeping.com/family/work-careers/1960-betty-friedan-article-3.

6 For fascinating histories of Friedan and her famous book, see Stephanie Coontz, *A Strange Stirring: The Feminine Mystique and American Women at the Dawn of the 1960s* (New York: Basic Books, 2011) and Daniel Horowitz, *Betty Friedan and the Making of the Feminine Mystique: The American Left, the Cold War and Modern Feminism* (Amherst: University of Massachusetts Press, 1998).

7 Connie Field, director, *The Life and Times of Rosie the Riveter* (1980); May, *Homeward Bound*, op. cit.

8 Karen Anderson, "Last Hired, First Fired: Black Women Workers During World War II," *Journal of American History*, Vol. 69, No. 1, June 1982, pp. 82–97.

9 Richard Drinnon, *Keeper of Concentration Camps: Dillon S. Meyer and American Racism* (Berkeley: University of California Press, 1989).

10 Valerie Matsumoto, "Japanese-American Women During World War II," *Frontiers: A Journal of Women's Studies*, Vol. 8, No. 1, 1984, pp. 6–14.

11 Zhao, Xiaojan, *Remaking Chinese America: Immigration, Family and Community, 1940–1965* (Rutgers: 2002), and Bao, Xiaolan, "When Women Arrived: The Transformation of New York Chinatown," in Meyerowitz, ed., op. cit.; Charlotte Brooks, *Between Mao and McCarthy: Chinese American Politics in the Cold War Years* (Chicago: University of Chicago Press, 2014).

12 Bao, Xiaolan, *Holding Up More Than Half the Sky: Chinese Women Garment Workers in New York Chinatown* (Urbana: University of Illinois Press, 2001).

13 Chiou-Ling Yeh, "'A Saga of Democracy': Toy Len Goon, American Mother of the Year, and the Cultural Cold War," *Pacific Historical Review*, Vol. 81, No. 3, August 2012, pp. 432–461; see photographs Chinese Historical Society of Southern California exhibit on Chinese Americans during World War II, http://www.chssc.org/history/ww2photos.html.

14 U.S. government, Office of War Information film, excerpted in Connie Field, "The Life and Times of Rosie the Riveter," (1980).

15 Crystal Galen, "Levittown: The Imperfect Rise of the American Suburbs," August 13, 2012 http://www.ushistoryscene.com/uncategorized/levittown/#identifier_0_2685; David Kushner, *Levittown: Two Families, One Tycoon, and the Fight for Civil Rights in America's Legendary Suburb* (New York: Walker Publishing Company, 2009).

16 Elaine Tyler May, op. cit.

17 *Kentucky New Era*, August 13, 1959, "Khrushchev's Visit a Must."

18 Elli Meeropol and Beth Schneider, "The Ethel Rosenberg Story," *Off Our Backs*, September 1975.

19 Sara Knox, "The Genealogy of Treason: Ethel Rosenberg and the Masculinist Discourse of Cold War," *Australasian Journal of American Studies*, Vol. 12, No. 2, December 1993, pp. 32–49.

20 Ethel Rosenberg to Julius Rosenberg, August 9, 1951. Robert Meeropol, ed., *The Rosenberg Letters: A Complete Edition of the Prison Correspondence of Julius and Ethel Rosenberg* (New York: Garland Publishing, Inc., 1994), p. 47.

21 Author's telephone interview with Martha Schaffer, March 11, 1989.

22 Sylvia Plath, *The Bell Jar*, p. 1 (New York: Harper and Row, 1971).

23 David K. Johnson, *The Lavender Scare: The Cold War Persecution of Gays and Lesbians in the Federal Government* (Chicago: University of Chicago Press, 2004).

24 Robert J. Corber, *Homosexuality in Cold War America: Resistance and the Crisis of Masculinity* (Durham, NC: Duke University Press, 1997).

25 Johnson, op. cit. p. 117.

26 May, op. cit., p. 13.; Johnson, op. cit.

27 Ellen R. Baker, *On Strike and On Film: Mexican American Families and Blacklisted Film-makers in Cold War America* (Chapel Hill, NC: University of North Carolina Press, 2007).

28 Jack Cargill, "Empire and Opposition: The *'Salt of the Earth'* Strike," in Robert Kern, ed., *Labor in New Mexico: Unions, Strikes, and Social History since 1861* (Albuquerque, NM: University of New Mexico Press, 1983), pp. 183–267; Mario T. Garcia, "Mexican-American Labor and the Left: The Asociación Nacional Mexico-Americana, 1949–1954," in John A. Garcia *et al.*, eds., *The Chicano Struggle: Analyses of Past and Present Efforts* (Binghamton, NY: Bilingual Press, 1984), p. 65–86.

29 *Salt of the Earth*, Michael Wilson screenplay. Copyright 1953. Published by *Feminist Press*, New York, 1978; Carl Weinberg, "Salt of the Earth: Labor, Film and the Cold War," *OAH Magazine of History*, October 2010.

30 Weinberg, op. cit. See, too, Dorothy Sue Cobble, *The Other Women's Movement Workplace Justice and Social Rights in Modern America* (Princeton: Princeton University Press, 2004).

31 Weinberg, op. cit.

32 ibid.

33 Horowitz, op. cit., and Erik McDuffie, *Sojourning for Freedom: Black Women, American Communism And the Making of Black Left Feminism* (Durham, NC: Duke University Press, 2011) p. 219.

34 Author's interview with Blynn Garnett, Corinth, Vermont, January 4, 1997.

35 Weinberg, op. cit.

36 For the first full revision and accounting of Rosa Parks' long career as an activist, see Jeanne Theoharis, *The Rebellious Life of Mrs. Rosa Parks* (Boston: Beacon, 2013).

37 See http://www.montgomeryboycott.com/profile_times.htm for profiles and interviews with Claudette Colvin, Mary Louise Smith, Aurelia Shines Browder Coleman (interview with her son).

38 *Montgomery Advertiser*, March 10, 1955.

39 *Montgomery Advertiser*, December 4, 1955; January 10, 1956; See also http://www.montgomeryboycott.com/profile_times.htm.

40 Dorothy Height, "'We Wanted the Voice of a Woman to Be Heard': Black Women and the 1963 March on Washington," in *Sisters in the Struggle: African American Women in the Civil Rights-Black Power Movement*, Bettye Collier-Thomas and V.P. Franklin eds., (New York: New York University Press, 2001).

41 The authoritative work on Baker is Barbara Ransby, *Ella Baker and the Black Freedom Movement: A Radical Democratic Vision* (Chapel Hill, NC: University of North Carolina Press, 2005).

42 Belinda Robnett, "African-American Women in the Civil Rights Movement, 1954–1965: Gender, Leadership and Micromobilization," *American Journal of Sociology*, Vol. 101, No. 6, May 1996, pp. 1661–1693; Karen Sacks, *Caring By The Hour* (Urbana: University of Illinois Press, 1988).

43 Septima Clark, *Echo in My Soul* (New York: E.P. Dutton, 1962); Septima Clark, *Ready From Within* (Trenton: Africa World Press Inc., 1990).

44 ibid. "Katherine M. Mellen, Septima B. Clark and the African American Freedom Movement," Unpublished Ph.D. Dissertation, University of Wisconsin at Madison, 1997, p. 138.

45 Memo to Ralph Tyler cited in Kathleen Charron, *Freedom's Teacher: The Life of Septima Clark* (Chapel Hill, NC: University of North Carolina Press, 2009), pp. 285–286. See Septima Clark Oral History Project, King Center, transcript 17, p. 39 cited in Robnett, op. cit.

46 For insight into Baker's desegregation work see Adina Back, "'Exposing the Whole Segregation Myth': The Harlem Nine and New York City's School Desegregation Battles," in Jeanne Theoharis and Komozi Woodard, eds., *Freedom North* (New York: Palgrave-Macmillan, 2003).

47 See Ella Baker Transcript, p. 10, Civil Rights Documentation Project, Mississippi Department of Archives and History. Archive number: OH 81-08.1 Interviewed by Anne Romaine on March 25, 1967. http://www.usm.edu/crdp/html/interviews/b-info.shtml.

48 Barbara Ransby, op. cit.

49 Chana Kai Lee, *For Freedom's Sake: The Life of Fannie Lou Hamer* (Urbana-Champaign: University of Illinois Press, 1999).

50 Kay Mills, *This Little Light of Mine: The Life of Fannie Lou Hamer* (New York: Plume Books, 1994); David Rubell, *Fannie Lou Hamer: From Sharecropping to Politics* (Englewood Cliffs, NJ: Silver Burdett Press, 1990).

51 The most extended reflection on how the Southern Civil Rights Movement paved the way for 1960s and 1970s feminism is Sara Evans, *Personal Politics: The Roots of Women's Liberation in the Civil Rights Movement and the New Left* (New York: Vintage, 1980).

4

EQUALITY NOW! – FEMINISM AND THE LAW

We, men and women who hereby constitute ourselves as the National Organization for Women, believe that the time has come for a new movement toward true
equality for all women in America, and toward a fully equal partnership of the sexes,
as part of the world-wide revolution of human rights now taking place within and
beyond our national borders.

> The National Organization for Women – Statement of
> Purpose – October 29, 1966[1]

This chapter, like the last, begins with the words of Betty Friedan, author of *The
Feminine Mystique*. Friedan's career spanned five decades, a political and personal
evolution that illustrates how the labor feminism of the 1940s continued to sim-
mer beneath the Cold War domesticity of the 1950s, exploding onto the political
stage in the 1960s, then driving the first self-identified women's rights movement
since American women won the right to vote. In the 1940s, Betty Goldstein, the
child of Russian Jewish immigrants, found her voice as a labor union journalist.
Fired by the United Electrical Workers when she became pregnant, Betty Friedan
(she was now married) turned herself full-time to child-rearing. Like so many
women who lost their jobs in the 1940s, she was angry about what had been taken
away from her.

By the mid-1950s, Friedan had managed to revive her career. Writing under
her married name she published in popular women's magazines, distancing herself
from the radical associations of her youth. Perhaps she did this because she feared
that she might be blacklisted or investigated. Perhaps she had shifted her political
views. In any case, Friedan wrote from the perspective of a middle-class wife and
mother. It positioned her well to agitate for change.[2]

The Feminine Mystique, published in 1963, forever altered the conversation about sex and gender in middle-class America. In that book, Friedan proposed the path of paid labor, career and work opportunities as a prescription for the dissatisfaction and isolation of American wives and mothers. By the mid-1960s, she understood the extent to which those paths were blocked by workplace discrimination against women. Friedan decided that her next book would explore legal obstacles to equality.

Civil Rights, Women's Rights and Sex Discrimination in the Workplace

Between 1963 and 1966, Friedan came to know a group of seasoned women scholars, attorneys and politicians whom she would later describe as Washington, D.C.'s "feminist underground." Among them was the visionary legal theorist Pauli Murray. This politically savvy network included Michigan Congresswoman Martha Griffiths, Labor Department researcher Catherine East and attorney Sonia Pressman. These women, all long-time activists, were deeply frustrated with the slow pace of change for women. They had come to believe that the time was right to wage a full frontal attack on legal inequalities based in sex. Active in, and politically informed by the strategies and successes of the labor and civil rights movements, these activists argued that women needed a civil rights movement of their own. Friedan later recalled that East and others in D.C.'s feminist underground "kept saying that what we needed is an NAACP for women. I thought of myself as a writer, not an organizer, but Catherine kept emphasizing that what was needed was outside pressure on government."[3]

Many of the women in this network had roots in the pre-World War II labor feminist coalition that had run the Women's Bureau of the Department of Labor since its creation. In 1961, pressure from this group, with its long-time focus on the status, wages and well-being of American working women, convinced President John Kennedy to create a President's Commission on the Status of Women. He appointed as its chair the most respected woman in American politics – former First Lady Eleanor Roosevelt.

At her behest, Kennedy directed the Commission to investigate sex discrimination in public and private employment and to recommend ways to combat it. He appointed politicians, the heads of major women's organizations, academics and labor union activists. These included several important black women leaders who were focused on how the Commission might push to open up job and career opportunities for the large percentage of African-American women who worked outside the home. From the beginning, there was tension between those on the Commission who wanted to support the increasing percentage of American women now working for wages and those who still felt that women's primary responsibilities must always be to husband and children.[4]

After two years of deliberation, the Commission published its final report, which documented systematic workplace discrimination against women in the U.S. This fact surprised no one who had been working on these issues in Washington. Still the report, published just six months after *The Feminine Mystique*, attracted considerable attention. The initial publication run of 83,000 copies was quickly snapped up, followed by an even more successful commercial edition – with a preface by famed anthropologist Margaret Mead. Few government reports are ever read by anyone outside Washington. The popularity of this one, coming so soon after Friedan's bombshell book, made clear that sentiment was building for some kind fundamental change in the status of women.[5]

Legal scholars Pauli Murray and Mary Eastwood played important roles in shaping the President's Commission recommendations. They argued strongly that federal and state governments must do more to combat employment discrimination against women. They knew that this was unlikely without pressure from the outside so they urged women activists to push the government by mounting lawsuits arguing that any law discriminating on the basis of sex violated the 5th and 14th amendments. Murray and Eastwood believed that these amendments contained such strong guarantees of equal treatment under the law for all citizens that they would be the foundation of any litigation strategy to overturn legal sex discrimination. "Equality of rights under the law for all persons, male or female," the President's Commission report concluded, "is so basic to democracy . . . that it must be reflected in the fundamental law of the land."[6]

The first victory in that campaign came in 1963. Women's Bureau and Women's Trade Union League activists had been campaigning for equal pay for women workers since World War II. By 1963, demographic changes in the nation's workforce had made the issue of equity for women workers impossible to ignore any longer. By 1963, 41.5% of mothers with children aged six or over worked outside the home, a 37% increase over the 1950 numbers. One in four mothers with children under six also worked. Clearly, economic realities for American mothers were shifting faster than popular culture gender norms.

Women's Bureau director Esther Peterson, formerly an AFL-CIO lobbyist and WTUL activist, had begun mobilizing support for an equal pay bill in 1961, writing to unions and women's groups to ask for documented instances of pay discrimination. There was much debate, and there were fierce attempts by business lobbyists to kill the bill. The final version was narrower and more watered down than women in the labor movement had hoped. Compromises hammered out to win votes weakened enforcement language, exempted workplaces with fewer than 25 workers, and substituted the phrase "equal pay for equal work," for the much more encompassing idea: "equal pay for comparable work." Because the labor force remained so sex-segregated, long-time activists had fought hard for a comparable work bill, but they did not prevail. Still, this was a political victory of profound significance. When the Equal Pay Act was signed by John Kennedy in

1963, it marked the first time in U.S. history that pay equity for women was enshrined in federal law.[7]

This position was strongly reinforced by the final report of the President's Commission. Marking a crucial shift from notions that it was somehow unnatural for women to work for wages outside the home, the Commission report concluded that employment discrimination against women was hindering American progress and planting seeds of anger that would soon lead to an uprising. "Barriers to women's employment and to their occupational progress generate feelings of injustice and frustration," it said. "Moreover, failure to use and develop the talents of women is a waste the Nation cannot afford. The public interest requires elimination of restrictions on the employment of women and assurance of fair compensation and equal job treatment on a merit basis."[8]

Toward that end, members of the Commission convinced President Kennedy to establish 50 State commissions on the status of women. These tapped local networks of women – union officials, women's club members, politicians and academics – putting hundreds of women to work on the local level on a range of issues from equal pay to discrimination in higher education. The results were significant.

Between 1963 and 1965, six states enacted minimum wage laws that covered women as well as men. Nine states extended existing minimum wage laws so that they now applied to all workers. Nine more states enacted equal pay for equal work, bringing to 35 the total number of states that mandated equal pay for men and women. Several states overturned laws that discriminated against women in the arenas of property, the courts and age of marriage/consent. State commissions also developed educational programs, lobbied for legislation and ran day-care centers. The country was literally abuzz with attempts to improve the status of women.[9]

In 1964, President Lyndon Johnson appointed a number of highly qualified women to senior posts in his administration – raising the profile of women in Washington. Much more importantly, Title VII of the Civil Rights Act passed by Congress in 1964 made it a violation of federal civil rights law to discriminate against women in the workplace. (It also prohibited workplace discrimination on the basis of race, religion and national origin.) This was, potentially, the most sweeping federal guarantee of women's rights since the 19th amendment gave women the right to vote.

Once again, though, compromises made in the name of passing the controversial bill seriously weakened the government's powers of enforcement. The bill did establish a federal Equal Employment Opportunity Commission (EEOC) to "investigate and conciliate" charges of workplace discrimination. The EEOC was empowered by Congress to issue rulings about whether a particular practice constituted discrimination. But, beyond that, it had but few powers of enforcement. The EEOC was, in the words of its own staff, "a toothless tiger."[10]

Toothless or not, American workers flooded the agency's offices with complaints. Expecting about 2,000 complaints to be filed in 1965, commissioners were overwhelmed when they received 8,852 complaints of workplace discrimination. What surprised them most about the first year's complaints was that one-third were from women, alleging sex discrimination. Expecting to deal with race discrimination, members of the Commission were somewhat baffled about how to respond. Even more vexing was the number of complaints that came from African-American women workers who argued that they were victims of double discrimination. This was uncharted terrain in the arena of workplace law, and the EEOC Commissioners scrambled to make sense of the evidence they were receiving.[11]

Under pressure to come up with guidelines interpreting what constituted sex discrimination, the EEOC Commissioners did so in 1965. These first guidelines were vague and weak. In particular, the EEOC angered activists by their failure to classify as discriminatory sex-segregated job listings, which reserved higher paid jobs "for men only." In October 1965, Pauli Murray publicly condemned the EEOC's stance. Her fierceness and powerful arguments helped catalyze a new women's rights movement.

Murray's career in civil rights and women's rights activism had been as long and storied as Friedan's. Her life, like Friedan's, illustrates how 1960s activism grew out of the radical movements of the 1930s, 1940s and 1950s, and how the labor, racial justice and women's rights struggles of those eras were inextricably linked. Murray herself forged many of those links. She has been described as "a one woman civil rights movement."[12]

The grandchild of slaves, the great-grandchild of a slave owner, Murray was always aware of herself as African-American, Native-American and Caucasian. Family gatherings, Murray would later write, "looked like a United Nations in miniature." Orphaned before she was 12, Murray was raised by her intellectually omnivorous school-teacher aunt. After graduating from high school in North Carolina, she moved to New York City to attend Hunter College, "the poor girls' Radcliffe." Murray loved Hunter but poverty made her skip so many meals that, by the time she graduated, she was suffering the effects of long-term malnutrition. While recovering, she lived for a time in a New Deal work camp for homeless women just outside the city. The camp had been established after Eleanor Roosevelt criticized New Deal youth programs for catering almost exclusively to young men.[13]

The two women met for the first time when the First Lady visited the camp dining hall and Murray was the only woman in the room who did not stand to greet her. Camp administrators were furious. Shortly thereafter, they expelled Murray from the camp. Administrators claimed that it was because they had found a copy of Karl Marx's *Das Kapital* in her room. Perhaps that was the last straw. To ensure that she had not been misunderstood, Murray wrote Roosevelt to explain her refusal to stand. It had been a protest, Murray wrote, against the President's failure to seriously address the condition of African-Americans in the Jim Crow South. To Murray's surprise, Mrs. Roosevelt replied. The two began a decades-long friendship chronicled in their letters. Murray described their early relationship as "confrontation by typewriter."

Roosevelt soon drew Murray into her circle of politically active women in New York City. In 1938, when Murray attempted unsuccessfully to integrate the University of North Carolina, Roosevelt was her most visible and forceful supporter. For the next quarter-century, the two worked together on a range of issues: fighting the poll tax that excluded poor and black voters, drawing attention to the plight of sharecroppers and finally, guiding the President's Commission on the Status of Women.[14]

Murray was as radical in her personal life as she was politically. When she was expelled from the WPA camp in 1935, she left with a white woman named Peg Holmes and the two traveled cross-country together, with Murray dressed in men's clothes and passing as a man. In language that foreshadowed transgender identity politics of a later period, Murray described herself as a man trapped in a woman's body. She crossed the country several times in the 1930s, dressed as a man, hopping freight trains and sleeping in hobo camps. It is difficult to imagine the courage and bravado she had to summon to wander through the American Southwest in the mid-1930s, a cross-dressed, mixed-race woman traveling with her white female lover. Though Murray is best known as a feminist legal theorist, her early life most definitely politicized the personal.

In a photo album from that time, entitled "The Life and Times of An American Called Pauli Murray," the young radical joyously documented her transgressive behavior. Included in that album are various shots of Murray in men's clothes. In the most daring of these, she wore a male sailor's uniform while cradling Holmes in her arms. These shots were labeled – "An armful: Pauli and Peggie." Murray also included photographs of herself as "The Dude," "Peter Pan," and "The Crusader." For the last of these she donned a trench coat and carried a briefcase. Perhaps the recent college graduate was already imagining her later career as a crusading litigator and legal scholar.[15]

In 1936, Murray returned to New York and took a job with the Works Progress Administration teaching English and organizing techniques to garment workers, domestic workers and transit workers. Her supervisor was Ella Baker. Murray came into contact with young Socialists and Communists who sparked her interest in analyzing the economic and legal structures that created inequality. Interested in furthering her understanding of the connections between class and race, Murray sought admission to the University of North Carolina graduate program in sociology. She was denied on the basis of race, though her white great-great grandfather had been a university trustee.

In the aftermath of that failed struggle, Murray turned to pacifism and civil disobedience. At first she was a solo operator. In 1940, she was jailed for refusing to give up her seat on a segregated bus in Virginia while on a trip to raise legal funds for a black sharecropper unjustly accused of murder. Then she began to strategize more broadly about the use of civil disobedience to combat segregation. In 1941, she enrolled at Howard University law school, where she was the only woman in her class and faced sexism both from faculty and students. There, in 1942, she collaborated with fellow pacifists Bayard Rustin and James Farmer, to found the Congress of Racial Equality, CORE. Murray, Rustin and Farmer applied the strategies of non-violent resistance that Mahatma Gandhi had pioneered in India's anti-colonial struggle to fighting Jim Crow in the U.S. Among their more famous protests was a silent sit-in at a segregated Washington, D.C. cafeteria.[16]

A believer in fighting on many fronts at once, Murray continued her education in law to enhance her arsenal of weapons as a civil rights advocate. Having graduated first in her law class at Howard, and the only woman, she was eligible for a postgraduate legal studies program at Harvard. But she was denied because she was a woman. That rejection was one of those electric moments, convincing her that she would have to fight both sex and race discrimination. Admitted to the University of California, Berkeley postgraduate program, she wrote her M.A. thesis on employment discrimination on the basis of sex and race.

In 1950, Murray published her first book: *States' Laws on Race and Color.* Future Supreme Court justice Thurgood Marshall, the man who argued the case that led to the landmark *Brown v. Board* decision in 1954, called Murray's analysis "the bible of the civil rights movement." Respect for her mind did not necessarily improve Murray's treatment by men in the movement. Murray responded angrily when she found out that "not a single woman was invited to make one of the major speeches" at the 1963 March on Washington. Though planners of the march called this an "omission," she believed it to be "deliberate," calling the decision "bitterly humiliating," and "a typical response from an entrenched power group."[17]

By the mid-1960s, Murray was calling legal discrimination against women "Jane Crow" and unapologetically comparing it to the legal edifice of racial inequality. She would spend the rest of her legal career trying to overturn it. She did so through her work for the President's Commission on women and by lobbying to pass the Equal Pay Act. In 1965, Murray and Mary Eastwood, who worked in the Office of Legal Counsel of the Department of Justice, published a ground-breaking article called "Jane Crow and the Law: Sex Discrimination and Title VII." This article laid out a thoughtful, provocative legal strategy for ending sex discrimination under the law.[18]

"During the 1960s," Murray and Eastwood began, "more concern for the legal status of women has been demonstrated than at any time since the adoption of the Nineteenth Amendment." The inclusion of sex along with race, color, religion and national origin in Title VII of the 1964 Civil Rights Act had been a crucial turning point. Women must push to ensure that it is actively enforced, Murray and

Eastwood argued. But they must then go further, building a new campaign on "the extent to which the Constitution may protect women against discrimination." They believed that it was unnecessarily divisive to pursue an Equal Rights Amendment to the Constitution banning sex discrimination. Women were already protected under the 5th and 14th amendments.

Murray had long made the argument that 5th amendment guarantees of due process and 14th amendment guarantees of equal protection under the law should be used to nullify laws that discriminated on the basis of race. Now she and Eastwood proposed that the women's rights movement use the same strategy to overturn laws that discriminate against women.

> That manifestations of racial prejudice have been more brutal than the more subtle manifestations of prejudice by reason of sex in no way diminishes the obvious fact that the rights of women and the rights of Negroes are only different phases of the fundamental and indivisible issues of human rights.[19]

Laws that classified half of the human race as a singular group, Murray and Eastwood argued, were not legally "reasonable" because "women vary widely in their activities and as individuals." Stepping boldly away from the defense of protective labor laws for women, the two concluded that:

> although the classification by sex doctrine was useful in sustaining the validity of progressive labor legislation in the past, perhaps it should now be shelved alongside the "separate but equal" doctrine . . . [J]ust as separate schools for Negro and white children by their very nature cannot be "equal," classification on the basis of sex is today inherently unreasonable and discriminatory.[20]

"A Civil Rights Movement for Women," The Founding of NOW 1966

This vision of legal change was on Pauli Murray's mind when she attended the June 30, 1966 convention of the 50 State Commissions on the Status of Women. Many of the delegates were restless and angry that the EEOC had yet to seriously address sex discrimination in the workplace. Their feelings on that subject were reinforced by the frustration of two EEOC Commissioners – Aileen Hernandez and Richard Graham – who described their work at the agency as exercises in futility. Sex discrimination was viewed as a joke by many of the men on the Commission. Hernandez, the only woman on the Commission, recalled that any attempt she made to address prejudice against women workers was greeted either by "boredom" or "virulent hostility."[21]

The climate on the EEOC that first year was epitomized by the attitude of the agency's first director, Franklin D. Roosevelt Jr. On the day the Civil Rights Act of 1964 went into effect a reporter asked Roosevelt: "What about sex?" He answered, "I'm all for it." A year later Herman Edelsberg, who became EEOC director, told a reporter who asked about sex discrimination: "There are people on this Commission who think that no man should be required to have a male secretary – and I am one of them."[22]

Congresswoman Martha Griffiths called the male leadership of the EEOC "negative and arrogant." But these men were hardly alone. The *Wall St. Journal* ran a piece suggesting that the main result of Title VII would be that the Playboy club could be forced to hire shapeless male bunnies. The *New York Times* opined that outlawing sex discrimination was as unenforceable as outlawing sex.[23]

Just before the 1966 convention of state commissions on women, Richard Graham, who had tried to move the EEOC to a more enlightened place on matters of sex discrimination, was forced off the Commission. Conference delegates hoped to use the gathering to protest Graham's dismissal. The delegates simmered with frustration. Sensing an opportunity, Friedan invited 15 of them to her hotel room. After a long discussion that night, the delegates proposed that a resolution be put before the larger gathering insisting that the EEOC enforce the sex discrimination provisions of Title VII. When they were told that the state commissions had no standing to pass any kind of resolution, the crisis reached a breaking point.

Meeting over lunch, Friedan, Hernandez, Murray and others decided that women would have a better chance of bringing legal change if they formed an independent political group and applied pressure from outside the halls of government. Betty Friedan scribbled the letters "NOW" on a napkin as the women talked. The name stuck. NOW stood for National Organization for Women. The name intentionally left an opening for men to join. Over the summer, 300 women and a handful of men did just that.[24]

In October 1966, 30 of the founding members of NOW came to Washington to elect officers and draft a statement of purpose. Friedan was elected President; Hernandez and Graham were elected Vice Presidents. United Auto Workers' activist Caroline Davis was made Secretary Treasurer. Friedan wrote the group's Statement of Purpose in close consultation with Pauli Murray.

The founders of NOW envisioned a dramatic restructuring of American gender relations – on the social, political and economic fronts. And they promised protests, lawsuits, lobbying and media campaigns to achieve that end. They articulated strategies for women to achieve equality in the workplace, in higher education and under the law. They also called for transformation of women's roles in political parties and government, in the family, in organized religion and in the media.

Reflecting the roots of NOW's founders in the labor movement and in the civil rights movement, the group's 1966 Statement of Purpose focused heavily on workplace discrimination. "Despite all the talk about the status of American women in recent years," it began, "the actual position of women in the United States has declined, and is declining, to an alarming degree . . . Working women are becoming increasingly – not less – concentrated on the bottom of the job ladder." And women of color, Friedan and Murray argued, experienced "double discrimination . . . Two-thirds of Negro women workers," were concentrated, "in the lowest paid service occupations." Discrimination, not lack of capacity, was the reason.[25]

As a partial remedy for this situation, NOW proposed to fight discrimination in education, in the professions and in wages. Women made up fewer than 4% of lawyers and 7% of physicians in 1965. This was partly because they were not admitted to the professional schools at the same rate as men and partly because of the prejudice they encountered in the professions. Women received one-third the number of Bachelor's and M.A. degrees as men in 1965, but earned only one-tenth of the number of Ph.Ds. NOW promised to fight "quotas against the admission of women to colleges and professional schools; lack of encouragement by parents, counselors and educators; denial of loans or fellowships." Even when men and women performed the same jobs, there was a wage gap. "Full-time women workers today earn on the average only 60% of what men earn," the document noted. "And that wage gap has been increasing over the past twenty-five years." (In 2013 American women earned 77 cents on every dollar that men earned.)

Part of the reason women were so disadvantaged in the workplace, NOW founders believed, was the presumption that they would take 10 or 15 years away from wage work to have children. Times had changed. NOW called for the creation of government-subsidized child-care centers that would enable women to return to wage work soon after their children were born. Transformations in technology had reduced the time it took to perform household labor and also lightened the physical labor necessary to perform many jobs. These changes could open doors for women in all kinds of previously male-dominated trades, NOW's founders believed. But this would not happen unless federal and state governments punished discriminatory hiring and promotion.

To achieve that goal, women would need more political power. NOW demanded an end to "separate and not equal" ladies auxiliaries in political organizations. Women deserved "representation according to their numbers in the regularly constituted party committees" and "in the selection of candidates . . . political decision-making and running for office themselves."

As a journalist who had spent a good part of her career writing for mainstream women's magazines, Friedan realized the important role that popular culture played in shaping women's consciousness. As she had in *The Feminine Mystique*, she used NOW's Statement of Purpose to reject demeaning representations of women in media, school texts and religious documents.

IN THE INTERESTS OF THE HUMAN DIGNITY OF WOMEN, we will protest, and endeavor to change, the false image of women now prevalent in the mass media, and in the texts, ceremonies, laws, and practices of our major social institutions. Such images perpetuate contempt for women by society and by women for themselves.

NOW's declared war on negative media images of women foreshadowed the future of the women's rights movement. However, in the end, NOW's primary focus and most lasting contributions would be in the arena of law. The founders believed that their first task was to ensure that Title VII was being properly enforced. In the longer term, they sought to unlock the potential for women in 14th amendment guarantees of equal treatment under the law. NOW's Statement of Purpose called for "recognition of the economic and social value of homemaking and child-rearing" and "a re-examination of the laws and mores governing marriage and divorce."

The 1966 NOW manifesto concluded:

> WE BELIEVE that the power of American law, and the protection guaranteed by the U.S. Constitution to the civil rights of all individuals, must be effectively applied and enforced to isolate and remove patterns of sex discrimination, to ensure equality of opportunity in employment and education, and equality of civil and political rights and responsibilities on behalf of women, as well as for Negroes and other deprived groups.

This belief in the power of the law as a tool for social change was about to produce a rights revolution for American women.[26]

Ruth Bader Ginsburg and the Struggle For Legal Equality for Women[27]

NOW began its combined protest and litigation strategy almost immediately. Workplace discrimination remained at the heart of NOW's vision for improving women's position in American society. But liberal feminists in NOW and in Washington also focused on women's reproductive rights, gender and poverty and continued Murray's quest for broad equality under the law. In these campaigns, they worked closely with the American Civil Liberties Union Women's Rights Project. The founder of that project, a young Jewish law professor from New York named Ruth Bader Ginsburg, was the person most responsible for realizing Pauli Murray's strategy of testing the protections of the 5th and 14th amendments before the U.S. Supreme Court.

Raised by a union garment worker in a working-class Brooklyn neighborhood, Ruth Bader was educated in the 1940s and 1950s in Brooklyn public schools. She would later say that, though her mother died too young, she instilled in Ruth a fierce sense of women's strength and independence. Bader ran with that. She graduated first in her class, at Cornell. She married Martin Ginsburg and bore a child before she had earned her B.A. Admitted to Harvard Law School as a young mother, Ginsburg was one of only 8 women in a class of 500. Chastised by her dean for taking what could have been a man's spot in the law school, she responded by becoming the first woman to make *Harvard Law Review*. When her husband was offered a post at Columbia, Ginsburg transferred to Columbia Law. There she graduated first in her law school class – while raising a young child and nursing her husband through a bout of cancer.

Despite her brilliance, Ginsburg had a difficult time finding a New York law firm willing to hire a woman. So she took the academic path, teaching at Rutgers Law School in the 1960s and then Columbia in the 1970s, where she became the first tenured woman professor of law. In 1972, she founded the ACLU Women's Rights Project. As its director she argued six cases before the United States Supreme Court and wrote briefs for many others. An admirer of Pauli Murray's legal scholarship, Ginsburg shared Murray's belief that the rights guaranteed in the 5th and 14th amendments were the clearest path to establishing legal equality for women.

Her first signal victory before the U.S. Supreme Court came in 1971 in *Reed v. Reed*. Idaho couple Sally and Cecil Reed separated after their son died tragically at the age of 16. Grief drove them against each other and each parent sought to be the executor of the child's small estate. Citing an 1864 Idaho law that automatically gave preference to men when choosing an executor, the Idaho Supreme Court ruled in favor of Cecil. Sally appealed. Ginsburg wrote the brief for Sally Reed. She argued that legal discrimination on the basis of sex violated the 14th amendment's guarantee of equal treatment. Her argument was affirmed unanimously by the U.S. Supreme Court.

In his ruling, Chief Justice Warren Burger was brief and blunt. "To give a mandatory preference to members of either sex over the other . . . is to make the very kind of arbitrary legislative choice forbidden by the Equal Protection Clause of the Fourteenth Amendment." Acknowledging her intellectual debt to Pauli Murray and Dorothy Kenyon, an industrial feminist from the Women's Trade Union League/Women's Bureau network, Ginsburg added their names to hers, as co-authors of the landmark brief.[28]

The idea that sex discrimination was unconstitutional gained significant political traction in 1972 with the passage of Title IX of the Elementary and Secondary Education Act. What Title IX said was simple. It was against federal law to discriminate on the basis of sex in any educational institution that received federal funds. Looking back four decades after the law's passage, most people know Title IX as the law that allowed girls and women to participate in school sports, and that requires colleges and universities to provide equal funding and facilities to male and female athletes. But the law actually covered many of the areas that the NOW had prioritized six years earlier: admissions quotas, professional education, equity in testing, math and science education, hiring and promotion. One section of the bill, little talked about in 1972, would galvanize a new women's movement 40 years later. This was the section of Title IX that prohibited sexual harassment and mandated that educational institutions make sure that women and minorities were not forced to learn in a "hostile environment." (There will be more on that later.) Patsy Mink of Hawaii, the first woman of color elected to Congress, and Edith Green of Oregon, a long-time women's rights activist, were the lead sponsors of Title IX.[29]

Indeed, Title IX did have a very dramatic effect on girls' and women's participation in school sports. In 30 years, girls went from 7% to 41.5% of varsity high school athletes, and from 16,000 to 150,000 inter-collegiate athletes. Those numbers continued to rise in the 21st century. The backlash to Title IX was immediate and fierce. High school and college administrators insisted that having to fund female athletes would damage revenue-producing boys' and men's sports. By 2013, the bill had weathered more than 20 major court challenges. And women students continued to press Title IX cases against their institutions.[30]

1972 also saw the first major breakthrough for those who advocated using the 5th Amendment to challenge sex discrimination. That year, Ginsburg argued *Frontiero v. Richardson*, citing 5th amendment guarantees of due process under the law. The plaintiff was Sharon Frontiero, an officer who sued the U.S. military because it refused to grant her husband a dependent allowance unless the couple provided documentation proving that he was economically dependent on her. Men in the service received automatic allowances for their wives, Frontiero argued. She believed this was discriminatory.

Military administrators insisted that it would be too costly to ask men for proof that their wives were dependent since there were so many men in the armed services. Ginsburg, in her first oral argument before the court, argued that this violated the 5th amendment's guarantee that all citizens receive due process. Speaking without notes, she cited both court precedent and American women's history so cogently that the justices did not ask a single question. One observer described her performance as mesmerizing. Five justices voted in Frontiero's favor, affirming Ginsburg's interpretation of the 5th amendment. They cited the Reed decision as precedent. In *Reed*, the court had ruled that administrative convenience was not a legitimate reason for legal discrimination.[31]

By 1973, Ruth Bader Ginsburg had proven Murray's contention that significant women's rights victories could be won by citing the 5th and 14th amendment protections. Still, she could not get a majority of justices to agree that sex discrimination cases deserved the same strict scrutiny as the court applied to race. In *Frontiero*, the court's most liberal justice, William Brennan, wrote a concurring opinion in which he argued that sex discrimination should receive strict scrutiny. He lost that argument five to four.

Ginsburg came just a little bit closer to that goal in her 1976 challenge to a Texas law that allowed women to buy low-alcohol beer at 18, while men had to wait until 21. In that case, the court established "intermediate scrutiny" for sex discrimination. States would now have to prove that discriminatory laws had a "substantial relationship" to "an important state interest" for a discriminatory law to stand. Over the next few decades, especially after 1993 when Ginsburg became the second female justice on the U.S. Supreme Court, the court's scrutiny of sex discrimination has slowly ratcheted up. Still, sex discrimination continues to be treated differently from race under the law. It is not clear, when, or if, that will change.[32]

Title VII and the Battles Over Workplace Discrimination

The struggle to end workplace discrimination on the basis of sex brought women together across lines of race and class and sometimes even political ideology – uniting conservatives and progressives. For women of all kinds were a permanent and growing part of the paid labor force by the late 1960s. And they all wanted fairer treatment and wage equity with men.[33]

The first victories in the campaign to make paid labor and the professions friendlier to women came soon after NOW was founded. In December 1967, NOW launched the first women's rights protests since the suffrage era, setting up picket lines in front of EEOC offices in five cities, to demand an end to sex-segregated want ads reserving better-paid jobs for men. NOW chapters lobbied for years for local laws banning sex-segregated ads and mounted suits to try to outlaw the practice nationally. The issue finally reached the Supreme Court in 1973.

The *Pittsburgh Press* had continued running sex-segregated ads even after a city ordinance was passed banning the practice. Pittsburgh NOW sued. The newspaper argued that the right to run sex-segregated ads was protected under the 1st Amendment guarantee of a free press. NOW lawyers mounted evidence showing that the newspaper ran fewer ads for women-only jobs and that most of these paid less than those advertised for men. In *Pittsburgh Press v. the Pittsburgh Commission on Human Relations*, the Supreme Court struck down sex-segregated help wanted ads, ruling that they discriminated on the basis of sex, violating Title VII of the Civil Rights Act.[34]

At the same time as they launched court suits, working women continued to bring cases of sex discrimination before the EEOC. In 1967, unionized airline flight attendants, who had been unable to resolve their grievances through collective bargaining, convinced the EEOC to hold hearings on sex discrimination in the airline industry. In 1968, the Commission found that discrimination against women airline employees was systemic and severe. Flight attendants testified to demeaning work requirements and discrimination on the basis of sex, age and body type.

In 1967, TWA introduced paper uniforms for some of its stewardesses, requiring them to dress as either "serving wenches" or toga-clad "Romans." Male customers amused themselves by burning these paper uniforms with cigarettes and spilling drinks on them to see if the paper would dissolve. Another airline gave "little black books" to male customers as they boarded so that they could write down flight attendants' names and numbers. Policies mandating termination of stewardesses who married, became pregnant, gained weight or passed the age of 32 were widespread throughout the industry.

Stewardesses for Women's Rights, a feminist labor union, fought sexist airline advertising. Particularly notorious was an ad campaign for National Airlines, featuring actresses who purred into the cameras: "Hi, I'm Maggie, Fly Me." Stewardesses for Women's Rights also protested a Braniff Airlines ad campaign called the "Air Strip" which featured young women changing uniforms mid-flight in the aisles as male passengers watched.[35]

In 1970, the EEOC ruled that airlines could no longer fire flight attendants on grounds of marital status or age. That was just the first victory. Flight attendants continued to fight corporate policies that allowed managers to fire women for becoming pregnant or gaining weight. It took Congressional action to address the first issue. Weight restrictions that applied only to female employees lingered into the 1990s.[36]

In the same period, NOW and the labor feminist coalition in Washington fought discrimination in hiring and promotion in both public and private employment. Esther Peterson of the Women's Bureau, along with NOW leaders, lobbied President Johnson to add women to his 1965 Executive Order mandating that federal contractors take "affirmative action" to recruit, hire and promote underrepresented groups. In 1967 Johnson agreed, extending the order to cover the hiring and promotion of women. This was a momentous decision.

Affirmative Action programs had a dramatic impact on women's success in both public and private employment. Between 1967 and 1984, employment of women grew by 15.2% in companies covered by Affirmative Action regulations, while there was only a 2.2% increase in companies that did not do business with the federal government. In major banks, the percentage of women managers grew by 20% in just a few years. Percentages of women police and firefighters doubled; the numbers of women hired in traditionally male trades grew as well. Representation of women in medicine and law also grew dramatically. Affirmative action regulations governing loans sparked a veritable explosion in the number of woman-owned businesses. By the turn of the 21st century, woman-owned businesses in the U.S. employed 27 million people.[37]

Throughout the 1960s and 1970s, women activists succeeded in expanding protections against workplace discrimination. In 1971, in *Phillips v. Martin Marietta*, the court ruled that it was a violation of Title VII for employers to refuse to hire mothers of young children if it had no such restriction on employing fathers. Passage of the Equal Employment Opportunity Act in 1972, a victory won by an extremely broad coalition of women activists spanning the political spectrum, amended Title VII to finally give the EEOC powers of enforcement in workplace discrimination cases. And, in 1974, in *Corning Glass Works v. Brennan*, the court ruled that paying women day inspectors less than men were paid was a violation of the 1963 Equal Pay Act.[38]

1975 was a banner year for women's rights decisions. In *Cleveland Board of Education v. LaFleur*, the court struck down a rule of many school districts across the U.S. requiring that pregnant women teachers had to take unpaid leave. This policy had been the target of many campaigns by unionized teachers but it took a court decision to strike it down. Ginsburg and others argued successfully that policies such as this constituted an infringement on women's 5th and 14th amendment due process rights.

In *Weinberger v. Weisenfeld*, Ginsburg argued successfully that the Social Security Administration could not distinguish on the basis of sex in the kind and amount of benefits it paid to widows, widowers and seniors. And in *Taylor v. Louisiana*, the court vacated state laws that kept women off juries or created obstacles to their jury service.[39]

One area of employment discrimination against women that proved difficult to legislate under Title VII or the Bill of Rights was pregnancy. In a series of decisions during the 1970s, the court sustained corporate policies that denied disability insurance to pregnant employees, ruling that pregnancy discrimination was not the same as sex discrimination and thus did not violate Title VII. In 1975, the Supreme Court struck down state laws that prohibited women from receiving unemployment benefits for 12 weeks before pregnancy and for 6 weeks afterwards. Still, many employers continued to fire women for becoming pregnant, forced them to take unpaid leave during pregnancy, and denied medical coverage for pregnancy and childbirth.[40]

In 1976, women activists decided to turn to Congress for relief. They sought an amendment to Title VII that would protect pregnant women and working women who decided to get pregnant. A broad coalition that transcended divisions of race and class, as well as politics, lobbied Congress to make workplace pregnancy discrimination illegal. In 1978, they were finally victorious. The Pregnancy Discrimination Act was passed with bipartisan support. The law was clear. It was illegal to fire, harass or refuse to hire a woman because she was pregnant or might become pregnant. It also required that accommodations be made for pregnant women who could not perform certain tasks, as accommodations were made for any other kind of disability.

The Pregnancy Discrimination Act was a remarkable victory in the degree to which it united women across so many lines of difference. And yet the kind of discrimination it sought to eradicate remains one of the most persistent and intransigent. Like so many other workers' rights laws, the Pregnancy Discrimination Act has largely been enforced by women who have brought suit against employers. In the first few years, these suits were extremely effective. By the late 1980s, the number of women fired from their jobs for becoming pregnant had dropped to an all-time low. But by the early 1990s, the numbers began to rise again and a new generation of women mounted law suits. These suits have continued into the 21st century. Since 2000, most of the cases have involved women who work in low-wage jobs in fast food restaurants and big box retailers. The Pregnancy Discrimination Act, like many of the advances in women's legal rights since the 1960s, has done the most good for the most disfranchised Americans.

Sexual harassment in the workplace proved equally thorny to litigate and to legislate. In January 1972, Diane Williams began working at the Department of Justice. Her supervisor, Harvey Brinson, made repeated sexual overtures. She firmly but politely resisted. After nine months on the job, he fired her. Williams brought the case to the EEOC, charging sex discrimination. In 1973, the EEOC ruled that she had not shown Brinson to have violated Title VII. Williams took the case to court and in 1972 in *Williams v. Saxbe*, a U.S. District court in Washington, D.C. ruled that, because her supervisor had made having sex with him a condition of her continued employment, this was a violation of Title VII's ban on sex discrimination in the workplace.[41]

NOW and the ACLU Women's Rights Project pressed the EEOC to specifically recognize sexual harassment as a violation of Title VII and to establish regulations governing workplace sexual harassment. In 1980, the agency finally did so. But it was not until 1986, 14 years after Diane Williams first filed suit, that the U.S. Supreme Court made its first significant ruling on sexual harassment. In *Meritor Savings Bank v. Vinson* the court ruled that an employer did not need to threaten an employee with termination for his or her behavior to violate Title VII. If an employee could show that an employer, or other employees, had created a "hostile working environment," that was sufficient. But to prove that one worked in a hostile working environment could be a harrowing undertaking, as the women employees of the Eveleth Taconite mine would find out.[42]

Lois Jenson, a single mother who desperately needed a job, found work at the Eveleth Taconite mine in northern Minnesota in 1975. The response of her male colleagues was hostile, to say the least. It took her nine years to complain to the Minnesota Department of Human Rights. A week after she did, she came out of work to find her tires slashed. In 1987, the Minnesota Department of Human Rights ordered the company to pay Jensen $6,000 in punitive damages and $5,000 more for mental anguish. The company refused. In 1988, Jensen and one other woman employee filed a lawsuit in federal court. In 1991 a judge granted class action status on behalf of the women employees of the Eveleth mine. This was the first class action lawsuit against sexual harassment. The women had to prove that their male co-workers were sexually harassing, stalking, and intimidating them.

Jensen left her job at Eveleth in 1992, unable to bear the mistreatment any longer. Soon thereafter she was diagnosed with post-traumatic stress disorder. A Minneapolis federal district court ruled that the company should have prevented the systemic and egregious harassment and appointed a special magistrate to determine punitive damages owed to the women. Over the next four years, he permitted the women to be grilled about their personal lives. They were ordered to give the company's lawyers access to their medical records. Finally, the magistrate decided that the women were just being "histrionic" and awarded them $10,000 each.

The plaintiffs appealed and the verdict was overturned in 1997. But, before a new damages trial could begin, 15 women workers settled out of court with Eveleth for $3.5 million. Patricia Kosmach, one of the original two defendants, was not among those who received money. She had died of cancer in the time it took to litigate the case. Despite the clear ruling in *Meritor* that creating a hostile work environment was a violation of Title VII, the Eveleth case demonstrated how difficult and damaging it could be for women workers to get the courts to protect their rights. Women workers and some men have continued to litigate sexual harassment cases into the 21st century. The Eveleth mine case was a turning point and an inspiration. It was even made into a gripping Hollywood film, *North Country* with Charlize Theron. But the film, like the case itself, was more than a story of justice long denied. It was also a cautionary tale.[43]

Battles Over Reproductive Rights

Like workplace discrimination, reproductive rights was a major arena for legal and political struggle during NOW's first decade. The legal gains from the mid-1960s to the mid-1970s were dramatic. The first landmark case was mounted in the early 1960s by women's rights attorneys at the ACLU. They represented Estelle Griswold, the director of Connecticut Planned Parenthood and Dr. Lee Buxton, a professor at Yale Medical School who were arrested, tried and convicted for providing birth control to married couples. The two were indicted under an 1879 law that made it a crime both for couples to use birth control and for anyone to provide birth control devices, even to married couples. The two appealed their convictions. In 1965, their case reached the Supreme Court. Twenty-eight states had laws that made it illegal for married adults to use contraception. The Griswold decision would determine their fate.

In 1965, in *Griswold v. Connecticut*, the Supreme Court ruled 7–2 that the state's contraception law was an invasion of marital privacy. The majority argued that, although no right to privacy was specifically granted by the Bill of Rights, the 1st Amendment guaranteed the right to private thoughts and free exchange of information. The 4th Amendment protected against unlawful search and seizure, and the 5th and 14th protected against violation of citizenship rights. Taking those amendments together, the court ruled that the Constitution guaranteed the right to marital privacy.

This decision paved the way for a 1973 decision, in *Baird v. Eistenstadt*, overturning the conviction of a Boston pharmacist who had provided birth control devices to unmarried students. This was against the law in Massachusetts. The

Baird decision established that every individual citizen had the right to contraception, regardless of whether they were married. In 1973, a woman's right to private consultations with her physician became the basis for *Roe v. Wade*, which guaranteed women the right to legal abortions through the 24th week of pregnancy when the fetus could conceivably live outside the mother's body. In 1977, the right to privacy was again cited in a decision protecting the right of minors under 16 to birth control.[44]

Ruth Bader Ginsburg recognized the importance of these decisions. They transformed the landscape for American women, especially, as she often noted, poor women who did not have the means to travel abroad for abortions or to states where abortion was legal. But she also criticized the legal basis for these decisions, especially *Roe v. Wade*. These rulings, she believed, should have been rooted in the citizenship rights guaranteed women by the 5th and 14th amendments. The Roe decision seemed overly concerned with the rights of male physicians, Ginsburg said. "The view you get is the tall doctor and the little woman who needs him."[45]

Twenty years later, when Ginsburg was a nominee for the Supreme Court, she was still waiting for the case that would guarantee full equality for women under the law. Reproductive rights, she argued, were just part of a larger package of human and citizenship rights that women had already been entitled to as U.S. citizens. She told the U.S. Senate in her confirmation hearing:

> The decision whether or not to bear a child is central to a woman's life, to her well-being and dignity. It is a decision she must make for herself. When Government controls that decision for her, she is being treated as less than a fully adult human responsible for her own choices.[46]

Women of Color and the Struggle Over Sterilization Abuse

The right to choose when and whether to have children was a central focus of feminist legal strategies in the 1960s and 1970s and successful litigation of that right is widely thought of as one of the signal (if most controversial) victories of that era. For poor women that was even more crucial than for women of means. This was especially true for women of color. African-American women and Native-American women fought hard for access to birth control and were often denied. Alversa Beals, a sharecropper in Sondheimer, Louisiana, begged for birth control in Louisiana in the 1950s and Las Vegas in the 1960s, finally refusing to leave her physician's office without a tubal ligation. She had, by then, conceived 11 children. Ruby Duncan, who also grew up picking cotton in Louisiana, tied herself to a Las Vegas hospital bed in 1967, after bearing her 7th child, insisting she would not leave the hospital until her tubes were tied. These stories were not uncommon for poor women in the 1960s.[47]

But poor women and women of color had an equally pressing reproductive rights issue that galvanized them politically in the 1960s and 1970s – sterilization abuse. By the 1970s, a majority of states had laws allowing forcible sterilization of the "unfit." Involuntary sterilizations had long been challenged in the courts. In 1927, the U.S. Supreme Court ruled in *Buck v. Bell* that forced sterilizations were constitutional. Famously, Justice Oliver Wendell Holmes dismissed the Buck family's arguments against the practice, noting impatiently that "three generations of imbeciles is enough." The Bucks were white and their case was about the legality of sterilizing people with mental disabilities. Through the 1960s, state sterilization laws affected poor women of all races almost equally. That changed in the aftermath of the civil rights movement, when public assistance rolls grew, and racist sentiments stirred up political opposition to federal poverty programs.

Small numbers of women and girls were sterilized by state order every year during the 20th century. Then, in the 1960s and 1970s, various states began experimenting with larger scale programs paid for by federal public health and anti-poverty dollars. These new programs targeted African-Americans, Native-Americans and Latinas disproportionately. Through the 1970s, large numbers of women of color were sterilized routinely and without informed consent.[48]

One of the most infamous and important cases came out of Montgomery, Alabama in 1973. Morris Dees and the Southern Poverty Law Center brought suit on behalf of Minnie Lee and Mary Alice Relf, two African-American girls who had been sterilized without parents present at the ages of 12 and 14. Montgomery welfare department officials had convinced the girls' mother to sign a consent form to have them injected with Depo Provera, a then-untested drug she was told would temporarily prevent them from conceiving children. She was not informed that the drug had not yet been approved for human use by the Food and Drug Administration. In fact, tests on African-American teenage girls were part of President Richard Nixon's anti-poverty program, overseen by Secretary of Health, Education and Welfare Secretary Casper Weinberger. Public health clinics in those years also inserted untested intrauterine devices (IUDs) in poor women who came to them for health care, and performed tubal ligations and hysterectomies without warning patients in advance.[49]

In March 1973, Katie Relf, then 17 and a resident of Montgomery public housing, was picked up by staff from a nearby family planning clinic and driven without her mother's knowledge to have an IUD inserted. A few months later, a family planning clinic nurse arrived at the Relfs' house and picked up Katie's younger sisters, telling their mother they were being taken for birth control injections. Their mother, who was illiterate, was asked to put her X on a consent form for the injections. Mary Alice and Minnie Lee Relf were instead driven to a hospital. The girls were left alone, until a nurse told Minnie Lee to sign another consent form stating that she was 21 years old. Minnie Lee refused. Borrowing change from someone on the ward, she called her mother and asked her to take them home. Another clinic employee attempted to pick up Katie and drive her to the hospital but she locked herself in her room. The younger girls were both anesthetized and surgically sterilized that day. When attorneys later asked Minnie in court if she planned to have children, she said yes. She had not consented to, and did not understand that doctors had performed, surgery that would make her forever unable to bear a child.[50]

The Relf case brought the problem of abusive state sterilization programs to light. A month after the Relfs were sterilized, Massachusetts Senator Edward Kennedy invited the girls' parents to testify before Congress. With the help of attorney Morris Dees, the Relfs also sued the federal government and won. In his ruling, Judge Gerhard Gesell estimated that between 100,000 and 150,000 poor women had been "improperly coerced" into sterilizations in the first few years of the 1970s. "The dividing line between family planning and eugenics is murky," Gesell wrote. In his decision he prohibited the use of federal dollars for any sterilization performed without the patient's informed consent. Gesell also banned local welfare departments from threatening to cut off public assistance to mothers who would not submit to sterilization.[51]

The Relf decision was an important turning point, but hospitals across the country continued to violate Gesell's injunctions. The 1970s saw a calculated effort by some state and federal officials to control the numbers of children being born to low-income women of color. In the Southeast, poor African-American women were sterilized. In the Northeast, women of Puerto Rican descent were targeted. In the Southwest, Chicana and Native-American women went into public health facilities for other reasons and left permanently unable to bear children.

Women of color felt betrayed and violated by these involuntary sterilizations. Their sense of humiliation and anger was deepened by the fact that so many white feminists seemed unable to grasp the seriousness of this issue. "Nobody realizes more than poor women that all women should have the right to control their reproduction," said Johnnie Tillmon, the President of the National Welfare Rights organization. For many white feminists, the battle for reproductive rights and reproductive choice was about access to contraception and safe, legal abortion. For poor women of color, reproductive rights were about a woman's freedom to decide when and whether to have children. The issue of sterilization abuse galvanized women's rights activism among women of color with the same passion that the desire for birth control and safe, legal abortion evoked among white feminists in the 1960s and 1970s.

In New York City and in California, Latina women were at the forefront of the battle against sterilization abuse. In New York, Dr. Helen Rodriguez-Trias was a key figure. Born in 1929, raised in both New York and Puerto Rico, Rodriguez-Trias came to understand racism and sexism from an early age. She turned to medicine, she would later say, because "it combined the things I loved most: science and people." While studying for her degree in medicine at the

University of Puerto Rico, Rodriguez-Trias bore four children and opened up Puerto Rico's first center for newborn babies. During its first three years the infant mortality rate at the hospital was cut by 50%.

Returning to New York in 1970, Rodriguez-Trias became head of pediatrics at Lincoln hospital in the poorest section of the South Bronx. There she advocated on behalf of health care workers and tried to raise consciousness of the hospital staff about health issues in New York's low-income Puerto Rican community. After attending a conference on abortion at Barnard College in 1970, she became a leading activist for free abortions and increasing access to birth control for poor women. She was inspired, she said, by "the experiences of my own mother, my aunts and sisters, who faced so many restraints in their struggle to flower and reach their own potential."

Rodriguez-Trias was deeply disturbed by U.S. sterilization campaigns in Puerto Rico, where a stunning one-third of women of child-bearing age were sterilized between 1938 and 1968. Returning to New York, she helped organize "one of the first consciousness-raising groups of Latino women . . . A number of incredible things emerged from women talking about their experiences," she later recalled. "We shared and we became very bonded. That was the beginning of my identification with women's issues and reproductive health."[52]

During the 1970s, she founded the Coalition to End Sterilization Abuse (CESA), and co-founded the Committee for Abortion Rights and to End Sterilization Abuse, (CARASA). Working with young women from the Puerto Rican civil rights group – the Young Lords – Rodriguez-Trias campaigned successfully to convince NYC to enact a mandatory waiting period between childbirth and sterilization. This prevented hospitals from sterilizing poor mothers while they were still under anesthesia after giving birth. The coalition also persuaded city government to mandate that, before sterilizations could be performed, hospitals must provide counseling for women in their native language.[53]

In Los Angeles ten Mexican-American women, who had been sterilized within hours of giving birth, sued obstetricians at Los Angeles County Hospital. Supported by a broad coalition of Chicana feminist organizations, including Comisión Feminil Mexicana National, the Chicana Service Action Center, the Chicana Welfare Rights Organization and California branches of CESA, the ten mothers charged Dr. Edward James Quilligan, chair of obstetrics and gynecology, with performing surgical sterilizations on low-income Spanish-speaking women without getting their informed consent. The women lost their case, because the judge ruled that the doctors had intended no harm. Undeterred, the women and their allies mounted a grassroots campaign to educate poor Chicana women about the risks of sterilization. These campaigns were sufficiently successful that Quilligan later complained to the *New York Times*. "They come here in great fear, feeling that we are going to grab them and sterilize them."[54]

The situation for Native-American women was even worse. In 1972, Indian nurses working for the Indian Health Service in Oklahoma organized protests against involuntary sterilizations of Native women. Dr. Connie Uri, a Chocktaw/ Cherokee surgeon, was asked to come to Oklahoma to investigate. Uri found records of sterilization of minors, sterilization consents extracted while a woman was still under anesthesia and other human rights violations. Uri had become an activist around this issue after treating a 26-year-old woman who told her that, at the age of 20, with two children and an alcohol problem, she was persuaded by an Indian Health Service physician to have a "reversible" procedure to stop her from conceiving. Without informed consent, the physician instead performed a complete hysterectomy.

Six years later, married and sober, the young woman hoped to start a family. She came to Uri for help but there was nothing Uri could do. "At first," Uri recalled, "I thought I had discovered a case of malpractice." She would soon find that this was not an isolated case. "I began accusing the government of genocide and insisted on a Congressional investigation."[55]

South Dakota Senator James Abourezk demanded an investigation by the General Accounting Office, which found numerous violations of federal regulations protecting patients. Indeed, there was a federal regulation prohibiting the sterilization of minors. Investigators found that was continually being violated in Indian Health Service clinics. Uri and other native women leaders conducted their own investigations as well. A common theme among the women they interviewed was that clinic workers had threatened to take their children away if they did not agree to surgical sterilization.

Ultimately, investigations by native women activists revealed that, between 1970 and 1976 alone, Indian Health Service clinics and their contract physicians had sterilized at least 25% – possibly and as many as 42% – of Native-American women of child-bearing age. Between 1970 and 1980, the number of children born to Native-American women in the U.S. was reduced by one-third. Uri's charges of genocide were not hyperbolic.[56]

Gerhard Gesell, the judge in the Relf case, was unequivocal that the federal government had a responsibility to prevent physicians and local welfare departments from coercing low-income women into being sterilized. In 1975, following hearings convened by Senator Edward Kennedy, Congress passed a series of laws to protect patients from abuse by physicians. As a result of continuing activism, Congress passed the Indian Health Care Improvement Act in 1976, giving Native-Americans greater control over their health care. In 1979, the Department of Health, Education and Welfare issued new regulations on publicly funded sterilizations based on the New York City regulations Dr. Rodriguez-Trias had successfully campaigned for.

The new HEW rules included a 30-day waiting period to allow women to reflect on the long-term ramifications of sterilization, and to prevent physicians and welfare caseworkers from pressuring women to make the decision quickly. A new consent form had to be signed by the woman, her physician and by an interpreter, if her first language was not English. It required that a detailed oral explanation of the risks and benefits of the operation be offered to each woman, and that she be fully briefed on non-permanent, non-surgical family planning methods. Lastly, HEW prohibited health care providers from sterilizing anyone legally incapable of giving informed consent. These included people under 21, people in prison or mental institutions, and the mentally disabled.[57]

Broad coalitions, including women activists of many colors and classes, worked tirelessly throughout the 1970s to bring about these victories. But they did not come without cost. The sterilization abuse campaigns drove a wedge between feminists of color and many white feminists, between poor women and more affluent activists.

The National Organization for Women (NOW) refused to endorse any regulation its leaders felt would restrict women's access to sterilization on demand. So, as women of color fought for new laws and guidelines to prevent involuntary or coerced sterilizations, they came into conflict with almost all of the major national feminist organizations – including NOW and the National Abortion Rights Action League (NARAL). NOW and NARAL decried sterilization abuse, but worried that new regulations might limit women's access to contraception. The battles between feminists around this issue were deep and acrimonious. And they left lasting scars.

The Battles Continue

Campaigns to expand women's legal rights continued into the 1980s and the early 1990s. The most important piece of legislation in that later period was the 1994 Violence Against Women Act (VAWA) which recognized violence against women as a hate crime, provided funding for domestic violence shelters, rape crisis hot lines and educational programs. The bill was the product of a three-year-long Senate investigation of violence against women, spearheaded by Senator Joe Biden in response to two decades of activism by feminist anti-violence advocates. The law filled jurisdictional gaps, allowing for federal prosecution of sexual assault, domestic violence and stalking as violations of women's civil rights. It brought together for the first time law enforcement, social service agencies, and private non-profits to maximize the access to services by victims of violence.

VAWA has been an engine of change in the litigation and legislation of the rights of victims of hate crimes targeted at women. In the two decades since the passage of VAWA, states have passed 660 laws combating sexual assault, stalking, domestic violence, spousal and intimate rape. Federal and local governments have partnered with hundreds of private companies to establish programs to assist victims of domestic and sexual violence. The National Domestic Violence Hotline has fielded 16,000 calls per month, offering interpreters to women victims who spoke 139 different languages.[58]

Certain parts of the law have come under attack repeatedly since it was first passed. The section of VAWA that classified sexual assault as a violation of a woman's civil rights was struck down by the Supreme Court in 2001. And sections of the law seeking to aid undocumented immigrants so that they could report abuse or assault without fear of being deported became flashpoints in Congress during debates over the law's reauthorization. So did sections of the law that attempted to overturn federal laws banning tribal authorities from prosecuting non-native people who commit crimes on reservations. Resistance to this was fierce among conservatives in Congress, though most Native-American women who are victims of rape are assaulted by non-native men. Finally, sections of the bill that provided aid to victims of gay, lesbian and transgender victims of assault and domestic violence have sparked controversy and opposition. Still, in February 2013, a new version of the bill was finally passed, including those new protections as well as protections for undocumented immigrant women who are victims of violence.[59]

Legal rights for women continued to evolve in the half century that followed the passage of Title VII in 1964. It was not in any way a straight line forward. Title IX has been challenged repeatedly in court. Pregnancy discrimination and sexual harassment in the workplace continue to be litigated. The expansions in legal rights won by activist women during those years were nothing less than revolutionary. But once change is won it has to be sustained. The battle for equality under the law goes on.

Notes

1 National Organization for Women website, *Now's History*, http://www.now.org/history/purpos66.html.
2 Daniel Horowitz, *Betty Friedan and the Making of the Feminine Mystique: The American Left, The Cold War, and Modern Feminism* (Amherst: University of Massachusetts Press, 1998).
3 Anthony Ramirez, "Catherine East, Inspiration for Women's Group," *New York Times*, August 20, 1996.
4 The primary accounts of the President's Commission remain Cynthia Harrison, *On Account of Sex: The Politics of Women's Issues, 1945–1968* (Berkeley: University of California Press, 1989), e-book: http://ark.cdlib.org/ark:/13030/ft367nb2ts/; and Alice Kessler-Harris, *In Pursuit of Equity: Women, Men and the Quest for Economic Citizenship in Twentieth Century America* (New York: Oxford University Press, 2001).
5 Harrison, op. cit.
6 Cited in Harrison, op. cit., p. 134.
7 Harrison, op. cit., pp. 90, 102–104.
8 President's Commission on the Status of Women, Report of the Committee on Private Employment, 1963. 1.
9 Harrison, op. cit., p. 184.

10 Alfred W. Blumrosen, "Administrative Creativity: The First Year of the Equal Employment Opportunity Commission." *George Washington Law Review*, 38, 1970: pp. 694–751.

11 "Shaping Employment Discrimination Law," EEOC 35th Anniversary, http://www.eeoc.gov/eeoc/history/35th/1965-71/shaping.html; Alice Kessler-Harris, op. cit.

12 Glenda Gilmore, "Pauli Murray: A One Woman Civil Rights Movement," *Schlesinger Newsletter*, Radcliffe Institute for Advanced Study, http://www.radcliffe.harvard.edu/news/schlesinger-newsletter/pauli-murray-one-woman-civil-rights-movement.

13 Pauli Murray, *Song in a Weary Throat: An American Pilgrimage* (New York: Harper and Rose, 1987).

14 Thomas W. Patton, "What of Her?' Eleanor Roosevelt and Camp Tera," *New York History*, Vol. 82, No. 2, Spring 2006, pp. 228–247.

15 Sarah Azansky, *The Dream is Freedom: Pauli Murray and American Democratic Faith* (New York: Oxford University Press, 2010), pp. 11–12.

16 http://paulimurrayproject.org/pauli-murray/timeline/.

17 Marion Wright Edelman, "One Woman's Freedom Movement," *Huffington Post*, August 10, 2011; Kenneth W. Mack, "Remembering Civil Rights in 1963, Fifty Years On," *Huffington Post* January 27, 2013; Leila Rupp and Verta Taylor, "Pauli Murray: The Unasked Question" *Journal of Women's History*, Vol. 14, No. 2, 2002, pp. 83–87; Rosalind Rosenberg, "The Conjunction of Race and Gender," *Journal of Women's History*, Vol.14, No. 2, 2002, pp. 68–73.

18 "The Negro Women in the Quest for Equality," speech to the National Council of Negro Women, November 14, 1963. Reprinted as "A Female Civil Rights Organizer Condemns 'Jane Crow'" in *The Acorn*, June 1964; Pauli Murray and Mary Eastwood, "Jane Crow and the Law: Sex Discrimination and Title VII," *George Washington Law Review* 43, No. 2. 1965: pp. 232–256.

19 Murray and Eastwood, op. cit., p. 235.

20 ibid., p. 240.

21 Quote cited in Harrison, p. 187.

22 *Washington Post*, November 23, 1965.

23 Kathleen Barry, *Femininity in Flight: A History of Flight Attendants* (Durham, NC: Duke University Press, 2007), p. 152–155; Dan Goldstein, "Protecting the Rights of Blind Individuals," *Braille Monitor*, November 2008.

24 "The Founding of NOW" National Organization for Women website. http://www.now.org/history/the_founding.html; "Shaping Employment Discrimination Law," EEOC 35th Anniversary, http://www.eeoc.gov/eeoc/history/35th/1965-71/shaping.html.

25 ibid.

26 All quotes from NOW Statement of Purpose, adopted at NOW's first National Conference in Washington, D.C. on October 29, 1966, http://www.now.org/history/the_founding.html.

27 "Major Supreme Court Decisions on Women's Rights," ACLU Women's Rights Project, https://www.aclu.org/files/interactive/womensrights_scotus_0303a.html.

28 Supreme Court Historical Society, "Breaking New Ground: Reed v. Reed, 404, U.S. 71, 1971, http://www.supremecourthistory.org/learning-center/womens-rights/breaking-new-ground/#sthash.d0otA3oh.dpuf.

29 Barbara Winslow, "The Impact of Title IX," HISTORY NOW: American History Online, Gilder-Lehrman Institute for American History www.gilderlehrman.org/history-by-era/seventies/essays/impact-title-ix.

30 "Equal Access to Education: Forty Years of Title IX," United States Department of Justice, June 23, 2012.

31 Supreme Court Historical Society, "A Double Standard for Benefits – Frontiero v. Richardson, 411 U.S. 677 (1973)." http://www.supremecourthistory.org/learning-center/womens-rights/a-double-standard/#double.

32 "Tribute: The Legacy of Ruth Bader Ginsburg and the Women's Rights Project Staff," *American Civil Liberties Union Blog of Rights*, http://www.aclu.org/womens-rights/tribute-legacy-ruth-bader-ginsburg-and-wrp-staff.

33 "Equal Employment Opportunity Commission," Legal Information Institute Cornell University Law School, http://www.law.cornell.edu/wex/equal_employment_opportunity_commission.

34 *Pittsburgh Press, v. Pittsburgh Commission on Human Relations* (1973), supreme.justia.com/cases/federal/us/413/376/case.html.

35 Kathleen Barry, *Femininity In Flight: A History of Flight Attendants* (Durham, NC: Duke University Press, 2007); Dawn Klingensmith, "Skies were Often Overly Friendly," *Chicago Tribune*, March 7, 2007; "Fly Maggie," http://www.youtube.com/watch?v=pA10Q5YefQQ.

36 Barry, op. cit; Klingensmith, op. cit.

37 "Affirmative Action and What It Means for Women," July 1, 2000. National Women's Law Center paper, http://www.nwlc.org/resource/affirmative-action-and-what-it-means-women.

38 "Major Supreme Court Decisions on Women's Rights, 1971–2006," *ACLU Women's Rights Project*, https://www.aclu.org/files/interactive/womensrights_scotus_0303a.html.

39 "Major Supreme Court Decisions on Women's Rights, 1971–2006" op. cit.

40 "Pregnancy Discrimination Act: Why is Pregnancy Still a Job-Buster in the 21st Century Workplace?" *National Women's Law Center* June 18, 2013, http://www.nwlc.org/tags/pregnancy-discrimination-act.

41 *Williams v. Saxbe Civ. A. No. 74–186.* 413 F.Supp. 654 (1976); www.leagle.com/decision-result/?xmldoc/19761067413FSupp654_1972.xml/docbase/CSLWAR1-1950–1985.

42 Supreme Court of the United States 477 U.S. 57, *Meritor Savings Bank v. Vinson.* No.84–1979 Argued: March 25, 1986—Decided: June 19, 1986.

43 Clara Bingham and Laura Leedy Gansler, *Class Action: The Landmark Case That Changed Sexual Harassment Law* (New York: Anchor, 2003).

44 *Griswold v. Connecticut.* The Oyez Project at IIT Chicago-Kent College of Law http://www.oyez.org/cases/1960-1969/1964/1964_496.

45 Emily Bazelon, "The Place of Women on the Court," *New York Times Magazine*, July 7, 2009.

46 "Nomination of Ruth Bader Ginsburg, To Be Associate Justice of the Supreme Court of the United States," Before the Senate Comm. on the Judiciary 103rd Cong. 207 (1993).

47 Author's Interview with Alversa Beals, Las Vegas, Nevada, September 2, 1992.

48 Gregory Michael Dorr, "Defective or Disabled?: Race, Medicine, and Eugenics in Progressive Era Alabama and Virginia." *Journal of the Gilded Age and Progressive Era* 5, October 2006, pp. 359–392.

49 Joanna Schoen, *Choice and Coercion: Birth Control, Sterilization and Abortion in Public Health and Welfare* (Chapel Hill, NC: University of North Carolina Press, 2005).

50 Thomas Volscho, "Sterilization and Women of Color," September 22, 2007, *Racism Review*, http://www.racismreview.com/blog/2007/09/22/sterilization-and-women-of-color/.

51 Alexandra Minna Stern, "Sterilized in the Name of Public Health: Race, Immigration and Reproductive Control in Modern California," *American Journal of Public Health*, July, Vol. 95, No. 7, 2005 pp. 1128–1138; S.J. Torpy, "Native American Women and Coerced Sterilization: On the Trail of Tears in the 1970s." *American Indian Culture and Research Journal*, Vol. 24, 2000, pp. 1–22.

52 "Celebrating America's Women Physicians: Changing the Face of Medicine," *The National Library of Medicine*. https://www.nlm.nih.gov/changingthefaceofmedicine/physicians/biography_273.html.

53 Jessie Gonzalez Rojas and Taja Lindley, "Latinas and Sterilization in the United States," *Women's Health Activist Newsletter*, National Latina Institute for Reproductive Health May/June 2008; http://nwhn.org/latinas-and-sterilization-united-states; Rebecca M. Kluchin, *Fit To Be Tied: Sterilization and Reproductive Rights in America, 1950–1980* (New Brunswick, Rutgers University Press, 2011).

54 Kluchin, op. cit., p. 199.

55 Jane Lawrence, "The Indian Health Service and the Sterilization of Native American Women," *American Indian Quarterly*, Vol. 24, No. 3, Summer 2000, pp. 400–419.

56 Myla Vincenti Carpio, "The Lost Generation: American Indian Women and Sterilization Abuse," *Social Justice*, Vol. 4, No. 31, (98), 2004, pp. 40–53; Gail Mark Jarvis, "The Theft of Life," *Akwesasne Notes,* September 1977, pp. 30–32; James Robison, "U.S. Sterilizes 25 Percent of Indian Women: Study," *Chicago Tribune*, 22 May 1977, sec. 1, p. 36.

57 Gonzalez Rojas and Lindley, op. cit.

58 "The Violence Against Women Act: Ten Years of Progress and Moving Forward," *The National Task Force to End Sexual And Domestic Violence Against Women*, http://www.ncadv.org/files/OverviewFormatted1.pdf.

59 Annie Rose Strasser, Adam Peck and Josh Israel, "Congress Finally Reauthorizes Violence Against Women Act," *ThinkProgress* February 28, 2013, http://thinkprogress.org/justice/2013/02/28/1651051/vawa-passes/.

5

RAISING CONSCIOUSNESS, VENTING ANGER, FINDING SISTERHOOD

"The Revolution is What is Happening in Every Woman's Mind"

Goodbye to Hip culture and the so-called Sexual Revolution, which has functioned toward women's freedom as did the Reconstruction toward former slaves – reinstituting oppression by another name . . . Let it all hang out. Let it seem bitchy, catty, dykey . . . frustrated, crazy, nutty, frigid, ridiculous, bitter, embarrassing, man-hating, libelous, pure, unfair, envious, intuitive, low-down, stupid, petty, liberating. We are the women that men have warned us about.

Robin Morgan, "Goodbye to All That," *RAT* 1970[1]

We talk to each other about ourselves. That doesn't sound like much, but it turns out to be dynamite . . . The revolution is what is happening in every woman's mind."

Woman in a consciousness-raising group, 1969[2]

Radical Feminism and the Idea of Consciousness Raising

So now we get to the angry, hairy part of the story – radical feminism in the 1960s and 1970s. This is the brand of feminism that everyone thinks they know, and that most people since that time have shunned lest they be identified with it. This was the era when a small group of women activists tried to launch a feminist revolution. To most Americans, whatever their political persuasion, the legal battles of the 1960s and 1970s were at least understandable. By the 1970s, most people in the U.S. were willing to admit that women were entitled to the same citizenship rights as men. Radical feminists fought battles that were harder for many people to accept and integrate. The struggles they waged were more intimate, more destabilizing of marriages, family hierarchies and gender norms. Radical feminists fought over relationships, over sex, over media images of women. They waged their struggles in kitchens, bedrooms and classrooms. These conflicts exploded with unexpected force in the personal lives of millions in the U.S. – and around the world. In real and profound ways, nothing has ever been the same.

Who were the radical feminists of the 1960s and 1970s? The dominant image is that they were young, affluent and white. That is not entirely untrue. Most *were* of a younger generation than the women who had founded NOW. They did not come of age in the 1930s, as did the labor feminist generation, but in the 1950s and 1960s. Many were women who had been active in the civil rights movement, in the anti-Vietnam war movement, in Students for a Democratic Society (SDS). Their activism was deeply influenced by the vision of Ella Baker and Septima Clark. They believed that changes in consciousness mattered at least as much as changes in the law, perhaps more. As Kathie Sarachild described it: "We were applying to women and to ourselves as women's liberation organizers the practice a number of us had learned as organizers in the civil rights movement in the South in the early 1960's."[3]

The career of Robin Morgan, one of the best-known radical feminists of that era, in many ways encapsulated the movement's turn to consciousness-raising as a fresh political strategy. A child of the 1940s and 1950s, raised by a single mother in what Morgan would later call "an apostate Jewish household," she first became a public figure as a child star on radio and television. Morgan had her own New York radio show in the 1940s, and in the 1950s she played Dagmar Hansen on the sentimental hit television series *I Remember Mama*. Her experiences as a performer, and her ability as a child to reach large audiences through media, strongly influenced her later evolution as a political activist.[4]

As a young woman Morgan was radicalized by the social movements and burning issues that defined her generation. In the early 1960s, she joined the New York City Congress of Racial Equality. She also became a militant opponent of the Vietnam War, and was deeply involved in the student movement. Like a great many of the women who would galvanize and articulate radical feminism in New York in the 1960s, Morgan was also a journalist. A lucid and vivid writer, with a flair for the dramatic, she contributed to many different radical publications through the late 1960s and into the 1970s.

As the decade wore on, Morgan and many other young radical women felt increasingly uncomfortable about the rampant sexism they experienced in New Left organizations. In 1967, a group of women intellectuals, civil rights and anti-war activists founded a new political organization – New York Radical Women (NYRW). One of the group's co-founders was a young painter and political theorist from St. Louis named Shulamit Firestone who was, like Morgan, the child of a Jewish refugee from Nazism. This circle of radical women promised to use techniques and philosophies they had learned in the civil rights movement to promote the ideals of women's liberation. (The term women's liberation drew directly on the language of anti-colonial "liberation" movements then so popular among young Leftists.) Firestone soon began editing a publication called *Notes,* in which many of the slogans of the new feminist movement first appeared in print. It was in *Notes* that these activists first declared that "sisterhood is powerful," and debunked "the myth of the vaginal orgasm."[5]

Early radical feminists drew on lessons learned from the Youth International Party, better known as the Yippies. The Yippies were an attempt by activists Abbie Hoffman and Paul Krassner to use guerilla theater as a form of political protest. Women activists had quickly clashed with male Yippies over their treatment of women. But, they appreciated the political potential of the group's use of humor and irony. In 1967–1968, Yippies had nominated Pigasus the pig for president and pretended to levitate the Pentagon. Hoffman's most famous stunt was a protest at the New York Stock Exchange. When guards attempted to keep him out, he deflected their concern, saying, "I have no picket signs. I'm not here to make trouble." He then proceeded to rain down cash from the balcony so that news cameras would record floor traders crawling around on their hands and news to scoop up the currency. A new form of political protest was born.

Morgan and other radical feminists deployed vivid forms of political theater to draw attention to feminism. An important mentor in that regard and a link to Black Power organizations was flamboyant, militant African-American attorney Florynce Kennedy. In 1968, New York Radical Women and Kennedy organized a soon-to-be-world-famous protest at the Miss America Pageant in Atlantic City, New Jersey. They picked the pageant because it was watched by millions of viewers and they sought quick impact through high visibility.

That kind of media savvy became one of the hallmarks of women's liberation. Protester (and future novelist) Alix Kates Shulman recalled: "When I was growing up Miss America was the symbol of what every young girl wanted to be. That was the kind of attainment that everyone yearned for, to be considered beautiful. There was nothing else." To protest Miss America was gutsy, organizer Carol Hanisch felt. "Because up to this point we hadn't done a lot of actions yet. We were a very small movement . . . Miss America was this American Pie icon. Who would dare criticize this?"[6]

In a press release issued two weeks before the protest Morgan explained why she repudiated "the degrading mindless boob-girlie symbol." The pageant paraded women down a runway like cattle, she said, while male judges appraised their bodies. Also, New York Radical women saw the pageant as "racism with roses." No Black, Hawaiian, Puerto Rican, or Mexican-American woman had ever won, nor had there ever been a "true Miss America – an American Indian." The pageant was baldly commercial, too, using scantily women's bodies to sell merchandise. Finally, Morgan wrote, they rejected the use of "Miss America as Military Death Mascot . . . Last year she went to Vietnam to pep-talk our husbands, fathers, sons and boyfriends into dying and killing with a better spirit . . . We refuse to be used as Mascots for Murder."

The press release put Atlantic City police on notice that, if the protesters were arrested, they would "demand to be busted by policewomen only. In Atlantic City, women cops are not permitted to make arrests – dig that!" It also warned the press that protesters would give interviews only to women journalists. Like Eleanor Roosevelt, who 35 years earlier had closed her White House press conferences to men, New York Radical Women hoped to force newspapers to send women reporters to cover the event. Kennedy disagreed with that strategy and pointedly spoke to as many male reporters as she could find covering the event.[7]

On a bright sunny day early in September 1968, 400 women from across the country marched on the Atlantic City boardwalk, many in aprons and slippers, pushing mops and vacuum cleaners. A few blocks away Kennedy joined civil rights activists to crown the first Miss Black America. Protesters from New York Radical Women carried signs that said: "Welcome to the Miss America Cattle Auction," and "If you want meat go to the butcher!" They crowned a sheep Miss America. Then the women gathered in a circle to chant and toss "instruments of female torture" – bras, girdles, false eyelashes, and copies of *Playboy* and *Ladies Home Journal* – into a "freedom trash can." Carol Hanisch remembers that organizers had hoped to set the trash can on fire "but the police department, since we were on the boardwalk, wouldn't let us do the burning."

Writing in the *New York Post,* Lindsay Van Gelder tried to confer an air of legitimacy and seriousness on the action by comparing it to the burning of draft cards by male Vietnam draft resisters. Her article gave rise to the myth of feminist "bra burners." "The media picked up on the bra part," Hanisch later said. "If they had called us 'girdle burners' every woman in America would have rushed to join us."[8]

A smaller group of protesters waited inside the pageant hall. Alix Kates Shulman had bought a bloc of tickets, paying with a check from the joint checking account she held with her husband. (She did not tell him, she would later recall, because he would not have approved.) Toward the end of the pageant, as the newly crowned Miss America 1968 was giving her acceptance speech, the protesters unfurled a banner from the balcony that said "Women's Liberation." They also chanted "No More Miss America."

Carrie Snodgrass, Miss America 1968, was offended. She felt that the protesters were diminishing the hard work of thousands of contestants who enrolled in the pageant as a path to college scholarships. She resented what she saw as condescension toward other women's choices. Her feeling that these women were condescending and elitist resonated for many American women, who felt that these college-educated, sarcastic feminists did not speak for them. Even so, Snodgrass admitted decades later that the Miss America protest had sparked positive changes in attitudes toward women, and that she and millions of other women had benefited.[9]

To further the revolution in attitudes that they had so successfully begun in Atlantic City, Morgan and New York Radical Women created a feminist guerilla theater group they called WITCH – the Women's International Terrorist Conspiracy from Hell. The name paid homage to their idea that

> witches and gypsies were the original guerrillas and resistance fighters against oppression, particularly the oppression of women down through the ages . . . Witches were . . . the first birth-control practitioners and abortionists . . . They bowed to no man . . . WITCH lives and laughs in every woman. She is the free part of each of us, beneath the shy smiles, the acquiescence to absurd male domination . . . If you are a woman and dare to look within yourself, you are a witch . . . You are free and beautiful.

WITCH activists swore off conventional political actions, favoring "hexes" and "zaps." There was no national organization. "Covens" as chapters were called, arose in cities across the country and pursued their own ideas for actions.[10]

Between 1968 and 1970, WITCH turned up everywhere, as unpredictable as it was controversial. For Halloween 1968, NYC WITCH staged a hex on Wall Street. Wearing fright masks and rags, they called on supernatural forces to produce a decline in the Dow Jones Industrial Average. In December 1968, WITCH covens "hexed" the trial of the Chicago Eight anti-war protesters, and invaded a House Committee on Un-American Activities hearing. "Slowly, solemnly, the Witches filed around the Federal Building," Jo Freeman described these actions, "faces dead white, staring straight ahead, flowing black capes swirling around them. 'Our sister justice lies chained and tied,' they chanted. 'We curse the ground on which she died.'"

In 1969, WITCH members invaded a bridal fair at Madison Square Garden wearing black veils and singing a parody of the bridal march: "Here come the slaves! Off to their graves!" They handed out "Confront the Whoremongers" pamphlets and released white mice into the room to spark chaos. Finally, in 1970, Washington WITCH activists "zapped" a Senate hearing on family planning, chanting and throwing birth-control pills at Texas Senator Ralph Yarborough as he and other men spoke about and for women. WITCH, like many of the feminist organizations of the time was short lived but the movement continued to grow long after its demise.[11]

In the Fall of 1968, representatives of 200 women's groups from across the U.S. and Canada came together for the first Women's Liberation Convention. Among them were members of Women's Radical Action Project (WRAP) from Chicago, Redstockings from New York (a play on the phrase Bluestockings, used as a pejorative to describe intellectual women) the Union for Women's International Liberation from Los Angeles, and Women's Majority Union from Seattle. Young, militant women's liberation activists debated whether feminism should be their primary concern or a component of racial and economic justice, and anti-war organizing. Whichever side the activists took on that question, they all agreed that women's liberation should be focused on changing hearts and minds – which they intended to do through a process called "consciousness-raising."

The idea to use consciousness-raising as a political strategy for women's liberation had first come up at a meeting of New York Radical Women. Kathie Sarachild recalled:

> We were interested in getting to the roots of problems in society . . . We wanted to pull up weeds in the garden by their roots, not just pick off the leaves at the top to make things look good momentarily. Women's Liberation was started by women who considered themselves radicals in this sense.

Though these were women who had been active in the civil rights struggle, the anti-war movement and the labor movement, they had just begun to think about the particular ways that women were oppressed.

Sarachild recalled NYRW member Ann Forer explaining why it was difficult even for politically sophisticated women to acknowledge and identify the sources of women's oppression:

> "I think a lot about being attractive," Ann said. "People don't find the real self of a woman attractive". . . I just sat there listening to her describe all the false ways women have to act: playing dumb, always being agreeable, always being nice, not to mention what we had to do to our bodies, with the clothes and shoes we wore, the diets we had to go through, going blind not wearing glasses, all because men didn't find our real selves, our human freedom, our basic humanity "attractive." And I realized I still could learn a lot about how to understand and describe the particular oppression of women in ways that could reach other women in the way this had just reached me.

Everyone in the group was struck by Forer's insight, Sarachild said. They decided at that moment that what they needed was to "raise our consciousness some more."[12]

By summer of 1969, Redstockings, whose members sought to apply the insights of Marxian class analysis to the oppression of women, issued a manifesto about consciousness-raising as a political tool.

> Because we have lived so intimately with our oppressors, in isolation from each other, we have been kept from seeing our personal suffering as a political condition. This creates the illusion that a woman's relationship with her man is a matter of interplay between two unique personalities, and can be worked out individually. In reality, every such relationship is a *class* relationship, and the conflicts between individual men and women are *political*

conflicts that can only be solved collectively . . . Our chief task at present is to develop female class consciousness through sharing experience and publicly exposing the sexist foundation of all our institutions.

Consciousness-raising, the Redstockings insisted, was "not therapy" because that was about finding individual solutions to problems. "The time for individual skirmishes is past," they opined. "This time we are going all the way."[13]

The very informality of the process was key to its effectiveness. Consciousness-raising did not require incorporation or bylaws. It did not operate according to formal meeting rules. It was achieved through conversations among women that took place in classrooms and dorm rooms, at kitchen tables, in cars, cafés, and doctors' office waiting rooms about topics that had previously been considered personal and private. Everything from the politics of the vaginal orgasm, to shame about rape, physical abuse by boyfriends, husbands and fathers, humiliation at the hands of men with whom they attended school or worked in political movements were all fair game. That last issue was a deeply troubling problem for many women activists on the Left.

Just What Were Those Women So Angry About? Goodbye to the New Left

In a 1969 article called "The Revolution in Our Minds," Chicago activist Jo Freeman wrote that women in New Left and civil rights organizations were tired of men telling them that their concerns were bourgeois, personal or "counter-revolutionary." They were also tired of being expected to make coffee, type meeting notes and offer sex to movement men. It was a long slow burn but, by the late 1960s, relations between men and women in the student Left had frayed beyond repair. There were a few moments in particular that led young women in the movement to give up on former comrades, lovers and friends from the New Left. They were ready to form a movement of their own.

In 1967, Freeman and art student Shulamit Firestone attended a conference of New Left groups in Chicago. They had organized a women's caucus that presented resolutions calling for equal pay, child care and abortion rights, as well as equal representation for women in the leadership of New Left organizations. They presented their resolutions to the conference organizers and insisted that they be put up for a vote. The women had spent days hammering out carefully worded political positions. When their request was ignored, Firestone and other women rushed the podium demanding to be heard. "They just laughed at us," Freeman later recalled. The convention chair patted Firestone on the head and said, "Cool down little girl. We have more important things to do here than talk about women's problems." One month after the conference, Firestone moved to New York City, where she became a driving force in the creation of New York Radical Women and, later, Redstockings.[14]

It turned into a summer of great fertility for women's liberation in Chicago as well. A week after the convention, Jo Freeman and other New Left women in Chicago created the West Side Group – forerunner of what would become one of the most important and wide-ranging radical feminist groups of the 1970s – the Chicago Women's Liberation Union. That summer also saw the birth of women's studies, when neuroscientist Naomi Weisstein and civil rights activist Heather Booth offered the first course on women ever taught at the University of Chicago. It was not part of the regular curriculum, but snuck in through radical activist Staughton Lynd's summer school for organizers. (It would take a few more years and much more activism before the first women's studies department was established at San Diego State University in 1970.)[15]

Weisstein was, by 1967, used to her ideas being marginalized. A Harvard Ph.D., who wrote her dissertation on parallel processing, she had been told by professors there that she could not touch the school's testing equipment because she might break it. When she was a post-doctoral fellow at the University of Chicago, men put their hands on her knee and urged her to have babies instead of researching. When she protested, she was fired. One colleague attributed her anger to "man hating," another to "insatiable lust."

For a while, Weisstein became a guerilla activist, part of a brigade that went from newsstand to newsstand under cover of night pouring glue on magazines with degrading photographs of women. She started a women's liberation band that used rock music and comedy to attack the pervasive sexism of popular music. Ultimately, she published more than 60 scholarly articles, most famously "Psychology Constructs the Female." This scathing critique of sexist bias in psychology was one of the first idol-smashing feminist texts of the era. She also founded American Women in Psychology and Women in Eye Research – creating professional networks for women professionals in psychology and ophthalmology. Still, the contempt directed at her by liberal men haunted her always.[16]

The most public and infamous eruption of New Left contempt for feminists took place at an anti-Vietnam-war protest in January 1969. Activists were planning a rally to protest President Richard Nixon's inauguration. Only one speaker's slot was saved for a woman. Activists in the anti-war movement successfully lobbied the organizers for a second woman speaker. One slot went to anti-war, anti-poverty and student-movement activist Marilyn Salzman Webb; the other they gave to Firestone, affectionately known by her movement friends as "the fireball" and "the firebrand."[17]

Webb had intended to talk about child care, abortion and the need to bring critiques of colonialism home to the movement, to understand the colonization of women's bodies, and the mistreatment of women by movement men. But the booing began almost as soon as she began to speak. Soon all hell broke loose, she recalled. "People were yelling, 'Take her off the stage and Fuck her!' And 'Fuck her down a dark alley.'" Webb left the stage in tears. "These were supposed to be my brothers and sisters . . . Over thirty years later I can still feel the shock."

Firestone stood off-stage, urging Webb to continue. But she too found herself unable to withstand the abuse. This was the moment Webb "knew that we couldn't build a coalition with the Left. Women's liberation was going to be an independent movement." Firestone put it more bluntly in an essay published ten days later: "We have more important things to do than to try to get you to come around . . . Fuck off Left! You can examine your navel by yourself from now on. We're starting our own movement."[18]

At the heart of their newly independent women's movement was a new kind of political activity: women talking among themselves privately and testifying in public about previously taboo subjects. Through their conversations and testimony about sex, rape and domestic violence, among other topics, they found an answer to men who dismissed their concerns as trivial, personal and apolitical. That answer soon became a powerful slogan: "The Personal," they insisted, "IS Political!"

One young feminist described how matters that had previously been considered personal started to feel political for untold numbers of women over the next few years: "We talk to each other about ourselves," she said. "That doesn't sound like much but it turns out to be dynamite. As we exchange experiences we begin to realize that all these discontents we thought were individual, personal problems have common social causes. Women have been kept isolated from each other in their individual homes. We've been taught to see each other as enemies, as competitors. Now we're changing that. We're changing our attitude about ourselves, about other women, about society." As one activist put it in 1969: "The revolution is what is happening in every woman's mind."[19]

Radical Feminism and Mass Media

Because so many of the leaders of women's liberation were journalists, it made sense to them to protest where they worked. Magazine take-overs were a common form of protest in the early days of the new movement. In 1970, Robin Morgan and other New York women's liberation activists occupied *Rat* – a radical New York City newspaper – and renamed it *Women's LibeRATion*. The women were angry that *Rat* subsidized its publication by selling pornography. And its editors had been dismissive of requests to write about the women's liberation movement. Instead they had run scathing articles about "clit militancy," and "pussy power." In the first issue under the new editorial team, Morgan explained why she and other women activists had decided to leave the New Left.

Taking her title from Robert Graves' World War I memoir, Morgan declared "Goodbye to All That." Many have asked about the radical feminists of that time: "Just why were they so angry?" Morgan sought to explain. Citing years of derision and contempt directed at New Left women by their male comrades, colleagues and lovers, Morgan announced a divorce.

> There is something every woman wears around her neck on a thin chain of fear – an amulet of madness. For each of us, there exists somewhere a moment of insult so intense that she will reach up and rip the amulet off, even if the chain tears the flesh of her neck. And the last protection from seeing the truth will be gone.

Morgan listed just a few of the "intense" insults women in the New Left and hippie counter-culture had endured in recent years: promises that the revolution would bring "free grass, free food, free women;" women enduring rape at Woodstock and the Altamont music festival, or being called "uptight" if they resisted; paeans to "groovy" chicks who liked "titshakes instead of handshakes"; *Rat* editors printing covers of nude women to sell more copies; posters depicting aerosol cans that sprayed "Free Pussy." "Where is your sense of humor?" radical men asked. They'd lost it long ago, Morgan shot back. She concluded her 1970 essay in a howl of rage that epitomizes the fury of radical feminism in those years, – powerfully compelling to many women at the time but disturbing and alienating to most people, then and now.

> Goodbye. Goodbye forever, counterfeit Left . . . male-dominated cracked-glass mirror reflection of the Amerikan Nightmare. Women are the real Left. We are rising, powerful in our unclean bodies; bright glowing mad in our inferior brains; wild hair flying, wild eyes staring, wild voices keening; undaunted by blood – we who hemorrhage every twenty-eight days; laughing at our own beauty we who have lost our sense of humor; mourning for all each precious one of us might have been . . . had she not been born a woman; stuffing fingers into our mouths to stop the screams of fear and hate and pity for men we have loved and love still; tears in our eyes and bitterness in our mouths for children we couldn't have, or couldn't *not* have, or didn't want, or didn't want *yet*, or wanted and had in this place and this time of horror. We are rising with a fury older and potentially greater than any force in history, and this time we will be free or no one will survive. Power to all the people or to none. All the way down, this time."[20]

Anxious to finally control the means of publication, feminist journalists staged numerous sit-ins and take-overs of magazines and publishing houses in the early 1970s. These involved not only students and counter-culture activists but also professional women journalists employed by mainstream newspapers and magazines. A group of them – Lindsay Van Gelder of the *Daily News* who had covered the Miss America protest, Nora Ephron of *New York* magazine, *Associated Press* and *Newsweek* magazine writers, freelance journalists Claudia Dreyfus and Lucy Komisar – organized a new group called Media Women to address sexism and denigration of women in the mass media. One of their first actions was to distribute stickers that said "THIS AD INSULTS WOMEN." Across the city activists pasted these stickers over demeaning images of women.

Next they pushed into the mainstream. In the early 1970s, almost all of the editors of the nation's largest circulation women's magazines – *Good Housekeeping, Ladies Home Journal* and *Seventeen* – were men. Some among the Media Women decided that the next step was to put pressure on women's magazines to hire women editors, and to write stories about issues that mattered to women. Susan Brownmiller recalled that they wanted women's magazines to stop "pushing a happy home-maker line from the 1950s that was white bread formulaic." Building explicitly on the sit-ins of the civil rights era, they believed that the best way to pressure male editors and owners of these magazines was to "occupy" their corporate headquarters. *Some* women who were employed full time at newspapers and magazines felt they couldn't risk being part of such an action, that it would be perceived as a violation of professional ethics. The freelancers had no such qualms.[21]

They first turned their attentions to *Ladies Home Journal* editor John Mack Carter, a man who had built his entire career on women's magazines but who belonged to a professional organization of journalists that excluded women. Though the *Journal* boasted a circulation of nearly 28 million women, more than half of its articles were written by men and all but one of its editors was male. Though it had nearly 2 million black subscribers it had run only one article about black women in the preceding year.

On March 18, 1970, 100 women, including Brownmiller, Ti-Grace Atkinson and Shulamit Firestone, streamed into Carter's office to demand that the magazine hire a woman editor-in-chief. Their other demands, according to Brownmiller, were extensive. They wanted *Ladies Home Journal* to hire non-white women at all levels of the managerial and writing staff, to open a day-care facility on the premises for children of employees, to stop publishing ads that degraded women, and to stop promoting the ideals of "kinder, kirche and kuche" (children, church and kitchen), as women's only satisfying path. As the women laid out their demands to a baffled Carter, Marlene Sanders of ABC News arrived with a film crew, pointed a microphone at the editor and asked: "What is your response?" Carter, looking miserable, said nothing.

The occupation lasted for 11 hours. It eventually involved nearly 200 women who hung banners out the office windows for "The Women's Liberated Journal" and happily gave interviews to ABC and CBS television, the *Daily News, The Washington Post, The New York Times, Newsweek* and *Women's Wear Daily*. After extended negotiations, Carter and senior editor Lenore Hershey, one of the only women among senior staff, agreed to give the occupiers control of part of an upcoming issue and to consider opening a day-care center for women employees.

Soon after, when 150 Grove Press employees, many of them women, tried to organize a union, publisher Barney Rossett dismissed them. Many were fired by telegram. Robin Morgan led a march on Grove's offices. Grove was a small press that had made its name publishing controversial male authors including Samuel Beckett, John Rechy and Jean Genet. Rossett described Grove as a "revolutionary" publisher that was unafraid of flouting mainstream sensibilities. In 1959, Grove had published an unexpurgated version of D.H. Lawrence's racy classic, *Lady Chatterley's Lover*. When copies were seized by U.S. Postal Service for being "pornographic," Rossett sued the Postal Service and won. During the 1960s, Grove subsidized its more serious books by selling what Rossett called "European 19th-century erotica" and Morgan called "pornographic books that degrade women." Rossett may have been "radical" in the sexual content of the books he published, Morgan told reporters, but he was dismissive of the women who worked for him and, at times, overtly sexist.

As picket lines surrounded the building, Morgan led nine women into Rossett's office, at the flashy new Grove headquarters in Greenwich Village. The women demanded that Grove put some of its profits from pornography sales into a prostitute's bail fund, a child-care center for employees, and salary increases for Grove's lowest-paid clerical workers who happened to be all women. They also insisted that profits from the sales of works by murdered activist Malcolm X be diverted to much-needed projects in poor black communities in New York.[22]

"No more using of women's bodies to rip off enormous profits for a few wealthy capitalist dirty old straight white men," Morgan and the women occupiers insisted. Then they set out to enjoy themselves. They opened Rossett's liquor cabinet and toasted a new day for women. Rossett was not amused. He pressed charges against the nine former employees, who were arrested, booked and strip-searched. Although the women got little of what they wanted, they garnered sympathetic media attention. Press coverage commented on the hypocrisy of a self-proclaimed cultural radical insisting that protesting employees be arrested.[23]

These occupations served some practical purposes, improving working conditions for women at magazines, newspapers, television and radio stations. But, equally important, these demonstrations – like the Miss America protest – also raised consciousness. Protesters highlighted sexism and denigration of women in the publishing world that had previously been seen as normal – a routine part of office behavior, an accepted means of portraying women and of selling products. Suddenly women were starting to rethink what they were willing to read, to buy, to put up with. Media representations of women began to look different.

A Few More Books That Sort of Changed the World

Given the large numbers of journalists, historians and writers in the movement, it is not surprising that the written word was central to 1970s feminist efforts to raise consciousness about sex, gender and personal politics. In 1970, three feminist books were published that left an indelible mark on public discussions of men and women – even if most people never read them.

Shulamit Firestone's *The Dialectic of Sex*, a manifesto for feminist revolution published in 1970, sought to apply the insights of Marx, Hegel and Freud to explain the ways that sex had functioned historically and how it determined distribution of wealth and political power. *Dialectic* was both lauded for the crystal clarity of its analysis and excoriated for its outrageous proposals. Firestone suggested that childbearing was at the root of women's oppression and argued that harnessing technology to free women from the tyranny of childbirth – by making test-tube babies – was the way to create equality between the sexes. The audacious 25-year-old author interwove and extended the thinking of two of the 20th century's most important male thinkers with ease and grace. Despite, or perhaps because of, its science-fiction-like vision of the future, *Dialectic* became an instant classic. It continues be read in the 21st century.[24]

Kate Millett, who was, like Firestone, both an artist and a writer, published *Sexual Politics* that same year. *Politics* presented "a systematic overview of patriarchy as a political institution."[25] Millett's sweeping analysis critiqued male domination of women in the economic, psychoanalytic and literary spheres, exposing and attacking the egregious sexism in canonical male writers – from Freud and D.H. Lawrence to Henry Miller and Norman Mailer.

Like most of the writings by radical feminists, *Sexual Politics* was both praised and vilified. Helen Lawrence, reviewing for *Esquire*, argued that Millett, and her fellow radical feminists were "not normal women. I think they are freaks." Literary critic Irving Howe, writing in *Harper's*, condemned Millett's writing. She had, he said, "a talent for the delivery of gross simplicities in tones of leaden complexity." He also accused her of ivory tower elitism, a common charge against 1970s feminists. She failed to understand class he said. Working-class women were no more oppressed than their husbands and fathers.

The venom reviewers poured on *Sexual Politics* was, in part, a function of how threatening Millett's ideas were in a time when women were still routinely denigrated and sexualized in art, as in everyday life. But it was also a reaction to the book's success. *Politics* sold 22,000 copies in its first month and continued to sell briskly for years. Doubleday called it one of the ten most important books it had published in 100 years. Suddenly, the word "patriarchy" was being discussed in college classes, in coffee shops, among trade union women and women professionals. It was revelatory. Could male privilege be a system of political, social and economic power rather than simply the natural order?[26]

As the fires built, Robin Morgan collected in one volume – *Sisterhood is Powerful* – some of the most important writings of the new feminist theorists. The book exploded in the lives of women who came of age in the 1970s in much the same way that the *Feminine Mystique* had a generation earlier. *Sisterhood* was a "fat little book," its white cover emblazoned with a red clenched fist inside a woman symbol. It dealt with an incredibly broad range of issues – from sexism in the media to lesbianism, abortion, birth-control pills, sterilization abuse, the politics of the vaginal orgasm, the triple oppression that poor women of color experienced, the sexism and racism of the welfare system, and the daily humiliations experienced by those who were fat, female and over 40. The writers included old and young women, African-Americans, Latinas and Asians, working-class whites and well-paid professionals. The editors, writers, even the printers who physically put out the book, were all women.

If *Mystique* had caused a stir among housewives in affluent suburbs, *Sisterhood is Powerful* could be found on the bookshelves of high school and college age women across the country. In print for three decades, it raised consciousness in waves for several generations of women, particularly those who came of age between 1970 and 1985. Morgan would later say that *Sisterhood* "engendered arguments, divorces, marches, legislation, and entire fields of scholarship–as well as ridicule and derision in some of its original reviews ('shrewish,' 'strident women,' 'malcontent libbers')."[27]

Morgan and her publishers received thousands of letters from women who said the book had changed their lives. As courses on women became increasingly popular in the 1980s and 1990s, *Sisterhood* was widely assigned – a crucial historical document for understanding just what happened to women's thinking in the late 1960s. It quietly went out of print sometime early in the 21st century.[28]

Gloria Steinem, *Ms. Magazine* and the Rise of Feminist Media

Even more influential as a consciousness-raising tool, *Ms. Magazine* was the first magazine owned, edited and written completely by women. Founded in 1971, it was the brainchild of the most glamorous face of 1970s feminism – journalist and political activist Gloria Steinem. Steinem's early years had been as unconventional as Morgan's. Her childhood was spent traveling in a trailer with her parents – an antique dealer and a journalist. She did not attend school regularly until she was 11. She educated herself in those years by devouring the contents of public libraries in whatever town her parents parked the family for a while. After her parents divorced, Steinem lived in poverty with her sister and their mentally ill mother in Toledo, Ohio. Gloria danced in variety shows to help support the family, and entered beauty contests, where she was frequently the runner-up. Like Friedan, Steinem was awarded a scholarship to the most famous of women's colleges – Smith College – in Massachusetts, where she hid her poverty-stricken childhood from more affluent classmates.

Graduating in the early 1960s, Steinem moved to New York to become a freelance journalist. She quickly became frustrated by editors' refusal to assign her serious pieces. Her first break, an assignment to write about college women and birth-control pills, came in 1962. Editor Clay Felker would later say that he assigned her the story because he thought "she had great legs."

The following year, Steinem went undercover for *Show* magazine as a "bunny" at New York's Playboy Club. She wrote a gritty, sardonic story about her experiences that pierced the aura of glamor surrounding *Playboy*, which was then selling a million copies a month. Like other working "bunnies," Steinem detailed how she was forced to take a venereal disease test, was told by her supervisor which customers to date and which to politely stave off and had money deducted from her check for the cost of cleaning her bunny costume. She also deflated the sexual allure of the Club by including little details about life as a "bunny," including the things they used to stuff their bras: tissues, plastic dry cleaning bags, and gym socks.[29]

The piece made Steinem famous but her official conversion to feminism didn't come until six years later, when she covered a *Redstockings* abortion speak-out for *New York* magazine. Steinem had traveled to London for an abortion when she was 22 but she had never told anyone. She was stunned by the bravery of the women at the speak-out who publicly described their harrowing experiences seeking illegal abortions. After that, there was no turning back. Steinem became a true believer. In 1970 she co-founded Women's Action Alliance. In 1971, with Friedan, Fannie Lou Hamer, Myrlie Evers, and New York Congresswomen Shirley Chisholm and Bella Abzug, she co-founded the National Women's Political Caucus.[30]

Dismayed by the condescending coverage of women in politics, she began thinking about creating the first woman-owned, woman-run women's magazine. Early in 1971, Steinem and attorney Brenda Feigen hosted two meetings for women journalists. "All of them," Feigen later recalled, complained of the same thing. "We can't get real stories about women published." Steinem said they should publish a newsletter. Letty Pogrebin, who had done publicity for book publishers targeting women readers, said they should think bigger. Why not publish a slick publication? Why not appeal to the same women who buy popular women's magazines. "I think that being slick and being sold on newsstands was a stealth strategy to 'normalize' or 'mainstream' our message," Pogrebin said later.

That decision would make *Ms.* widely influential but it drove the more radical feminists from the group. They weren't interested in creating a magazine that *Ladies Home Journal* readers would like, recalled memoirist Vivian Gornick. They wanted to blow up the family. The radicals' distrust of Steinem deepened when she turned to Clay Felker, the editor of *New York* magazine, for help. Felker offered to subsidize the printing of the new magazine if he could run a 40-page insert in his magazine. That insert came out in December 1971. The first independent issue ran in January 1972.[31]

The founders debated names for the new magazine but decided on *Ms.* – a way to address women that did not reflect their marital status. The cover of the first *Ms.* featured a blue multi-armed woman juggling many domestic tasks. The image sort of looked like a Hindu goddess they thought. It was an intentional attempt to be, in Steinem's words, racially "multi-biguous."

The slick-looking magazine contained subtly and not-so-subtly subversive content. One provocative piece focused on housewives' epiphanies – the moments when a woman realized that she was carrying an unfair burden in the home. These "Aha" moments brimmed with edgy humor, but also with anger. Another controversial piece showcased the names of celebrities willing to say: "We Have Had an Abortion." Writer Nora Ephron remembered: "Gloria called me and said they were doing a statement that was inspired by what the Danes had supposedly done during World War II, wearing Jewish stars, daring the Nazis to arrest them." Ephron hadn't actually had an abortion, she said, but she wanted to express solidarity with women who had. *Ms.* dared police to arrest famous women for admitting to this still-illegal act.

The first issue also contained an anonymous interview with feminist author Anne Koedt about her attraction to other women. Steinem said: "Clay and many magazine people told me not to include a lesbian article in the first issue – and so, of course, we did." (Still, Koedt did not yet feel safe coming out in the piece.) Pogrebin wrote about raising her daughters in a non-sexist way. Finally, there was a piece called "Heaven Won't Protect the Working Girl," by Louise Bernikow, which explained working women's need for legal protections. "There is no job safe from the perils and humiliations of sex discrimination," she wrote.[32]

Ms. hit the publishing world like a tsunami, far outselling even publishing phenomena like *Mystique* and *Sexual Politics*. The premier issue sold 300,000 copies in eight days. Thousands of subscription cards poured in. There was a veritable flood of letters from readers. One brief letter spoke volumes about how average women responded to *Ms.*: "News-dealer (patronizingly): 'Is this the magazine you girls have been waiting for?' Us (proudly) 'No. It's the magazine we women have been waiting for.'"[33]

Again, the response of many men in media was overtly hostile. Abe Rosenthal, editor of the *New York Times*, told Steinem he'd never hire her again. Gossip columnist Earl Wilson's column on the *Ms.* launch party in 1972 focused on which of the women journalists attending were "well-stacked." When CBS journalist Dan Rather asked President Richard Nixon for a comment on *Ms.* he laughed uncomfortably. His private response to National Security Advisor Henry Kissinger was recorded on the Oval Office tapes that came to light after Watergate: "For shit's sake, how many people really have read Gloria Steinem and give one shit about that?" Even Felker figured the women would only publish one issue. What was there left to say?

Ms. writers had plenty to say but the ad department had such difficulty selling advertising that even they wondered if the magazine could survive. Auto manufacturers refused to place ads because they said that women didn't buy cars. When *Ms.* saleswomen showed them research to the contrary, Cathy Black recalls, admen were furious. "I had an ad-agency guy grab our research report out of my hands, throw it on the floor, and make a gesture as though he were going to spit on it." One representative for California avocado growers was particularly hostile: "Why the hell would I want to put an ad in a magazine for lesbians?"[34]

But *Ms.* did survive; before the year was out it even boasted ads from auto manufacturers and avocado growers. The magazine continues to publish in the 21st century, though since 1991 it has been ad free, raising revenues in ways that don't allow advertisers to influence editorial content. Both before and after 1991, *Ms.* published controversial articles on a wide range of topics, including domestic violence, sex trafficking, date rape, women workers in overseas sweatshops and the glass ceiling in corporate America. Both the immediate success of *Ms.* and its popularity over more than 40 years, illustrate a world forever changed by feminists of the 1960s and 1970s.

It is worth noting that *Ms.*, while the most famous and long-lasting feminist publication of the era, was just the most visible face of a booming international trend. Between 1968 and 1973, 560 feminist newspapers and magazines were published in the U.S. There were hundreds more in Europe, Latin America and Asia. Communications networks were essential to the rise of feminist activism in the 1970s and the periodicals of those years provide a fascinating window onto the thinking, aesthetics and sensibilities of the time. They extended the ripples started by small, informal consciousness-raising groups until they spread everywhere.

The World That Consciousness Raising Remade

The idea that the personal was political remade relations between women and men, women and media, women and work, women and government, women and the health care establishment. Through speak-outs on abortion, rape and domestic violence, sit-ins at media offices and the creation of new woman-run institutions – rape crisis hot lines, battered women's shelters and women's health clinics – feminists in the 1970s transformed the experience of American women on many levels.

The redefinition of rape and domestic violence, and the subsequent legal changes and revisions of police procedure were perhaps the most profound of the changes wrought by radical feminism. Prior to the 1960s, rape was seen as a woman's personal shame. Bringing charges against an assailant for rape often required that a woman submit to police and defense interrogations as if she were herself a criminal. The burden was on her to prove that she had not consented to or "invited" rape. When psychologists approached rape, it was to argue that rapists were mentally ill – men who were unable to control their sexual urges. Sometimes they were cast as men who had been damaged by an overbearing mother and/or a weak father. Rape, many at the time believed, was a crime resulting from out-of-control male sexual urges and female seductiveness.[35]

In the early 1970s, feminists began to redefine rape as an act of violence aimed at reinforcing male power over women. In *Sexual Politics*, Kate Millett argued that rape was not an act of aberrant individuals and unfortunate victims but a kind of violence specific to patriarchy and used to enforce its sex-based hierarchy – giving men greater ability to control women. Writing in the New Left magazine *Ramparts* in 1971 Susan Griffin applied that notion to an American context. She called rape "the all-American crime," offering statistics to show that it was, at that time, the most frequently committed violent crime in America.

"I have never been free of the fear of rape," she began.

> I, like most women have thought of rape as a part of my natural environment – something to be feared and prayed against like fire or lightning . . . At the age of eight my grandmother took me to the back of the house where the men wouldn't hear and . . . I learned not to walk on dark streets, not to talk to strangers.

Rape informed the way mothers and grandmothers raised little girls, she explained. Older women inculcated fear in young girls to control their behavior. As women matured, they internalized that fear and learned to police themselves. "Rape and the fear of rape are a daily part of every woman's consciousness," Griffin wrote.[36]

As consciousness-raising and the politicization of the personal changed women's understanding of rape, a new movement arose. The first impulse of this new movement was to try to exorcise the shame that haunted victims. A speak-out on rape was organized by New York Radical Feminists at Judson Church in Greenwich Village early in 1971. Rape survivors told their stories and listened to those of other women. The effect was electrifying and cathartic. From these speak-outs and the conferences that followed, came a feminist critique of the ways that police, the courts and hospitals treated victims of rape. There was also a ripple effect. Women began talking to each other about their experiences with rape, not in formal settings but in private kitchens and dorm rooms, in workplaces and houses of worship. They noted the commonalities in their experiences; they tapped shared anger and a collective desire for change.

One early empowerment strategy was teaching women to defend themselves. In 1969, Boston's Cell 16 pioneered feminist self-defense classes. Women taught martial arts to other women as a tool that would enable them to move through the world freely and without fear. Women in these classes were encouraged to transcend their reluctance to be aggressive. One famous anti-rape poster created by Betsy Warrior of Cell 16 showed a woman fighting off a rapist quite aggressively: kicking him in the groin and punching him in the face. Emblazoned on the poster was a new slogan: "Disarm Rapists: Smash Sexism."

The women's self-defense movement spread across the country in the 1970s and 1980s, spawning women's martial arts schools, classes on college campuses, and conferences built around women's self-defense. More mainstreamed by the 1990s, and far less ideological, self-defense classes, specifically geared to helping women fight off attackers, could be found among the physical education offerings at high schools, colleges and community centers.[37]

Women's Take Back the Night marches, which began in Philadelphia in 1975 after the murder of a young woman scientist a block from her home, fused the emotional release of personal testimony with the in-your-face empowerment spirit of the self-defense movement. The movement spread quickly to Europe where a massive "Reclaim the Night" march took place in conjunction with a 1976 International Tribunal on Crimes Against Women, which attracted delegates from 33 countries. The marches quickly spread to cities across the U.S. and around the world. The first march in Bombay, in 1978, filled the streets after a pregnant woman was raped. This form of feminist direct-action protest has survived and thrived in the 21st century as an annual event in thousands of cities and towns and on college campuses around the world.

One popular Take Back the Night chant − "Stopping the Silence, Stopping the Violence" − embodied the ethos of the marches. They were (and are) intended to literally take back the streets for women, to make going out at night safer. Anti-violence activist Andrea Dworkin described some of the marches she was involved in:

> In New Haven, Connecticut, 2000 women marched. Street prostitutes joined the March and old women in old age homes came out on balconies with lit candles. In Old Dominion, Virginia, blacks and whites, women and men, gays and straights, in the hundreds, joined together in the first political march ever held in Old Dominion, an oligarchical, conservative stronghold, as the name suggests. People marched fourteen miles, as if they didn't want to miss a footpath, under threat of losing their jobs and with the threat of police violence. In Calgary, Canada, women were arrested for demonstrating without a permit, the irony that a March is the safest way (arrests notwithstanding) for women to go out at night lost on the police but not on the women. In Los Angeles, California, the tail end of a double line of 2000 women walking on sidewalks was attacked by men in cars.[38]

In the second half of the 1970s, feminists began to work more institutionally, to create support systems for victims of crime − rape crisis hot lines, centers for women victims of violence. Anti-rape activists also worked to change the ways that police departments investigated rape, the ways that city and state authorities prosecuted the crime and to limit the kinds of defense tactics that put the victims on trial or, as many women said, made women feel raped a second time.

The energy and emotional fuel for the movement came out of women's personal experiences. Susan Brownmiller recalled being sensitized to the issue of rape when she heard three women in her West Village consciousness-raising group describe terrifying personal experiences with rape. Lee Abrams organized Bay Area Women Against Rape in Berkeley, California after her daughter was raped at Berkeley High School. Activists at the Crenshaw Women's Center in Los Angeles formed an anti-rape squad and set up a rape telephone hotline after one of their members was raped while hitch-hiking.[39]

Washington D.C. Rape Crisis Center, which opened in 1972, put together packets of safety information for individual women, and protocols for hospitals and police working with rape victims. As police and city authorities began to recognize the effectiveness of these approaches, what started as movement-based organizations began to receive funding from city and state authorities. In 1974, the first national anti-rape organization was founded in Washington, D.C. The Feminist Alliance Against Rape (FAAR) became a nationwide clearinghouse for local groups seeking to support rape victims.

In 1975, the most influential and controversial of feminist anti-rape tracts was published – Susan Brownmiller's *Against Our Will: Men, Women and Rape* – a sweeping history of rape from ancient times to Vietnam. Brownmiller argued that rape is about power not sex, that it has been, over the millennia, a consciously used means of enforcing male privilege as a system, that rape of civilian women has been used systematically by occupying armies as a weapon of war, that men have been socialized to rape and to take prurient pleasure in stories of rape, and that women have been socialized both to fear rape and, secretly, to fantasize about it. The single most explosive line in the book came toward the end of the introduction. "From prehistoric times to the present, I believe, rape has played a critical function. It is nothing more or less than a conscious process of intimidation by which all men keep all women in a state of fear."[40]

Brownmiller's book was explosive and powerful. It was loved and hated. It was enthusiastically received in some quarters, garnering a front-page review in the *New York Times Book Review* and serialization in four major publications. It was featured by book clubs. It was assigned in college classes, where it provoked a firestorm of emotion. I sat in one in the late 1970s in which students reacted as though a depth charge had been set off in our lives. Many of the women were electrified at all the ways that this book shed harsh light on our own experiences. One man threw the book angrily across the room, hurt and offended that Brown-miller seemed to be suggesting that all men used the threat of rape to intimidate women. Some walked out. Most of us stayed. The ensuing discussion was painful and divisive.

The book drew fierce criticism from some black feminists, including Angela Davis and bell hooks, who felt that Brownmiller said too little about the rape of black women as a cornerstone of white supremacy. *Against Our Will*, Davis argued, reinforced the stereotype of the black rapist by suggesting that white women who accused black men of rape were not always lying, and that those who were had often been coerced and were – in their own way – victims. Other critics felt that Brownmiller went too far in her fierce condemnation of Eldridge Cleaver's *Soul on Ice*, which she saw as an apologia for black men who raped white women. The argument delegitimized the entire Black Power movement, some critics felt.

Brownmiller would later explain what she had hoped to do with her controversial treatment of race and rape. She wanted to bring the Left, African-American activists and white feminists together to take on rape as a global human rights issue. "By pitting white women against black men in their effort to alert the nation to the extra punishment wreaked on Blacks," she wrote ". . . leftists and liberals . . . drove a wedge between two movements for human rights and today we are still struggling to overcome this historic legacy."

Critics tarnished the book's reputation and Brownmiller's as well. Still her sweeping, ambitious, flawed and provocative book became a feminist classic. *Against Our Will* was translated into 16 languages and read around the world. It continues to be a jumping off point for debates about the nature and history of rape; it still evokes epiphanies; it still sparks anger and frustration and probably, now and then, someone still throws it across a room.[41]

Tensions between white radical feminists and women of color in the 1970s did not quickly disappear. But fragile, complicated coalitions emerged around the issue of violence against women. Surveys showed that black women were as supportive of feminist goals generally as white women and certainly as concerned about sexual and domestic violence. But they often organized on their own – in groups like the National Black Feminist Organization (NBFO), created in 1973, and the Combahee River Collective, founded in 1975.

When the NBFO held its first convention in 1973, it ran well-attended workshops on black women and rape. Essie Green Williams, one of the organizers, argued that black women were ready to get involved in the anti-rape movement even if they were reluctant to publicly criticize black men. "At the same time that the black woman does not want to be another foot on the black man's head," said Williams, "she is trying to point out that a lot of the interactions that go on between black men and black women are very oppressive." Despite initial distance, black feminist groups began to work closely with white-run feminist organizations to produce literature, organize conferences and lobby for more generous funding of rape crisis centers and hot lines.[42]

By the mid-1970s national anti-rape networks had emerged and they began to transform treatment of victims and prosecution of perpetrators. In 1974, the Feminist Alliance Against Rape linked anti-rape groups nationally. NOW began to work on the issue through 300 local and state rape task forces. Robin Morgan co-founded the National Network of Rape Crisis Centers to coordinate lobbying and to act as a clearinghouse for information and resources for local groups. One of the first victories of these new networks was the creation of a National Center for the Prevention and Control of Rape at the National Institute for Mental Health. The new government agency channeled large sums into developing new treatments for traumatized sexual assault victims. The grass-roots feminist campaign against rape dovetailed with a growing law-and-order sensibility nationally. The result was more energetic prosecutions of rapists and reform of police practices for investigating rape.[43]

Activist and scholar Angela Davis has argued that some white anti-rape activists were too quick to ally with the social conservative campaigns for law and order that were popular in the 1970s. Those alliances were part of the reason some women of color distrusted the anti-rape movement initially. Black women feared that anti-rape activists would revive long-held stereotypes of black men as rapists, and that a heightened focus on arrest and punishment of rapists would disproportionately, and often unjustly, target black men. (The arrest, conviction and long-term imprisonment of five innocent black and Latino teenagers in New York 1989 for the rape of a white woman jogger in Central Park confirmed for many that those fears were justified.)[44]

Still, rape was an issue that transcended race and class, and both African-American women and Latinas participated in the movement to support survivors. African-American activist Loretta Ross recalled the Washington, D.C. anti-rape movement as a place where black and Latina women leaders worked alongside the white women who had founded the group. They were drawn in, she says in part, because the Rape Crisis Center focused not only on sexual assault, but domestic violence, sexual harassment on the job and also questions of poverty and racism. Nkenge Toure recalled that black women took information about resources available to rape victims out into the black community, fostering grass-roots organizing among black women who had never before associated themselves with feminism.[45]

Still some women of color continued to feel uncomfortable in white dominated rape crisis centers. In particular, in California, Chicanas complained about being lectured to by white women activists who felt they were not feminist enough. For these and other reasons, they preferred to organize resources for rape victims in their own community. In Los Angeles, in 1976, a group of Chicana activists set up the East Los Angeles Rape Hotline. The East L.A. hotline offered services in Spanish and English. In 1978, Nilda Rimonte set up a multi-lingual hotline for Asian and Pacific women – with counselors who could handle calls in Vietnamese, Korean, Laotian, and Tagalog. These groups built creative programs to educate their communities. The East L.A. group produced and aired a tele-novela about a Mexican-American family dealing with the rape of a teenage girl. They also staged theatrical productions free to the community that tried to reinforce belief in the honor and integrity of rape survivors.[46]

On the national level, NOW and other feminist groups lobbied for changes in rape law that would benefit all women. By 1980, almost all states had changed their rape laws and their courtroom practices in rape cases. Defense attorneys could no longer introduce a victim's sexual history as evidence of implied consent. The definition of consent was changed so that "submission" did not equate with consent and a woman could not be said to have consented if she was unconscious. States no longer required survivors to provide testimony from a witness to corroborate their accusations of rape. Rape within marriage became a crime in most states.[47]

During the 1970s and 1980s, many police departments began to hire female officers to conduct rape investigations. They also retrained officers and prosecutors investigating violent crimes against women, and hired investigators who were sensitive to victims rather than naturally allying with perpetrators. And, increasingly, public monies flowed to rape crisis centers. By the end of the 1970s, there were over 1,000 rape crisis centers in the U.S., many of them receiving critical funding from city, state and federal agencies.

These were huge transformations in the way rape was conceptualized and treated in the U.S. As these new institutions acquired public funding, they became more service-oriented, more professionalized and less focused on consciousness-raising and feminist principles. When a new generation of young activists began to fight against rape culture in the second decade of the 21st century, they found once again that they had to engage in consciousness-raising among survivors, among their peers, among college administrators and counselors and among police. Still, they inherited an infrastructure that could provide support and information, as well as changes in law enforcement, government and the courts that enabled them to start at a very different place than activists had in 1970.[48]

Politicization of violence against women in the 1970s also radically changed perceptions of domestic – or intimate – abuse. Along with the idea that the personal is political, the women's liberation movement focus on power relations within the home set the stage for activists to combat violence against women by husbands and boyfriends. Like rape crisis centers, the earliest battered women's shelters were creations of the 1970s women's movement, arising out of radical feminism's preoccupation with changing thought as well as law and material circumstances. Women's Advocates – one of the first shelters for battered women – founded in Minneapolis in 1971, grew out of a local consciousness-raising group. Myriad others did as well.[49]

The battered women's movement sought to create safe havens for women seeking refuge from violence in their homes. Activist-run shelters provided services for battered women – helping them to locate new housing, find jobs and get health care. But, at the same time, shelter staff encouraged victims to see battering not as a problem only in their personal relationships, but as part of a system of male control over women. During the 1970s, hundreds of volunteer shelters were founded by feminist groups across the United States, as well as in the UK and Europe.[50]

Again there was one book that changed public discussion on the issue of domestic violence – *Battered Wives* by Del Martin, first published in 1976. Martin was well known among gay and lesbian activists as one of the founders of the U.S. gay rights movement (see Chapter 7). Through the publication of *Battered Wives*, Martin helped launch another political struggle. The book was built around harrowing first-person accounts of intimate violence that were shocking to almost everyone who read them. Even people who thought they understood the problem were taken aback by the frightening stories Martin collected. The book opened with a letter from a woman whose college graduate husband had kicked her in the abdomen while she was pregnant. This was not an extreme case Martin wrote. "Time and again, battered wives tell of being hit or kicked in the stomach while pregnant."[51]

As shocking as these stories were, Martin argued that violence against women was not a problem caused primarily by mentally ill men. It transcended every class, race and ethnic culture, Martin wrote, because men were socialized to believe that male domination of women was the normal human state. And women were socialized to accept that. Martin's view of domestic partner violence as integral to a socio-economic system of domination allowed her to express sympathy even with batterers. "The economic and social structure of our present society," she wrote, "depends upon the degradation, subjugation, and exploitation of women. Many husbands who batter their wives in anger and frustration are really striking out against a system that entraps them, too."[52]

Battered Wives told real women's stories of attempting to get out of violent relationships. When they attempted to leave their abusers, the women in Martin's book encountered resistance from and obstruction by police, courts, pastors, even their own parents. None of this was a product of individual relationship issues or specific triggering events, Martin argued. It was rooted in long-held views about men's and women's proper roles in marriage, and it was reinforced by women's lack of economic power.[53]

Battered Wives critiqued the legal and social service systems, police and the courts. Martin suggested concrete ways that each could reform. She called on judges and counselors to de-emphasize reconciliation between husbands and wives, to push for jail time for abusers rather than granting them probation. And she asked police to enforce court orders intended to keep violent husbands away from their wives. Martin's book was the first to make it widely known that women were in greatest danger in the weeks and months after leaving their abusers. Funding shelters and enforcing restraining orders were the best ways that governments could protect women in those vulnerable times.[54]

As the issue finally began receiving attention, NOW established a national task force on domestic violence. This concern resonated internationally. Indeed, the movement gained strength in Europe before it did in the U.S. On March 4, 1976, 8,200 women from 33 countries came together in Brussels for the first International Tribunal on Crimes Against Women. The delegates developed multi-national strategies to combat rape, battering, forced sterilization, mutilation and economic and legal crimes against women. They sent a resolution on domestic violence – containing specific recommendations – to the governments of 40 nations. Smaller tribunals met in New York and San Francisco at the same time where women aired experiences with intimate violence and offered prescriptions for change.[55]

Between 1976 and 1979, domestic violence advocates launched successful lawsuits against police departments in Oakland, New York City and numerous other cities. Most of these cases were settled out of court but yielded significant improvements in how police approached domestic violence cases. Departments began training officers to better understand the dynamics of violent relationships and to treat battered women as crime victims rather than wives in a disagreement with their husbands.

Some municipalities instituted mandatory arrest policies that forced police to remove abusers from the home and keep them away from their victims for a set period of time. They also beefed up enforcement of restraining orders. In Chicago, women activists founded the Abused Women's Coalition and an allied Legal Center. It pioneered tactics for helping women who had left their abusers get back onto their feet – providing housing and legal assistance. The model was soon picked up elsewhere.[56]

As late as 1979, fewer than half of domestic violence shelters in the U.S. were receiving public funding. As a result, the vast majority of women seeking refuge had to be turned away. Hundreds of groups devoted to fighting domestic violence came together to lobby successfully for state laws that increased funding for services for victims of violence. By the early 1980s, there were 700 shelters in the U.S. serving around 225,000 women and children, many of them funded with public monies.

Still, a great many families' needs were going unmet. Drastic budget cuts in social services during the first years of Ronald Reagan's presidency in the 1980s, sharply reduced federal funding to battered women's services. In 1984, advocates successfully pushed through Congress the first federal legislation to increase funding for domestic violence services – the Family Violence Prevention and Services Act. Still, the scope was too limited. Studies in the late 1980s showed that increased funding was the highest priority for existing women's shelters.[57]

Campaigns to pass federal legislation intensified. In 1992, the U.S. Surgeon General released a report showing that domestic violence was the leading cause of physical injury among American women ages 15 to 44. The 1994 Violence Against Women Act substantially enhanced federal funding for education, advocacy and social services for survivors of domestic violence. Federal administrators acknowledged that the infrastructure now funded by government agencies was created and staffed by activists in the "battered women's movement."[58]

As of 2012, there were 1,500 emergency shelters for battered women in the U.S., most of them receiving some kind of funding from local, state and federal governments. These shelters provided vital transitional services but still remained far too few to meet the need of millions. At the turn of the 21st century, one American woman was being battered every 15 seconds – most of them by husbands and boyfriends. The psychological, physical and financial toll of that abuse has been enormous.[59]

In the late 1970s, attorneys partnered with psychologists to try to create some legal frameworks that acknowledged the toll battering took on victims. The most controversial dimension of their work was an attempt to reduce legal penalties for abuse victims who killed their batterers. In 1977, Francine Hughes, on trial for murdering her husband, introduced evidence that he had beaten her for 14 years.

She divorced him but he refused to move out of the home they shared. In a landmark decision, the jury accepted her plea of temporary insanity. Hughes' mental state at the time she killed her husband, defense attorneys argued, was rooted in damage from battering and fear for her life. Hughes was acquitted and allowed to go free. It was a decision that shocked many.

Over the next few years, attorneys for battered women began testing a strategy that became popularly known as "the battered women's defense." This defense sought to answer one of the most important questions asked to women who killed their abusers – why did they not simply leave. The idea for the new defense came from a 1979 book, published by psychologist Lenore Walker, that detailed "battered women's syndrome," a state of resignation and learned helplessness that women adopted in the face of escalating violence.[60]

The "battered women's defense" also drew on the therapeutic work that psychologist Bruno Bettelheim had done with concentration camp inmates. Interned for a year in Dachau and Bergen-Belsen in the late 1930s, Bettelheim noticed that inmates sometimes developed a pathological attachment to those who imprisoned them, harming them repeatedly and brutally but occasionally casting them a crumb of human kindness. In Bettelheim's recollection, interestingly, a woman inmate only returned to her healthy individual self by grabbing a gun and killing a particularly sadistic Nazi guard. Bettelheim's analysis of the psychology of victims of long-term violence was applied to housewives by Friedan in *The Feminine Mystique* and revived by advocates for battered women in the late 1970s.[61]

Activist attorney Michael Dowd argued that the idea was too reductive. Battered women failed to leave for a variety of reasons, he believed. Physical as well as psychological injury constrained them. Many suffered from legitimate fear that they would be in greater danger if they left. Most lacked the financial resources that would enable them to leave. Using evidence that violence in abusive relationships escalates over time, Dowd and other battered women's attorneys argued that existing legal standards for claiming self-defense were biased toward men. They argued for a "reasonable" battered woman's standard for claims of self-defense.[62]

In one of Dowd's most famous cases, the trial of a 29-year-old Queens mother charged with stabbing her estranged husband to death, Dowd introduced evidence that Karen Straw had been violently victimized for years. Straw's case, according to Holly Maguigan, another defender of battered women, was "emblematic of what happens to other women" who seek help from the legal system. Straw had pressed charges against her husband for assault and taken out a restraining order on him. Still, the police failed to protect her. It was a typical scenario, said Maguigan. "The police are called; they respond to the call. The complaint, if it is made, is not vigorously prosecuted."

Victims of domestic violence, Dowd and Maguigan argued, had few options other than to defend themselves. Straw's husband had beaten and raped her in front of her two children the night before she stabbed him. She had reason to fear for her life, Dowd told the jury. The prosecutor argued that Straw could have and should have fled. In a decision that vividly illustrated how quickly views of domestic violence were changing, the jury accepted Straw's assertion that she had acted in self-defense and acquitted her of all charges. After the verdict, Straw said quietly through tears: "I just hope that what I went through helps someone else going through this."[63]

In the years that followed, it became clear that a significant percentage of women in prison for murder were victims of long-term domestic violence and were there for killing their abusers. In 1990, citing a decision by the Ohio Supreme Court that same year allowing women defendants to introduce evidence of battering as part of their defense, outgoing Ohio Governor Richard Celeste granted clemency to 25 women then serving prison terms for killing their abusers. This mass clemency for battered women prisoners was unprecedented and sent shock waves through the legal system. Celeste and his wife Dagmar had been long-time activists in the battered women's movement. In the 1970s, they had even turned their Cleveland home into a shelter for battered women.[64]

In 1992, the *Boston Globe* published a study showing that as many as 90% of women in prison for murdering men had been victims of domestic violence who struck back at their abusers. That same year, the California state legislature passed a bill making evidence of domestic violence grounds for consideration of clemency. Illinois Governor Jim Edgar followed Celeste's lead in 1994, granting clemency to four women imprisoned for killing their abusive partners. He cited battered women's syndrome as the reason he believed they should have been acquitted in the first place.[65]

By 2000, scores of women incarcerated for killing their batterers had submitted petitions for clemency. Sixty-nine of them were freed – many of them in conservative states – including Arizona, Missouri, Louisiana, Kentucky, New Hampshire and Florida. Republican governors as well as Democrats had issued these pardons, sometimes of multiple women at once. In each case, the Governor claimed to feel compassion for the abuse these women had endured. Though these pardons remain controversial, overall the response has been positive and Lenore Walker noted that they send a message that women will not be expected to tolerate abuse without fighting back. The National Clearinghouse for Defense of Battered Women in Philadelphia notes that the gender biases of judges and juries continues to negatively affect battered women who find themselves charged by a justice system that had failed to protect them from their abusers. Still, the law and the response of law enforcement now reflect a far deeper understanding of domestic abuse than was the case before the battered women's movement.[66]

One final arena of women's lives that changed dramatically as a result of consciousness-raising was health care for women. Though there is not enough space in this small book to cover everything, it is important to briefly mention the accomplishments of the women's health movement. In the 1970s, feminists began to question a medical establishment dominated by men. Male researchers on health and disease developed studies and care protocols that did not include women.

Male doctors decided how women's health and illness would be diagnosed and treated, whether or not women could be prescribed birth control or be given abortions and whether they should be institutionalized against their will for mental illness.[67]

A grass-roots women's health movement developed, in large part sparked by the collection *Our Bodies Ourselves*, first published in 1971 by the Boston Women's Health Collective. The collective was created by a group of New Left women in 1969, after attending a feminist conference workshop called "Women and Our Bodies." For a time the women met to talk about their experiences with health care, abortion and birth control. Then they decided to publish a self-help manual that would give women greater control over their most essential possession – their bodies.[68]

By providing accurate medical information that non-professionals could understand and make use of, *Our Bodies Ourselves* empowered women to become informed health care consumers and to take charge of their own health care. *Our Bodies* urged women not to accept it when medical professionals tried to pathologize normal women's life experiences – from menstruation to childbirth, menopause to old age. Increasingly, many didn't. The book was transformative in many ways both in the U.S. and around the world. Translated into 25 languages, it was adapted for local use by women's groups across the globe. The English language version is in its 9th edition, released on the 40th anniversary of the original publication.[69]

The self-help philosophy of activists in the women's health care movement moved them to open woman-run health clinics across the country. Many were self-described "collectives" where women patients could be tended by midwives and even non-professional service providers, in addition to traditionally trained nurses and women physicians. These clinics offered gynecological exams, distributed birth control and sometimes performed abortions.[70]

In Chicago, the Jane Collective, a group of women without medical degrees, taught themselves to perform inexpensive, high quality abortions. They offered that service to Chicago-area women in the early 1970s, before *Roe v. Wade* made abortion legal nationally. In so doing, they knowingly broke the law, but they did so in the spirit of civil disobedience. Jane Collective members felt that laws criminalizing abortion were unjust and that they caused thousands of women to die unnecessarily every year as a result of botched abortions performed on the black market. The St. Mark's Women's Health Clinic in New York's East Village saw tens of thousands of women for free in the 1970s and 1980s. Similar clinics opened in those years in many parts of the country.[71]

Like other feminist institutions described in this chapter, woman-run health clinics saw their task as promoting consciousness-raising while providing service delivery. In Olympia, Washington, the Evergreen State College women's health center sported posters advocating that women do self-exams with plastic speculum, mirror and flashlight. On the ceiling in one of the exam rooms was a poster depicting a speculum with a raised fist. It said: "With My Speculum I Can Fight!" On another was a poster for Linda Gordon's 1976 history of birth control: "Women's Body, Women's Right."[72]

The women's health movement broke open the monopoly that men had on the medical profession. As late as 2008, three-quarters of American physicians were male, most of them white. By 2010, 30% of physicians were female. Among physicians under 40, nearly half were female and entering classes in medical school became half female in 2003. The increasing representation of women in medicine has also sparked a reassessment of the importance of midwifery as a health care profession. Every year since 1975 increasing numbers of expectant mothers in the U.S. have chosen midwives to deliver their children.[73]

Women's hands-on approach to caring for themselves has spread around the world since 1971. In the 2011 edition of *Our Bodies Ourselves*, editors cited the work of the Our Bodies Our Selves Global Network. "From distributing posters via canoes in rural Nigeria to setting up interactive websites in Israel and Turkey and reshaping health policy in Nepal and Armenia, their efforts exemplify movement building and the power of voices raised in action."[74]

The changes wrought by consciousness-raising and radical feminism in the 1970s had far greater impact than anyone could have predicted. The revolution they made long outlasted that turbulent time. Still, sexism and misogyny would prove more intractable than even these furious revolutionaries believed it to be, and the revolution they started would have to be revived again and again. Robin Morgan, who was involved in every arena of the movement during those years, reflected on its successes and how much work remains to be done. Given an award for her humanitarianism in 2007, she said:

> Forty years ago, I couldn't get credit or a driver's license in my own name when I was married; battery and rape victims were blamed (even in the law) for being victimized; rape in marriage was perfectly legal, as was date rape and acquaintance rape; girls and women didn't "do" sports; and the thought of a female secretary of state (two – white and black) and a major presidential candidate who's a woman – forget about it. It took one hundred years, basically, to win suffrage in this country. I'd say we're about halfway through the contemporary wave of feminism in the United States."[75]

Notes

1 Robin Morgan, "Goodbye to All That," *Women's LibeRATion*, January 1970.

2 Jo Freeman, "The Revolution is Happening in Our Minds," *REVOLUTION II: Thinking Female*, Vol. 48, No. 2, February 1970, p. 63.

3 Kathie Sarachild, "Consciousness-Raising: A Radical Weapon," talk to the First National Conference of Stewardesses for Women's Rights, March 12, 1973. Expanded and reprinted in *Feminist Revolution* (New York: Random House, 1978), pp. 144–150.

4 Paul D. Buchanan, *Radical Feminists: A Guide to An American Subculture* (ABC-CLIO, LLC: 2011), p. 127.

5 In Memoriam, On Shulamit Firestone, Part I. by Jo Freeman, *N+1* September 26, 2012, http://nplusonemag.com/on-shulamith-firestone-part-one; Susan Faludi, "How Shulamit Firestone Shaped Feminism," *The New Yorker,* April 15, 2013.

6 Nell Greenfield Boyce, "Pageant Protest Sparked Bra-Burning Myth," National Public Radio, September 5, 2008; http://www.npr.org/templates/story/story.php?storyId=94240375.

7 Robin Morgan, "No More Miss America," August 22 1968. Press Release. *Redstockings* web archive. http://www.redstockings.org/index.php?option=com_content&view=article&id=65&Itemid=103. See too Sherie Randolph, "The Lasting Legacy of Florence Kennedy" *Solidarity* Summer 2014.

8 Boyce, op. cit.; Lindsay Van Gelder, "The Truth About Bra Burners," *Ms.* September–October 1992, pp. 80–81.

9 Snodgrass interview, in Boyce, op. cit.

10 WITCH Manifesto, 1968, http://www.sccs.swarthmore.edu/users/00/afreima1/femspirit.html.

11 ibid.

12 Sarachild, op. cit.

13 *Redstockings Manifesto*, July 7, 1969, Redstockings Archive for Action, http://www.redstockings.org/index.php?option=com_content&view=article&id=76&Itemid=59.

14 In Memoriam, On Shulamit Firestone, Part I. by Jo Freeman.

15 "The Chicago Women's Liberation Union: An Introduction," The CWLU Herstory Website, http://www.uic.edu/orgs/cwluherstory/CWLUAbout/cwluintro.html.

16 Freeman, op. cit.; Jesse Lemisch and Naomi Weisstein, "Remarks on Naomi Weisstein," CWLU Herstory Website, Memoirs and Biographies http://www.uic.edu/orgs/cwluherstory/CWLUMemoir/weisstein.html.

17 Susan Faludi, op. cit.

18 Simon Hall, *American Patriotism, American Protest: Social Movements Since the Sixties* (Philadelphia: University of Pennsylvania Press, 2011), p. 62; Cathy Wilkerson, *Flying Too Close to the Sun: My Life as a Weatherman* (Seven Stories Press, Reprint edition, 2010), p. 242; as cited in Faludi, op. cit.

19 Jo Freeman, "The Revolution is Happening in Our Minds," p. 63.

20 Robin Morgan, "Goodbye to All That," *Women's LibeRATion,* January 1970.

21 Susan Brownmiller, *In Our Time* (New York: Random House, 2000), Bold Type Excerpt http://www.randomhouse.com/boldtype/1199/brownmiller/excerpt.html.

22 "In Your Face Women," PRX Radio; http://www.prx.org/pieces/87302-robin-morgan; Choire Sicha, "All the Young Dudes," *Slate Book Review,* January 9, 2012; http://www.slate.com/articles/arts/books/2012/01/richard_seaver_s_the_tender_hour_of_twilight_a_memoir_of_grove_press.

23 David Banash, "Join the Underground," *Pop Matters,* April 29, 2013. http://www.popmatters.com/pm/column/170895-join-the-underground-loren-glasss-history-of-grove-press/.

24 Faludi, op. cit.

25 Kate Millett, *Sexual Politics* (New York: Doubleday, 1970) p. ix.

26 Phyllis Jacobsen, "Kate Millett and Her Critics," *New Politics,* Fall 1970.

27 "Sisterhood is Powerful," *The Official Web Site of Robin Morgan;* http://www.robinmorgan.us/robin_morgan_bookDetails.asp?ProductID=9.

28 ibid.

29 Gloria Steinem, "A Bunny's Tale," *Show Magazine,* May 1963.

30 Carolyn Heilbrun, *Education of a Woman: The Life of Gloria Steinem* (New York: Ballantine Books, 1995).

31 Patricia Bradley, *Mass Media and the Shaping of American Feminism* (Oxford: University of Mississippi Press, 2003); Abigail Pogrebin, "How Do You Spell Ms? An Oral History," *New York Magazine*, October 30, 2011.

32 ibid.

33 Gene Corea, "Dear Gloria," January 28, 1972. Cited in Pogrebin, op. cit.

34 Pogrebin, Oral History; University of Southern California Anneberg Center "*Ms.* Then and Now," http://historyppf.uscannenberg.org/group4/profile-on-ms-magazine/.

35 Patricia L.N. Donat and John D'Emilio, "A Feminist Redefinition of Rape and Sexual Assault: Historical Foundations and Change," in *Journal of Social Issues*, Vol. 48. No. 1, 1992, pp. 9–22.

36 Susan Griffin, "Rape: The All-American Crime," *Ramparts Magazine*, September 1971, pp. 26–35.

37 Maria Bevacqua, *Rape on the Public Agenda: Feminism and the Politics of Sexual Assault* (Hanover: University Press of New England, 2000) p. 31.

38 Andrea Dworkin, "Letters From a War Zone, 1976–1989. Part I – Take Back the Night," http://www.nostatusquo.com/ACLU/dworkin/WarZoneChaptIb.html.

39 Bevacqua, op. cit., p. 32.

40 Susan Brownmiller, *Against Our Will: Men, Women and Rape* (New York: Simon and Schuster, 1975), Introduction.

41 Brownmiller, p. 254; Stevi Jackson, "Classic Review – Against Our Will," *Trouble and Strife,* Issue 35, Summer 1997, http://www.troubleandstrife.org/articles/issue-35/classic-review-against-our-will/.

42 Bevacqua, op. cit. p. 42.

43 Bevacqua, op. cit.

44 Sara and Ken Burns, *The Central Park Five* (2013), www.pbs.org/kenburns/centralparkfive.

45 ibid.

46 Nancy Matthews, *Confronting Rape: The Feminist Anti-Rape Movement and the State* (New York and London: Routledge, 1994).

47 ibid.

48 "Summary of the History of Rape Crisis Centers." *Office for Victims of Crime Training and Technical Assistance Center* website, https://www.ovcttac.gov/saact/files/summ_of_history.pdf.

49 Susan Schechter, *Women and Male Violence: The Visions and Struggles of the Battered Women's Movement* (Boston: South End Press, 1982).

50 Ann Jones, *Next Time, She'll Be Dead: Battering and How to Stop It* (Boston: Beacon Press, 2000).

51 Del Martin, *Battered Wives* (New York: Pocket Books, 1976), p. 60.

52 Martin, op. cit., p. xvii.

53 ibid.

54 ibid.

55 "A History of the Battered Women's Movement," Copyright © 1995–2008 Minnesota Center Against Violence and Abuse.

56 ibid.

57 H. Lien Bragg, "The Basics of Domestic Violence," in *Child Protection in Families Experiencing Domestic Violence* (Office of Child Abuse and Neglect, Children's Bureau, U.S. Department of Health and Human Services, 2003).

58 ibid.

59 Natasha Tracy, "Battered Women's Shelters," Healthy Place, America's Mental Health Channel, http://www.healthyplace.com/abuse/domestic-violence/battered-women-shelters-what-are-they-how-to-find-one/; *United Nations Study on the Status of Women, Year 2000.*

60 Lenore Walker, *Battered Woman* (New York: William Morrow Paperbacks, 1980).

61 Bruno Bettleheim, "Individual and Mass Behavior in Extreme Situations," *Journal of Abnormal and Social Psychology*, Vol. 38, 1943, pp. 417–452. Bruno Bettelheim, *The Informed Heart: Autonomy in A Mass Age* (New York: Board Books, 1960).

62 Michael Dowd, "Dispelling the Myths About 'Battered Women's Defense,' Towards a New Understanding," *Fordham Urban Law Journal*, Vol. 19, Issue 3, Article 2, 1991.

63 Julie Johnson, "Queens Woman Acquitted of Killing Husband," *New York Times*, October 1, 1987.

64 "Ohio Governor Grants 25 Abused Women Clemency," *New York Times News Service*, December 22, 1990.

65 Allison Bass, "Women Far Less Likely to Kill than Men; No One Sure Why." *The Boston Globe*, February 24, 1992, p. 27; Carl Ingraham, "Wilson Signs Bill on Clemency for Battered Women," *Los Angeles Times*, September 29, 1992; Associated Press, "Illinois Governor Frees Four Women Who Killed Abusive Mates," May 14, 1994, *Los Angeles Times.*

66 Linda Ammons, "Why Do you Do the Things You Do? Clemency for Battered Incarcerated Women: A Decade's Review," *Journal of Gender, Social Policy and the Law*, Vol. 11, No. 2, 2003.

67 Barry S. Levy and Victor W. Sidel, eds., *Social Injustice and Public Health*, 2nd edition (New York: Oxford University Press, 2013).

68 Kathy Davis, *How Feminism Travels Across Borders; The Making of Our Bodies Ourselves* (Durham: Duke University Press, 2007), p. 1.

69 Boston Women's Health Book Collective, *Our Bodies Ourselves*, 9th edition (New York: Simon and Schuster, 2011).

70 Wendy Kline, *Bodies of Knowledge: Sexuality, Reproduction and Women's Health in the Second Wave* (Chicago: University of Chicago Press, 2010).

71 ibid.; Sandra Morgen, *Into Our Own Hands: The Women's Health Movement in the United States, 1969–1990* (New Brunswick: Rutgers University Press, 2002).

72 Author's observation.

73 NBC News, "More Mothers Choose Midwives For Delivery," September 28, 2006. http://www.nbcnews.com/id/13062835/ns/health-pregnancy/t/more-mothers-choose-midwives-delivery/#.UgKdXlOG6Is.

74 *Our Bodies Our Selves*, 9th edition, Introduction; Davis, *How Feminism Travels Across Borders*, op. cit.

75 Pat Willis, "Robin Morgan, 2007 Humanist Heroine," *The Humanist* (November/ December 2007), http://www.thehumanist.org/humanist/PatWillis.html.

6

WOMEN'S MOVEMENTS FOR REDISTRIBUTIVE AND SOCIAL JUSTICE

Other Faces of Radical Feminism

I have been asked whether being a woman has made it difficult for me in my exercise of leadership. For years I never thought about that. We were too busy organizing struggles . . . I am sort of a born again feminist.

> Dolores Huerta, Co-Founder United Farm Workers of America[1]

I grew up thinking all grandmothers wrote letters to the president. She told us about the stars, about the sacred Black Hills. She was the one who told me about treaty rights. There were no strong, stoic Indian grandfathers in our lives. There were strong grandmothers.

> Madonna Thunderhawk, Co-Founder, Women of All Red Nations[2]

Welfare's like a traffic accident. It can happen to anybody, but especially it happens to women. And that's why welfare is a women's issue. For a lot of middle-class women in this country, Women's Liberation is a matter of concern. For women on welfare it's a matter of survival.

> Johnnie Tillmon, President, National Welfare Rights Organization,
> "Welfare is a Women's Issue," *Ms.* 1972[3]

Perhaps the single most commonly held fallacy about radical feminism in the third quarter of the 20th century is that it was an outburst of anger by young, white, affluent women that held little appeal for other women and made little sense to anyone else. The reality was far more complicated. The players were far more diverse than that. The picture of that era becomes both clearer and more crowded when we step away from the idea that feminism was a unitary ideology and we look instead at protests by very different kinds of revolutionary women. Moved to action by their class and race positions, and by their responsibilities as mothers, these radical women were all essential players in the women's revolutions that swept the world in the 1960s and 1970s. Though they did not think of themselves as feminists initially, all of them were keenly aware of the ways that sex interacted with class and race to structure hierarchies of power that affected their lives every day. By the end of this time period all of them had begun to consider themselves women's rights activists. Some became full-fledged feminists.

PART I: SCENES FROM "OTHER" WOMEN'S REVOLUTIONS

The Native-American Movement and Its Women Leaders

San Francisco, 1964: Hundreds of thousands of Native-Americans relocated to California as part of the federal termination program that, from the 1950s to 1970, moved Native-Americans off reservations to cities. By the end of the termination era, California had the largest Native-American population in the country. Young activists from many different tribes met each other in California and began to network. In the San Francisco Bay Area, Native-Americans from across the U.S. began to build alliances with African-American, Asian-American and Latino/a civil rights activists. They shared language, political vision and strategies, and made California fertile ground for Indian activism. Among the leaders of these new movements were many women.[4]

In March 1964, Lakota Sioux organizer Belva Cottier and 40 American Indian activists announced that they were reclaiming Alcatraz Island as native land. A rocky outcrop in the middle of San Francisco Bay, Alcatraz had for many years been home to an infamous prison. Driving claim stakes into the rocky ground, the activists offered the U.S. government 47 cents an acre – a total of $9.40. At the same time, Cottier filed a claim in court under the 1868 Fort Laramie treaty that entitled Indians to abandoned federal property. The island had been declared "surplus" federal land earlier that year.[5]

Nisqually River, Yelm, Washington, October 13, 1965: As 50 women and children lowered their fishing nets into the Nisqually River, 20 minutes north of the state capital of Olympia, Washington, dozens of game wardens and police surrounded and arrested them. The Medicine Creek Treaty of 1854 guaranteed that Indian fishing grounds throughout the Northwest would be preserved, but state officials in Washington routinely arrested Native fishermen and women for fishing on their own lands. On this day in 1965, Janet McCloud, a descendant of Chief Seattle, was leading a "fish-in" to protest.

McCloud had grown up in poverty and homelessness, but as a young adult had settled on the Nisqually with her husband, truck driver Don McCloud. Her first adult spark to activism came when game wardens broke into the McCloud home in 1961 looking for deer meat. This was common procedure in Washington at the time. McCloud became angry and asked to see a search warrant. The wardens told her that they had a warrant to search the home of "John Doe" living near the Nisqually. In other words, they could enter anyone's home on the reservation any time they pleased.[6]

By the mid-1960s, McCloud had begun to argue that federal laws criminalizing traditional Indian ways of living constituted a form of cultural genocide. To fight these illegitimate federal intrusions, she organized a series of protests to reassert Nisqually rights to harvest their own, long-held, fishing grounds. To live according to the old Indian ways, McCloud said, meant that the Nisqually had to engage in civil disobedience. In response to their Fall 1965 "fish-in", McCloud recalled, "wardens were . . . shoving, kicking, pushing clubs at men, women and children. We were all vastly outnumbered, yet we were all trying to protect one another."[7]

The protesters had expected that their action would spark conflict. Comedian and activist Dick Gregory had come to offer support and was arrested. As he fasted in an Olympia prison cell, McCloud gathered women and children "off the rez" to protest. They set up a teepee on the grounds of the state Capitol. On the orders of the governor, state troopers tore down the teepee and – as "Bull" Connor had during Martin Luther King's children's march into Birmingham, Alabama – they turned high power water hoses on the child protesters. State police then arrested adults and children alike, using clubs on anyone who resisted. McCloud was outraged but also inspired.

> You never hear about some people in the "official' history," she recalled. "But we'd all be dead if it wasn't for the struggle. We were fast on our way to becoming alcoholics. I've always been grateful for those bumps in the head – because it woke me up"[8]

McCloud knew from personal experience how emotionally taxing activism could be, and she understood that federal authorities would show no restraint in their battle against native civil rights leaders. So, she and Don decided to turn their land by the beautiful Nisqually into a spiritual center, a place of retreat and recuperation for activists in the burgeoning Native-American movement. Eight years later, American Indian Movement leaders came to Nisqually to plan an occupation of Wounded Knee. Twenty years later, in 1985, a new and lasting civil rights organization was founded there – the Indigenous Women's Network – which would continue into the 21st century, promoting leadership and community action among native women the world over. The McCloud land came to be described by Indian activists as "the center of everything." And McCloud was given a new Indian name – *Yet Si Blue* – "the Woman Who Speaks Her Mind."[9]

San Francisco, 1969–1971: 100 Native-American students from several University of California campuses occupied Alcatraz Island for a second time. The prison had been shut down several years earlier and there was no running water or electricity. Similar conditions prevailed on most Indian reservations, occupiers told the press. The occupation lasted 19 months. Fifty-six thousand Indians from various tribes across the country came to stay for a while. So did some very famous movie stars, including Jane Fonda, Marlon Brando and Anthony Quinn.

Though they got little attention from media at the time, native women ran much of the occupation. They staffed the kitchen, taught school for the children and delivered health services. The occupation focused national attention on Native-American issues and sparked the rise of a pan-Indian civil rights movement that would spread across the country. It also became a founding ground for a Native-American women's movement. Among its leaders are the women listed below.

La Nada Boyer Means, a Shoshone woman, stayed on Alcatraz from the beginning to the end of the occupation. She was the first Indian student to be admitted to U.C. Berkeley and she organized the first native student organization in the U.C. system. She would become a founding member of the American Indian Movement (AIM).

Madonna Thunderhawk, a Lakota Sioux, came with her three-year-old daughter because she believed "the struggle is intergenerational." Thunderhawk would help found AIM. Soon after, she co-founded one of the first native feminist organizations – Women of All Red Nations.

Blackfoot physician Dorothy Lone Wolf Miller tended to the physical needs of occupiers. She secured grants to set up and run a school and health clinic on Alcatraz. For years after the occupation ended, she remained a key player in Native-American health care activism.

Sac Fox activist and World War II veteran, Grace Thorpe, daughter of Olympian Jim Thorpe, found a generator for the occupiers and made connections with film stars Fonda, Brando and Candace Bergen, who brought much-needed funds to the occupiers and also attracted media attention. As a result of Thorpe's efforts, the band Credence Clearwater Revival donated a boat to ferry people and supplies back and forth to the island. After Alcatraz, Thorpe had a decades-long career as an environmentalist. She protested the poisoning of native lands, and ran the National Environmental Coalition of Native-Americans.

Wilma Mankiller, 23 at the time of the occupation, coordinated support for the protest in San Francisco. After the occupation, she founded a native youth center in San Francisco to provide support, tutoring and after-school activities to native youth in the city. She would become best known for her decade as principal chief of the Cherokee from 1985 to 1995. She was the first woman to lead a major Indian nation. A self-described feminist who became a board member of the Ms. Foundation, Mankiller would later say that the Alcatraz occupation made her who and what she became.[10]

November 1972 (all across the U.S.): 500 Indian activists left from the West Coast for a caravan to Washington, D.C. called the Trail of Broken Treaties. Their aim was to repeal a 1871 law that rescinded the sovereignty of Indian nations to negotiate treaties with the U.S. government. They demanded enforcement of existing treaties. With no place to stay, they decided to occupy the Bureau of Indian Affairs.

As was the tradition in Native-American activism, the protesters came as families – elders, women, children and men. On the first night, 71-year-old Pawnee Martha Grass spoke to protesters gathered in the auditorium about the long history of broken treaties. "There are nothing but crooks and liars up here. They will steal you blind," she said. Looking out at the weary crowd, she told them how inspired she was by the activism of the young people.

Among the youngest at the occupation were Lydia and Hope Heis, 14 and 16. Lydia explained that she had come because she was usually "surrounded by white people in white school . . . they kept saying they were the best and Indians were nothing. I'm not worried anymore though because Indians will get their rights." Sixteen-year-old Mary Brave Bird had escaped from a reservation boarding school where the Bureau of Indian Affairs sent young Indian children to school them in English and Christianity, and to encourage them to forget Indian traditions. She had found in the American Indian Movement hope and affirmation. It had, she said, changed her life.[11]

On November 4, 1972, a federal judge ordered the Indian occupiers to leave the BIA building. In direct violation of the court order, they remained for nearly a week. Comanche activist La Donna Harris, wife of Oklahoma Senator Fred Harris and founder of the largest War on Poverty organization run by Native-Americans, Oklahomans for Indian Opportunity, came to negotiate with the protesters. By the third day, the occupiers had erected a 20-foot teepee on the lawn in front of the Bureau. Men, women and children hung out of windows. Others stood atop the roof armed with roof tiles and buckets of water, prepared to fight anyone who tried to evict them. President Richard Nixon, hoping to avoid a fight, promised to respect Indian land and water rights. It quickly became clear, however, that nothing was going to change. The movement continued to build.[12]

Wounded Knee, South Dakota, 1973: Three months after the BIA occupation, more than 200 activists, including Madonna Thunderhawk, 17-year-old Mary Brave Bird and 19-year-old Lorelei DeCora – the youngest member of the American Indian Movement board of directors – hiked and drove to the site of the 1890 Wounded Knee massacre where 300 Sioux elders, women and children were shot dead by the U.S. army. They decided to occupy that emotionally powerful site after numerous attempts by traditional women elders on the Pine Ridge reservation to unseat corrupt tribal chairman Dick Wilson had failed. Sioux activists believed Wilson and his friends had grown rich diverting federal dollars meant for the tribe while most reservation dwellers languished in poverty without sufficient food, heat or water.

Women elders also protested the violence of Wilson's "GOON (Guardians of the Ogalala Nation) squad." GOON was responsible for a series of brutal attacks on young AIM activists and on elders fighting to revive traditional Lakota ways of living. Pine Ridge had the highest murder rate and was one of the poorest counties in the U.S. Though the reservation also had the highest ratio of FBI agents to regular citizens, nearly 200 of its residents had disappeared without a trace since Wilson's first term in office. Reservation dwellers asked federal authorities for help in finding their "disappeared" loved ones. But the FBI and U.S. Attorney's offices in South Dakota insisted there were no grounds to open a criminal investigation.

By January 1973, residents of Pine Ridge were growing weary and angry. When a white businessman stabbed 20-year-old Wesley Bad Heart Bull to death and was given one day in prison, AIM activists brought Wesley's mother Sara to protest. In the course of the rally she was thrown down the steps of the Custer courthouse by police. Sara was then tried and convicted for rallying without a permit. When the judge gave her 1-to-5 years in prison, angry AIM members set the courthouse and other buildings on fire.

One month later, on February 27, 1973, 250 AIM members, equal numbers of women and men, lay claim to the hamlet of Wounded Knee on the Pine Ridge reservation, demanding that Dick Wilson step down as tribal chairman, and that his successor be determined by a free and fair election. Madonna Thunderhawk recalled: "I was ready to do whatever it takes for change. I didn't care. I had children, and for them I figured I could make a stand here."[13]

Within hours, state police and federal marshalls surrounded the occupiers. "They were shooting machine gun fire at us, tracers coming at us at nighttime, just like a war zone," one occupier recalled. To the Vietnam vets among them, the Wounded Knee siege felt eerily like what they had just experienced, except this time men in U.S. military uniforms were firing at them. The occupiers held off federal authorities for 71 days. Media from around the world covered the siege. Indians from around the country flocked to support the occupiers.

Mary Brave Bird gave birth to a child at Wounded Knee, a moment of joy, an act of resistance, in the midst of a siege that left the occupiers without supplies or a way out. Two activists died in the shooting and one federal agent was paralyzed. Dozens of AIM members and occupiers were indicted in the aftermath on charges related to the occupation. Most charges were dropped when a federal judge ruled that there was improper collaboration between local tribal officials and the FBI. But the battle did not end there.[14]

In the years that followed, a virtual civil war broke out between Dick Wilson and AIM. Sixty AIM members were murdered. AIM activists believed that local FBI agents supplied GOON with both intelligence on its members and armor piercing bullets. In 1975, a shoot-out between the FBI and Lakota activists resulted in two agents' deaths and the death of a Lakota man, Joe Stuntz. No one was prosecuted for his death. AIM member Leonard Peltier was tried, convicted and sentenced to two life terms for the FBI agents' deaths. He maintains his innocence and insists that he was railroaded. He remains in prison as of 2014.

Violence engulfed the Lakota community in the ensuing decades, a good deal of it targeting women. Although 21st-century evidence shows that the majority of assaults on Native-American women are made by non-Native men, domestic violence was endemic to reservation life in Pine Ridge. After the siege ended, Janet McCloud called together AIM's male leaders and told them that they needed to deal with it. Rally Indian men, she challenged them, to take the lead in fighting domestic violence against Native women. She also challenged AIM to root out sexism in its own ranks. By 1978, AIM had dissolved, but Native women's groups took the struggle into the next millennium.

Rapid City, South Dakota, 1974: To create an alternative path for the Native-American civil rights movement, McCloud, Madonna Thunderhawk and Lorelei DeCora convened a native women's conference in Rapid City, South Dakota. More than 300 women from 30 tribal communities attended. At the conference, they founded a new federation – Women of All Red Nations (WARN). Native health and safety were the group's first concerns. Along with domestic violence, WARN chose to focus on the involuntary sterilizations of Native women at Indian Health Service clinics. They also worked to develop culturally sensitive approaches to fighting alcohol and drug abuse among poor women on reservations.

The organization championed Native sovereignty and self-government as AIM did. But, for women, WARN leaders insisted, their key demand was the right to physical safety and bodily integrity – freedom from assaults, from involuntary sterilization, and from exposure to environmental toxins. WARN helped pioneer the environmental justice movement, protesting contamination of land and water on Indian reservations, collecting and publicizing data on the high rates of miscarriages and birth defects that pollution caused. On the Pine Ridge reservation, Thunderhawk created a group home for children whose parents were imprisoned or disappeared after the Wounded Knee occupation. DeCora opened a clinic on her Winnebago reservation in Nebraska.

"When we were at Wounded Knee," she recalled, "I became a medic and I was only 19 years old, and what I saw set the tone for the rest of my life. I saw how dependent Indian people are on non-Indian people for our own health." In later years, DeCora developed a highly regarded and innovative program using traditional Winnebago spiritual and medicinal practices to treat the Type II diabetes that was so common among her people. She says of activism:

> It's a hard life. It's easy to just think of yourself and drive a nice car and have nice things, but the reward is that when the day comes that I have to die or Madonna has to die, and our ancestors are there in the spirit world, we can stand in front of them and say, "I didn't just look the other way. I did what I could."[15]

Washington, D.C, 1978: In 1978, the year that AIM disbanded as a national organization, McCloud and WARN leaders walked 3,000 miles from several sites on the West Coast to Washington, D.C. Thirty thousand people rallied there, protesting proposed new bills to limit Native-American treaty rights. McCloud's speech highlighted the forced sterilization of Indian women. She also condemned 11 proposed bills that would abrogate Native-American fishing, hunting, land and water rights. When she left the capital, McCloud drove across the country to the office of Seattle's representative in Congress. In front of invited press, she ripped up copies of the bills. McCloud continued to lead protests for Indian land and water rights over the next decade.[16]

Yelm, Washington, 1985: 11 years after the founding of WARN, a new international indigenous women's federation was created on Janet McCloud's land after a gathering of more than 200 indigenous women leaders from around the world. One of the founders of the Indigenous Women's Network was Minnesota activist Winona LaDuke, descendant of Anishanabe spiritual leaders on her father's side and Jewish immigrant labor activists on her mother's. IWN engaged Indian women from the Pacific Northwest to Nova Scotia and from New Mexico south into Latin America. Their goal was to promote the vision of the Elders, enabling Native women to control their own bodies, the education of their children and the health of their communities. It was a decidedly feminist vision and one that the organization has promoted for nearly three decades.[17]

"Since the early 1970s," IWN activists wrote in 2006, in *Indigenous Woman* – the only magazine written by and for Native women –

> we have asserted ourselves in ongoing dialogues and are assuming greater authority in the governance of our Nations and communities. By caring for our children, we are often the first to realize threats to our communities' health – and the first to recognize solutions. We see our communities in a holistic fashion, seeing issues of education and illiteracy, environmental and personal health, natural resource management, housing, economic development, preservation of Native language and culture, and spirituality as inter-related and interdependent. We cannot – and should not – fix the one without somehow addressing another.

Nearly 1,000 miles away in Southern California a similar movement for dignity and subsistence took root among Mexican and Mexican-American women in the 1960s and continued into the 21st century.[18]

Women and the United Farm Workers

Delano, California, September 20, 1965: Well before dawn, Esther Uranday and scores of Mexican-American grape pickers woke up the owners and foremen at *Pagliarulo and Son* farm to announce that they were joining with Filipino farm workers who had gone on strike a few days earlier. The union had only $70 in the strike fund at the time. Its leaders and members had many children to feed, recalled Dolores Huerta. And yet, said Uranday, "we headed off into several other farms, picketing and showing our demands. I am sure it must have been quite a sight for all those growers to see these farm workers waking them up at 3 a.m., ready to do battle with them. It must have been quite a wakeup call."[19]

Back then, recalled grape picker Hortensia Mata, "I wasn't aware and didn't even know what a strike was. . . . That day my life was changed forever . . . The hardships were tremendous," she says, "especially when we had nothing to eat . . . The fight in the fields was especially difficult because the police sided with the growers and every time we tried to put something together the police struck it down."[20]

As the strike dragged on, Dolores Huerta, co-founder of the fledgling farm workers union, launched an exhausting round of speeches at Bay Area churches, universities, women's and peace groups. She convinced listeners that this strike was as much a matter of fundamental justice as the Southern civil rights movement. The farm workers desperately needed the support of more affluent Californians, to donate money and walk picket lines. In 1966, union president Cesar Chavez led male and female farm workers on a 300-mile march from Delano to the state capital in Sacramento. Alarmed, a few growers moved to settle the strike. Huerta, as lead negotiator, won the workers a 35-cent-per-hour raise. The battle had begun.

Building on their success in the Delano strike, the farm workers' union struck the large and powerful DiGiorgio Fruit Co. To try to break the strike, the company had begun running buses from Mexico to bring in non-union labor. In 1966, Huerta put her body on the line to stop them. She traveled to Juárez, Mexico where she walked back and forth along the border carrying a picket sign and leaflets in Spanish and English. "I was there for a whole month picketing the border, passing leaflets in Juárez, Mexico, and asking people not to work for DiGiorgio. Sometimes they were sending two buses every other day to bring in scabs and break the strike. Our work was effective." Still, the strike dragged on and on, passing two, then three years. In a mad whirl of voter registration, Huerta and other activists made the farm workers a significant constituency in the California Democratic Party. In June 1968, she walked to the podium with Presidential candidate Robert F. Kennedy, the night he won the California primary. She was standing next to him that same night when he was shot and killed.[21]

Huerta headed east in 1968 to coordinate a national boycott of grapes. She hoped to harness consumer power to force the growers to negotiate. Dividing New York City into eight districts, she found local activists to coordinate the boycott in each. They planned a day of coordinated action across the city. One hundred housewives walked into chain grocery stores in different neighborhoods, picked up bunches of grapes, then asked to speak to the manager. In loud voices intended to be overheard by other shoppers, the women said that these grapes had been picked by scab labor – strike breakers – forced to work under terrible conditions. Huerta found volunteers from the city's activist churches, student groups, synagogues and peace organizations who then picketed supermarkets, leafleting shoppers and explaining the conditions under which farm workers lived and labored. The grape boycott became a national phenomenon.

Over the next two years, farm workers traveled to most of the nation's major cities to organize for the boycott. By 1969, a Louis Harris poll estimated that 17 million Americans had stopped buying California table grapes. The big supermarket chains pressured California growers to settle. They finally did, in 1970. Organizer Jesse de la Cruz recalled: "When the strike finally ended in 1970, I was exhausted, physically and emotionally scarred. It had been five long years but we finally accomplished what we had set out to do."[22]

Back in California, between 1970a and 1973 Huerta negotiated historic contracts with grape and lettuce growers. Farm workers won raises, the right to organize, drinkable water in the fields, bathroom breaks, and promises from growers that they would refrain from using pesticides that could and did harm farm workers and their families. Ever the coalition builder, Huerta gave a great deal of credit to the allies she and others in the union had worked so hard to rally. "Just as we had our share of enemies, we also had our share of friends. These included the Puerto Ricans who taught us how to strike, the Jewish people with their generosity and the Black Panthers . . . Without the contribution of all of these groups the boycott and strike wouldn't have been a success."[23]

What the farm workers achieved was historic. From 1970 to 1973, the UFW rode high, representing 60,000 grape and lettuce pickers across California, more than half of them women. The contracts that Huerta negotiated dramatically improved farm workers' wages, working and living conditions. Just as importantly, they radically reduced farm workers' exposure to dangerous pesticides.

And then, in 1973, the UFW contract expired and California's biggest growers recruited the Teamsters Union to challenge the UFW for the right to represent farm workers. Twenty-seven growers announced that they had signed contracts with the Teamsters. The terms they offered were better than the conditions workers had known before the UFW, but far less generous than the deals that Huerta had negotiated after the grape boycott. Before the Delano strike, 3 million American farm workers earned average yearly wages of $1,389.00. A third of them had no toilets, a quarter had no running water. 1,000 a year died from pesticide poisoning. The average life expectancy was 49. The grape boycott and the contract that Huerta negotiated in 1970 changed that – doubling their wages, banning child labor, restricting pesticide use. But in 1973, the contract expired, growers signed with the Teamsters, and the UFW was forced back on strike.[24]

Coachella Valley, California, 1973: Nineteen-year-old Alicia Uribe picketed in front of the Mel-Pak vineyards on a 90 degree April day, carrying her red and white United Farm Workers' flag. Along the road 100 UFW picketers stood on cars, waved their flags and shouted "Huelga" – Strike! Many did not speak English. Out of the desert dust came a white sedan. It pulled up alongside Uribe. A pair of brass knuckles rocketed through the window and shattered the bones in her face. "Los Teamsters," the other picketers said. It was just the first of many times during the 1973 strike that the Teamsters would break up picket lines comprised largely of women and teenagers.

The UFW decided on a strategy of pulling workers off farms that had signed with the Teamsters. This strategy was carried out primarily by young women organizers. A week into the strike one young woman stood outside the Bobara ranch with a bullhorn. She spoke to workers in the fields. "Remember when we were under contract and we used to have a 15 minute rest period every four hours. I haven't seen anyone resting. Aren't there rest periods anymore?" And the workers sat down and took a break. She reminded them that under the UFW they could go to the bathroom any time they wanted to. "Don't the Teamsters let you?" A small number of workers headed to the porta-san toilets on the edge of the fields. Teamster officials ran into the fields warning workers to stay where they were. After a tense pause, the workers continued walking. The young woman with the bullhorn chanted the UFW slogan: "Si Se Puede" (Yes We Can).[25]

The Teamster organizing style was very different from that of Huerta, Cesar Chavez and Jesse de la Cruz. "The Teamsters never came into the fields to talk to us," said Rosario Pelayo. "Our foreman was a teamster and he just signed us all up without telling us. The day before the strike the Teamsters came and broke all our union flags. We had flags on our cars and on the grape rows but they tore them all down." When she and others continued to organize for the UFW, the owner chased them out of the fields with a sharpened grape stake. She and 85 others on her farm walked out to protest the owners' decision to sign with the Teamsters. Pelayo, her husband and six children had to live on $50 a week UFW strike benefits. "It's difficult," she said, "but we have to struggle. It's our life."[26]

On June 23, 1973 the strike erupted into open warfare between the Teamsters and the United Farm Workers. Seventy-five muscular Teamsters with pipes and tire irons snuck up behind 100 United Farm Workers' pickets, most of them teenage boys, women and young children. The Teamsters lobbed firecrackers and split heads. Five UFW pickets were hospitalized, 20 more had to seek medical treatment, one UFW member's house was burned down, and someone shot at Cesar Chavez. In the weeks that followed, thousands of farm workers were arrested for violating injunctions against picketing. Two were shot and killed on the picket lines.

California, 1973–2011: Over the next two years, tapping Huerta's extensive network of allies, and banking on the respect that had been earned through the UFW's commitment to non-violence, the farm workers lobbied the California legislature for protection. In 1975, they won passage of the landmark California Agricultural Labor Relations Act. The CLRA gave farm workers the right to secret ballot elections to choose between the two unions. The bill required employers to negotiate with any union the workers chose. The UFW won overwhelmingly.

For a time, the Teamsters appeared likely to withdraw from the grape and lettuce fields. But, in a concession to growers, the law banned secondary boycotts, robbing the UFW of their most potent weapon. The 1968–1970 grape boycott had enabled the union to rally support from millions of sympathetic consumers. With the threat of consumer action removed, the growers dragged their feet, refusing to sign contracts. In 1982, Republican George Dukmeijan was elected governor. He appointed growers and their representatives to enforce agricultural labor relations under the CLRA. Once again, the UFW found itself forced to turn to civil disobedience.

In 1988, Chavez went back to Delano. There he launched a long hunger strike, hoping to inspire the field workers to carry on until the UFW won a new contract. In San Francisco, a frustrated and exhausted Huerta hurled her body against a line of riot police to draw the attention of visiting Presidential candidate George H.W. Bush to the plight of California farm workers. Club wielding police attacked the 58-year-old grandmother viciously, breaking several of her ribs and so severely damaging her spleen that it had be removed. Videotape captured police ramming a club into Huerta's doubled-over torso. It took her two years to recover fully. She sued the San Francisco Police Department and won a large financial judgment in compensation for her wounds. She donated most of it to the farm workers' health benefits fund. The rest became seed money for the Dolores Huerta Foundation, which continues to fund grass-roots leadership and organizing projects into the 21st century.

In the decade after Cesar Chavez' death in 1993, Huerta and the farm workers union turned back to field-based organizing and won contracts for grape pickers, lettuce, strawberry and mushroom pickers in California, Arizona and Washington State. In 2011 the farm workers marched for 13 days to the state capital in Sacramento, where they lobbied to pass legislation to guarantee fairer treatment of the state's farm workers. In 2012, President Barack Obama gave Dolores Huerta the Medal of Freedom, the highest civilian honor that a president can bestow. He was grateful, he joked, that Huerta had let him use the farm workers' slogan. "Si Se Puede – Yes We Can."[27]

In the second decade of the 21st century, the farm workers union was still fighting for cold, clean water to drink in the fields, the right to unionize and the right to stay safe from pesticide poisoning. But Lucila López, a mother of four who worked picking grapes from the early 1990s into the 2010s, believed that the farm workers' best hope was to keep the struggle going. "When we are treated badly, we should blame ourselves," she said in 2011. "We shouldn't be afraid to stand up for our rights."[28]

Women in the Welfare Rights Movement

In cities across the U.S. during the 1960s, one more group of poor women launched a campaign for dignity and justice. Theirs was a movement made up entirely of mothers, founded and led by a migrant laundry worker from Los Angeles named Johnnie Tillmon.

Watts, Los Angeles, 1963: Tillmon was born to sharecropping parents in Arkansas. Like so many black migrants who left the South in the two decades after World War II, she had picked cotton throughout her childhood. At 18, she left for Little Rock, where she worked as a maid, a dishwasher and a short-order cook. She also inspected bomb fuses in a defense plant. (It was incredibly dangerous and not a job that many white people would accept.) Like many women who would become politically active in those years, she was a devoted member of her local Parent Teacher Association. In 1960, when her marriage to James Tillmon failed, she moved to California, hoping to find opportunities there for herself and her six children.[29]

Tillmon moved to the Watts section of Los Angeles where she found few jobs open to a single black mother besides domestic and laundry work. Tillmon worked at a commercial laundry, pressing 150 shirts an hour as a line operator. In her off hours she organized neighbors in the public housing project where she lived. The women planted around their apartments, creating green space where their children could play. By 1963, severe and chronic arthritis forced Tillmon to quit her job. Hospitalized for a variety of ailments, she had no choice but to apply for public assistance.[30]

She recalled her shock at how much people seemed to change their view of her as soon as she began receiving government aid. After a lifetime of hard work, she was now treated as someone trying to get something for nothing. She felt that her dignity had been stripped away. Women on aid lost their right to privacy, she recalled. State welfare policies required caseworkers to search aid recipients' homes in the middle of the night, looking for evidence that a man was living there. Angered at the indignities of life on "welfare," Tillmon rallied the women in her project to form a group they called ANC Mothers Anonymous. (ANC was the name for California's public assistance program).

Tillmon would later explain the group's name. "We got a dictionary," she said, "and we found out that anonymous meant nameless. We understood that what people thought about welfare recipients . . . was that they had no rights, they didn't exist." A woman on welfare, said Tillmon, became "a statistic and not a human being." ANC Mothers Anonymous was the first welfare rights group formed in the United States but it quickly became a prototype and inspiration for a new national movement.[31]

ANC Mothers called for livable welfare allotments, job training, and subsidies for daycare so that mothers of young children could look for jobs. Polling local aid recipients about what kinds of jobs they wanted to do and what kinds of jobs they felt needed to be done in their community, Tillmon came up with a list of 600 jobs that women on welfare thought they were qualified for. To break down resistance among local employers to hiring poor mothers, Tillmon enlisted the help of local school principals and public housing managers. At the same time, she pushed welfare mothers to become politically active on their own behalf. ANC mothers met with their elected representatives, ran voter registration drives and educated their neighbors about the politics of housing, education and health care. Some became so passionately engaged that they ran for office themselves. There was much talk in the 1960s about energizing the poor to engage politically. Few were as effective at it as Johnnie Tillmon.

ANC Mothers Anonymous was a path-breaking organization in 1963. It provided a model for poor women's mobilization that encouraged alliances with middle-class people but insisted that leadership and voting membership stay in the hands of poor mothers. The key, Tillmon argued, was helping poor mothers to find work that paid them enough to support their children. "Everybody is dying for a job," she said. "Everybody is saying, yes, we want to be trained for something that pays decently."[32]

Washington, D.C., Spring 1966: In 1966, Tillmon took her fresh political vision to Washington, D.C. There she met with former chemistry professor and civil rights activist George Wiley, and with New York welfare rights organizer Beulah Sanders, a magnetic woman with strong ties to labor, tenant rights and anti-Vietnam War organizations. Sanders had, with funding from the 1964 federal Community Action Program and support from anti-poverty activists in the student movement, built the largest welfare rights coalition in the nation. It was called Citywide and it represented African-American, white and Puerto Rican welfare mothers from the Bronx to Brooklyn. Tillmon, Wiley and Sanders began to plan a strategy for mobilizing poor mothers.[33]

Each brought different strengths to the movement. Tillmon could organize from the bottom up like no one else. Sanders was a consummate coalition builder, able to forge unity across race, class and political causes. She also understood how to tap federal monies through the War on Poverty. Finally, she was a fire-breathing speaker, utterly unafraid to speak truth to the most powerful of white male politicians. Wiley brought ties to the Southern civil rights movement and to wealthy donors. Working with social scientists Richard Cloward and Frances Fox Piven, Wiley was able to tap educated and affluent progressives who could provide access to politicians and agency officials as well as to young anti-poverty activists.

Two more key alliances shored up the welfare rights movement. The first was with activist attorneys who would launch a revolutionary litigation strategy to hold the federal government accountable for the promises it made in the Economic Opportunity Act of 1964. The second was with the National League of Women Voters. The primary liaison in Washington between welfare rights activists and the League was Maya Miller, a wealthy and fiery activist from Carson City, Nevada who saw the issue of child poverty as one of the paramount human rights issues of the 1960s. The mostly white, mostly married, mostly middle-class women of the League of Women Voters related to the welfare activists in a way that no one else did – as mothers. They understood and supported these women's struggle to provide an adequate minimum standard of living for their children.[34]

Tillmon and Sanders understood that welfare mothers were organizing across the country in small, militant groups. Piven and Cloward believed that, through a "politics of turmoil" that brought poor mothers onto the streets to protest, the welfare rights movement could revolutionize American politics. In 1966, the activists called together a meeting intended to create a federation of those groups. They declared June 30 a national day of protest for an adequate minimum income for all Americans.

Twenty-five Cities Across the Country, June 1966: On June 30, 1966, 6,000 women and children in 25 cities rallied in front of city, state and federal offices. In New York, Beulah Sanders led 1,500 mothers and their children through the streets in the rain to protest at City Hall. They met with the city welfare commissioner who promised to provide clothing grants for the next school year. In Boston, welfare mothers and their children rallied on the Common, asking that they not be penalized for working and that caseworkers stop referring to their children as "illegitimate." In Philadelphia, 150 women and children held a "sleep out" at state offices, demanding a benefits increase that the state had agreed to ten years earlier. Poor mothers and their children also rallied in Chicago, Louisville, Baltimore, San Bernardino and other cities across the U.S.

In all of these protests, the women sought higher monthly cash assistance, and special grants to enable mothers to buy new school clothes for their children each Fall. They also asked for Food Stamps so that poor mothers could buy food for their children in stores like other parents, instead of having to wait for handouts of government cheese, dried milk, canned meat and peanut butter. Poor mothers had not protested in such a coordinated national action since housewives' councils boycotted meat, milk and bread to lower staple food prices during the Great Depression. The 1966 welfare rights protests were modest in size. But they made the evening news on two of the three major television networks, focusing national media attention on this provocative new movement.[35]

Later that summer, welfare mothers met with civil rights workers, student activists, academics and social workers in the first national welfare rights convention in Chicago. As the women swapped stories with each other, Tillmon recalled, "we forgot about . . . shame. And as we listened to the horrible treatment and conditions all over the country, we could begin thinking . . . that maybe it wasn't us who should be ashamed."[36]

Cities Across the Country, 1967: Armed with the core belief that, as mothers trying to ensure adequate food, clothing and shelter for their children, they had nothing to be ashamed of, a national movement of poor women took the country by storm and by surprise in the late 1960s and early 1970s. During the summer of 1967, families receiving public assistance protested in 40 cities. Two thousand mothers and children led by Beulah Sanders demanded to speak to New York City Mayor John Lindsay. They wanted to know where the clothing grants were that they had been promised the previous year. They also demanded the right to have telephones in their apartments. Caseworkers had ruled phones a luxury; the mothers felt otherwise.[37]

Representatives from mothers' groups across the country came to Washington, D.C. that August to found the National Welfare Rights Organization (NWRO). Tillmon was elected chair, Sanders vice-chair. Delegates selected an inter-racial national board of six African-American mothers, two white women, and one Puerto Rican woman. NWRO's logo was two linked circles – uniting the civil rights and the anti-poverty movements. The women of NWRO described their organization as a "union" for poor women and children. And, like trade unionists had always done, they attracted members by organizing around basic needs.

> How do you get the money to live next week? How do you get clothing to send your kids back to school? How do you get them into a school lunch program? . . . How do you get back on welfare if your check is cut off?[38]

None of those issues were abstract. In summer 1967, Congress proposed freezing the number of families receiving public assistance and imposing new work requirements on mothers already receiving aid. Tillmon and Sanders urged the Senate Finance Committee to listen to the testimony of poor mothers before voting on the proposal. When committee members refused, the women convinced New York Senator Jacob Javitz to help them secure a hearing room on Capitol Hill for a "People's Hearing." They sent invitations to every sitting member of Congress. Not a single one came.[39]

So, a few months later, welfare mother activists came to Senate hearings on the new welfare proposals en masse, demanding to testify. Senator Russell Long of Louisiana, one of the most powerful Senators in the history of the institution, interrupted Tillmon's testimony to ask why he should budget more money in aid when he could no longer find someone willing to iron his shirts for the wage he had always paid. Tillmon replied that she had ironed shirts for 18 years – and when she was too sick to continue working, she couldn't find someone to help her feed her children. She had no choice but to apply for public assistance. All but two members of the Senate Finance Committee walked out while Tillmon and other women were testifying. Upset, the mothers staged an impromptu sit-in, refusing to leave the witness table until all 17 members of the committee returned to hear their testimony.

Long was dismissive. The women, he said, were "brood mares." Besides, he opined: "If they can find the time to march in the streets, picket, and sit all day in committee hearing rooms, they can find the time to do some useful work. They could be picking up litter in front of their houses, or killing rats instead of impeding the work of Congress." Capitol police warned the women they would face six months in jail if they didn't leave the room peacefully. As they streamed out, they shouted, "We won't iron your shirts for you anymore, Senator Long." The following June, on NWRO's annual day of protest, Tillmon organized a series of actions she called "Brood Mare Stampedes."[40] Across the country, activist welfare mothers watched these news stories with interest and amusement. Powerful politicians seemed actually afraid to meet face-to-face with welfare recipients. Photographs of fist-waving, chanting welfare mothers appeared on the front pages of the nation's largest newspapers.[41]

The coverage had negative as well as positive effects for the women and their families. It played into stereotypes of black women as angry and ever hungry for public aid, the insatiable poor draining the resources of hard-working taxpayers. But, after decades of scholarly analysis and politicians' pronouncements objectifying poor black mothers, Americans were finally seeing their faces and hearing their voices. And some important people began to listen.

Washington, 1968: Most notably, the leaders of the Southern civil rights movement finally began to show interest in welfare mothers. The social stigma attached to poor, single mothers had long made the Reverend Martin Luther King Jr. and other middle-class black leaders uncomfortable about allying themselves with the welfare rights movement. For years, poor women had accepted their invisibility to mainstream civil rights activists. But, when King ignored welfare as an issue in his 1968 Poor People's Campaign, Sanders and Tillmon asked to meet with him.

Sitting next to King with her grandchild on her lap, Tillmon asked him for his position on several pieces of welfare legislation then being considered in Congress. When he answered vaguely, Mrs. Tillmon "jumped on Martin like no one ever had before," King's assistant Andrew Young would later recall. She said: "You know, Dr. King, if you don't know about these questions, you should say you don't know, and then we could go on with the meeting." An awkward silence followed, and then King, not usually receptive to criticism from women, apologized. "You're right Mrs. Tillmon," he said. "We don't know anything about welfare. We are here to learn."[42]

Organized labor, too, finally began to respond to overtures from welfare activists. Beulah Sanders negotiated with District Council 37, the largest public employees' union in New York City, to develop job training and placement programs for welfare mothers. Sanders also forged alliances with social workers' unions in the city to advocate for more generous welfare payments.[43]

New York and Other Cities, 1969–1970: In the summer of 1969, 300 social workers sympathetic to the welfare rights movement walked out of a national social work conference in Manhattan and marched down Seventh Avenue to the Sears and Roebuck on 31st Street. There they publicly destroyed their Sears credit cards, as a gesture of support for the city's welfare mothers who said that Sears discriminated against families on public assistance by denying them credit. Tired of waiting for city and state officials to approve special grants for school clothing for their children, furniture and household appliances, the members of Citywide marched into Sears, applied for credit, listing NWRO as their guarantor, and then ordered clothing and furniture. Like any inquiring shopper, they tried out sample vacuum cleaners, sewing machines and record players. "Sears has got to learn one thing," Sanders said. "They have to deal with the poor."[44]

Organizers didn't ignore the specter of credit card debt. "We weren't stupid in what we asked for," recalled Roxanne Jones, the former dancer and waitress who led NWRO in Philadelphia. The group requested only $50 in credit and each cardholder could increase her debt limit only if she paid off her monthly bills. By the end of 1969, Sears, E. J. Korvettes, Gimbels, Abraham and Strauss and Marshall Field department store in Chicago had granted the women credit.[45]

For Sanders, Tillmon, Jones and other welfare rights leaders, these protests had a common purpose – establishing visibility and a public voice for poor women. Sanders testified before President Richard Nixon's Commission on Income Maintenance, a blue ribbon committee exploring options for welfare reform. She said: "Everybody from President Nixon on down is talking about us. Everyone has their own plan on what to do with welfare recipients." Pointing out that Senator James Eastland of Mississippi had received hundreds of thousands of dollars in crop subsidies from the U.S. Department of Agriculture, she questioned who was really dependent on welfare. "The only thing you can really do," she told the Senators, "is get up off your 17th century attitudes, give poor people enough money to live decently, and let us decide how to live our lives."[46]

President Richard Nixon, hoping to resolve the welfare crisis, introduced the Family Assistance Plan in 1969. FAP offered a guaranteed minimum income for all Americans, established uniform eligibility criteria across the states, for the first time included the working poor among those eligible for public assistance and allowed aid to families with fathers still living at home. It would have been revolutionary except for one thing – the plan offered a family of four only $1,600 a year. NWRO estimated that, in 1969, a family of four required a minimum of $5,500 a year to live decently. Had it passed, the FAP would have dramatically increased the incomes of most recipients of public assistance in the South, but it would have cut benefits significantly in New York, Illinois and California – home to nearly half of the nation's recipients of public aid.

Not surprisingly, the plan sparked opposition on both sides of the aisle and at both ends of the American political spectrum. Southern politicians predicted that FAP would drain the pool of labor for low wage jobs. "There's not going to be anybody left to roll these wheelbarrows and press these shirts," said Georgia Congressman Richard Landrum. On the other side, liberal Michigan Congressman John Conyers called FAP "the greatest welfare cutback in modern times." NWRO leaders launched a no-holds barred attempt to "ZAP FAP." Interestingly, Johnnie Tillmon, ever the pragmatist, had a more nuanced response. She praised President Nixon for trying to establish a minimum annual income for all Americans, then urged him to raise it to a level that families could live on. Nixon did a 180 degree turn and withdrew support from the plan entirely. In May 1970, welfare mother protesters occupied the offices of the Secretary of Health, Education and Welfare, Robert Finch. They proclaimed that they could run the welfare system better than he.[47]

Many years later, Tillmon wondered to interviewers whether welfare rights activists had not scuttled their best chance to pass a minimum income bill that later could have been adjusted upward. After another failed attempt by Jimmy Carter in the late 1970s, no American President would again introduce the idea. Indeed, by the 21st century, it would seem positively utopian.[48]

In the courts, 1968–1973: The welfare rights movement was quite a bit more successful in the courts than in Congress. Aided by the Legal Services Corporation, established under the 1964 Economic Opportunity Act, welfare mothers sued successfully in the late 1960s to overturn a variety of regulations they felt to be discriminatory. In *King v. Smith* (1968), the court overturned the "man in the house rule" that had spawned the hated dawn and middle of the night raids of welfare recipients' homes and bedrooms. In *Shapiro v. Thompson* (1969) the court overturned residency requirements blocking poor mothers from moving to states that gave more generous allotments. And, in *Goldberg v. Kelley* (1970), poor mothers won the right to hearings when a state or local welfare official sought to terminate their benefits.

Poor mothers also sued the federal government to release funds for Food Stamps, the Women and Infant Children nutrition and pre-natal care program, as well as for free school breakfasts and lunches. Finally, welfare mothers across the country applied for funds made available through the federal War on Poverty to establish community programs run by poor women for poor women and their children. By the end of the 1960s, poor mothers themselves were providing desperately needed services in poverty-stricken communities across the country. And they were doing a really good job.[49]

Las Vegas March 6, 1971, "We Can Do it And Do it Better!": On a sunny Spring day in 1971, the Las Vegas Strip was filled with marching, chanting welfare mothers from across the United States. Tourists gaped as the demonstration headed south down the famous strip of desert highway, past wedding chapels and glittering hotels. Arm in arm, black and white, Latina and Native-American mothers marched alongside an interesting array of allies: activist priests, film stars Jane Fonda and Donald Sutherland and civil rights leader Ralph David Abernathy. This rag-tag army of anti-poverty warriors was led by Ruby Duncan, a 37-year-old hotel maid and mother of seven, who had moved from Louisiana to Las Vegas in the early 1950s to escape life as a cotton-picker. Walking six to eight abreast, the marchers sang "We Shall Overcome" and carried signs that demanded "Give Us Back Our Checks."

The marchers were protesting a decision by Nevada welfare administrator George Miller to cut one third of the state's recipients off the rolls entirely and to reduce the checks of another third. Nevada already had the second lowest monthly payments in the country, behind only Mississippi. Duncan had traveled to Washington, D.C. to meet with Sanders and Tillmon. The two had patiently explained that the only way to make the state listen was "to hit them in the pocketbook." Returning home to the Strip Duncan looked around and realized: "This is the main vein of Nevada. This is *the* pocketbook."

"When the marchers turned into Caesars," Duncan recalled, "one cop threw up his hands. 'Oh my God,' he said. 'Where do you think you're going?'" Duncan turned a 100-watt smile on him. The march was going exactly where she intended it to: straight into Caesars Palace – the gilt and red-velvet heart of Vegas. The marchers streamed into the casino, with its Roman centurion guards and wise-cracking, toga-clad cocktail waitresses. Welfare recipient Essie Henderson noticed that "the fur salon was taking all the furs off and hiding them. They couldn't imagine that we weren't there to steal." Laughing at their sudden power, the women broke into song, creating their own version of an old labor and civil rights anthem: "We Are into Caesars Palace, and We Shall Not Be Moved."

From 1971 to 1974, Las Vegas welfare mothers marched, rallied, and mounted class-action law suits to try and move first the state then the federal government to provide better food aid, clothing assistance and medical care for their children. By 1974, they had lost faith in the promises of politicians and welfare professionals. "We can do it and do it better," they promised. And they did.

These women and their allies would build an alternative welfare system run by poor mothers for poor mothers and their children. They ran it successfully in West Las Vegas for over 20 years, not closing their doors until the 1990s. They provided a model for poor women's community action across the country. In the poorest neighborhood in the city, they opened the first medical clinic, library, public swimming pool and job training programs for teens and poor mothers. They built low-income housing, fitted old homes with solar panels to lower energy costs, published a community newspaper, and managed a range of federal programs including the Women and Infant Children Nutrition Program, Early Periodic Screening and Diagnostic Testing for poor children, and a Comprehensive Education and Training Act grant to employ local young people. By the late 1970s, the organization they created, Operation Life, was the largest employer on the West Side of Las Vegas. And the clinic they ran screened the highest percentage of eligible children of any federally funded pediatric facility in the nation.

In the mid-1970s Operation Life was lauded as an example of good management by Republican conservative Department of Health and Welfare (HEW) Secretary Casper Weinberger. In 1980, Ruby Duncan, the movement's leader, was appointed by President Jimmy Carter to attend the White House Conference on Families. She was also appointed to federal commissions on community development, housing and health care. She was one of the only poor women of color on any of these commissions and was also one of the only poor women of color elected to the board of the National Organization of Women (NOW).

Operation Life was just one of many similar community projects run by poor mothers in the 1970s. In Baltimore, poor mothers opened Self-Help Housing and food cooperatives. In Durham, North Carolina, poor black and white mothers opened a successful and long-running clinic together. In Memphis, poor mothers did pioneering work to combat infant mortality and hunger, riveting the attention of the nation and paving the way for the passage of the Women and Infant Children Nutrition Program that still exists today. In every way, this movement of poor mothers, its members, leaders and the alliances they built force a rethinking of the contours and parameters of 1970s feminism, as well as civil rights, black power and poverty politics.[50]

PART II: RETHINKING POOR MOTHERS' ACTIVISM AND FEMINISM IN THE 1970S

How do these three movements force us to rethink feminism in the 1970s? They do so in a number of ways. First, they make clear that women's activism was as often galvanized by concerns of class and race as by questions of gender inequality. Second, they make clear that gender inequality cannot be understood without seeing the ways that class and race intersect with sex. Finally, they make clear that motherhood was, as it had always been, one of the primary motivations for women to become politically active.

There was a great deal that the movements led by Native-American women, Mexican-American women farm workers, and African-American welfare mothers in the 1960s and 1970s had in common. These movements were all led by, and mounted on behalf of, the most disfranchised and impoverished people in the U.S. These were all fundamentally subsistence movements – motivated by the great need of participants for access to the essential sustainers of life – clean water, decent housing, food, protection from exposure to poisons, an income sufficient to sustain life. They were also united by a shared sense that participants in these movements had been unjustly denied the most basic trappings of human dignity enshrined in the Constitution – the rights to privacy, to control their own bodies, to associate with whomever they chose, to raise their children as they saw fit, and to live free from state-sanctioned and state-supported violence.

There were differences as well. Native-American women activists were drawn into the American Indian Movement, and other Indian civil rights actions, initially by profound anger at the policies of the 1950s that had cut off federal funds to tribal authorities and relocated reservation dwellers to cities where a sense of Indian community was difficult, if not impossible, to sustain. An unintended consequence of these relocations was that young Indian students in colleges and urban settings across the U.S. came into contact with civil rights, labor and feminist activists of many races and ethnicities whose thoughts and political actions sparked new kinds of organizing among Native-Americans in the 1960s and 1970s.

The farm workers' union that began in the mid-1960s, built on the multicultural class-consciousness deployed by progressive labor organizers from the 1930s on. An important influence was the vibrantly multi-ethnic United Cannery and Packinghouse Workers' Union, in which Mexican-American women organizers had played a major role. It is significant that the 1965 Delano strike began when Huerta, Caesar and Helen Chavez and other unionized Mexican-Americans decided to support a walkout by Filipino farm workers. Several previous attempts to organize farm workers in California during the 20th century had failed, in part because of the challenges of organizing Mexican, Japanese and Filipino farm workers together.[51]

But the farm workers' movement was every bit as much, if not more, influenced by race-based civil rights consciousness. Huerta's father had been a miner in New Mexico and experienced the race prejudice against Mexican miners and the dire living conditions portrayed in the film *Salt of the Earth*. Her brother was one of many Mexican boys beaten by police and military during the 1940s California "zoot suit" riots. Like Native-American activists in California during the same era, Dolores Huerta, Caesar Chavez and other leaders of the United Farm Workers union were heavily influenced both by the rhetoric and the non-violent direct action protest strategies of the African-American freedom struggle in the 1950s and 1960s. Chavez modeled his 1966 march from Delano to Sacramento on Martin Luther King's march from Selma to Montgomery. Huerta modeled her coalition-building and use of boycotts on the successful strategies of the Southern civil rights movement.[52]

But Huerta also drew on the bread and roses strikes of the 1910s, when affluent women came out to support immigrant working girls. Harnessing the power of women consumers was a strategy that had worked for the labor movement from the union label campaigns of the 1910s through the staple food boycotts and rent strikes of the Great Depression. The farm workers union was, in that sense, a full fusion of labor, race and working-class feminist traditions and political strategies.

The welfare rights movement, begun by Southern migrant mothers, spread through the country in the late 1960s and 1970s, becoming the largest and most important subsistence movement by poor mothers in the U.S. since the Great Depression. The Las Vegas mothers' movement was one brilliant example, but thriving welfare rights movements also took root in Brooklyn, Chicago, Cleveland, Washington, D.C. and many of the nation's largest cities, as well as Indian reservations and rural Mississippi cotton counties. Welfare rights was without question a motherist movement, sparked by poor women's concerns about fulfilling their maternal responsibilities to feed, clothe, shelter and educate their children. In that way, it fit into a long tradition of mothers' activism.

But the welfare mothers struggle was also an extension of the civil rights movement, made up overwhelmingly of African-American women and driven by a demand for rights and services. Like the Southern black freedom struggle of the 1950s and early 1960s, it was a response to promises made by an activist liberal government in the mid-20th century that expanded citizenship rights for the disfranchised. Title IV of the Social Security Act of 1935, one of the crowning achievements of Frances Perkins and the industrial feminist coalition in Washington,

D.C., guaranteed government support for poor families with dependent children. The Economic Opportunity Act of 1964 funded community action programs to help mobilize the poor on their own behalf, and created the Legal Services program, through which the welfare mothers' lawsuits around man in the house rules, residency requirements, the right to hearings, Food Stamps, WIC and the school lunch program were launched.

These federal assistance programs were aimed broadly at the poor. But, in practice, they mostly served poor mothers and their children, creating a sense that poor mothers had rights worth fighting for and some support from the federal government. Las Vegas welfare rights activist Alversa Beals recalls that it was like an electric shock going through her body the first time she heard the words "welfare and rights in the same sentence." Her colleague in the Las Vegas movement, housing activist Emma Stampley recalled: "They said it was a movement for women and kids. And I thought, 'I'm a woman. I got kids. I gotta go!'"[53]

There were strains of motherist activism in the American Indian Movement and the Mexican-American farm workers' movement as well. "We are caretakers," said Yvonne Swan (formerly Wanrow) of the women in AIM. They saw their job both as taking care of children and protecting the mother of everyone and everything, Mother Earth. "We're survivors of abuse as women, as is Mother Earth, as is Grandmother Moon. So we identify with all the female part of creation."[54]

One of the founders of AIM and Women of All Red Nations, even carries the name Madonna. And many of her organizing activities have focused on children. Thunderhawk started a home and school in South Dakota for children of Indian activists indicted and/or imprisoned. She took in runaways and other native children with no place else to go. Thunderhawk also described herself as mothering the next generation of political activists: "You have to think and plan for seven generations ahead," she said. "When I saw the real meaning of land struggle I knew I had to raise my children and grandchildren to continue the struggle . . . I knew it was ongoing."[55]

In the farm workers' movement, many of the activists were mothers who also brought their children with them to the fields, to picket lines and boycotts to support their strikes. To some extent this was part of the migrant lifestyle that farm worker families had to adopt to survive, moving from town to town, region to region, following crops. Huerta, who was a single mother of 11 children, made her family a part of her work. She noted that this practice rarely earned her criticism from other poor mothers in the movement. "Poor people have to haul their kids around from school to school," she said of the migrant workers she organized. "Women have to go out and work and they've got to either leave their kids or take them out to the fields with them. So they sympathize . . . with my problems in terms of my children."[56]

Women in the movement moved their children to different parts of the country to live for a while during the organizing campaign for the grape boycott.

Maria Luisa Rangel moved nine children to Detroit. Juanita Valdez moved eight to Cincinnati to work on the lettuce boycott. They worked for the movement as families. Many UFW women who remained in California blended their work as mothers and family caretakers with work for the union – walking picket lines, caring for those wounded in battles with police, company guards and rival Teamsters' union muscle.

This blending of family and political work made their contributions to the farm worker's movement difficult for historians to see. To appreciate the contributions made by thousands of grass-roots women activists in the farm workers' movement, historian Margaret Rose has argued, we need to expand our understanding of politics and labor activism. To see their contribution to the 1970s women's movement, we similarly need to broaden our definition of feminist activism to include these women who occupied federal lands, picketed and fought hand to hand with armed men, and who sat in at the offices of male welfare administrators to demand food and shoes for their children.[57]

Seeing these movements and their members as part of the history of modern feminism is not only about broadening definitions of feminist activism to include other kinds of women's movements. These subsistence movements and the women who led them were affected by the rhetoric and activism of radical and mainstream feminists. And women leaders in these movements saw themselves as feminists.

Johnnie Tillmon, founder and president of the National Welfare Rights Organization, published an essay in *Ms. Magazine* in 1972 explaining why the mistreatment of poor mothers on public assistance was inextricably linked to the denigration of women generally. Her aim was to get middle-class women to see welfare as an issue of concern for feminists. "I'm a woman. I'm a black woman. I'm a fat woman. I'm a middle-aged woman. And I'm a woman on welfare," she began. "In this country if you're one of those things you count less as a human being. If you're all of those things, you don't count at all. Except as a statistic."[58]

Tillmon knew all too well that one of the major difficulties that welfare rights activists faced was finding allies. One reason for that, she argued in her *Ms.* essay, was the lies that politicians tell about welfare recipients – that they are lazy, stupid, incompetent and immoral. "There are a lot of other lies that male society tells about welfare mothers . . . If people are willing to believe these lies, it's partly because they're just special versions of the lies that society tells about all women." And the point of telling such lies, she said, was to justify men's control of women.

Women on A.F.D.C. (Aid to Families With Dependent Children), she argued, experienced an extreme form of that control: "The truth is that A.F.D.C. is like a super-sexist marriage," she wrote.

> You trade in a man for *the man*. But you can't divorce him if he treats you bad. He can divorce you, of course, cut you off if he wants. But in that case,

he keeps the kids, not you. *The man* runs everything. In ordinary marriage, sex is supposed to be for your husband. On A.F.D.C. you're not supposed to have any sex at all. You give up control of your own body. It is a condition of aid. You may even have to agree to get your tubes tied so you can never have more children just to avoid being cut off welfare. *The man*, the welfare system, controls your money. He tells you what to buy, what not to buy, where to buy it, and how much things cost. If things – rent for instance – cost more than he says they do, it's just too bad for you.

Politicians insisted that mothers on welfare did not want to work. But poverty was not a result of women not working. Millions of people worked for wages that do not support them, Tillmon argued, and most of those concentrated in low wage jobs were women. (That remains just as true in the 21st century.) The denigration of women's work had to become a feminist issue, Tillmon argued, or the vast majority of American women would never be liberated.

President Richard Nixon liked to talk about the dignity of work, Tillmon wrote. But

> there is no dignity in starvation . . . Either it breaks you and you start hating yourself or *you* break it. There's one good thing about welfare. It kills your illusions about yourself, and about where this society is really at . . . You have to learn to fight, to be aggressive, or you just don't make it.

In the final analysis, she argued, "it is we poor welfare women who will really liberate women in this country" by making clear the value of mothering work. If I were president, Tillmon wrote,

> I'd just issue a proclamation that 'women's' work is *real* work . . . I'd start paying women a living wage for doing the work we are already doing – child-raising and housekeeping . . . For me, Women's Liberation is simple . . . no woman can be liberated until all women get off their knees. That's what the National Welfare Rights Organization is about – women, standing together on their feet.[59]

Winona LaDuke felt that the Indigenous Women's Network was also a feminist organization. The point of IWN, LaDuke recalled, was "to encourage women's participation at the local, national and international levels. We wanted to talk about organizing, and strategies that are working and challenges that we're facing – and despair and hope and all those pieces." What started as a retreat to talk and regroup, became the most lasting native women's civil, political and economic rights organization in U.S. history – run by and for women and to promote women – a clearly feminist agenda.[60]

Women in subsistence movements broke gender barriers by taking on roles usually reserved for men. Dolores Huerta was described by growers as crazy and violent for being a tougher negotiator than many men. And she decided that was a good thing. Early in the 1960s, she wrote to Caesar Chavez that she had learned to "speak on a man to man basis" to growers, government officials and lobbyists. She and Chavez worked closely, but Huerta also battled with him on a regular basis. And it was Huerta, not Chavez, who became the acknowledged master of union contract negotiation, a province usually reserved for men. Chavez, she would say, did not have the patience for it.[61]

For "born again feminists" like Huerta, Wilma Mankiller and Ruby Duncan, it made sense to work directly with mainstream feminist groups. They recognized, as so many leaders of poor women's movements before them had, that middle-class and affluent feminists could provide crucial support for poor women's struggles. Wilma Mankiller served on the board of the Ms. Foundation, funding woman-led and conceived projects across the world. She focused on helping poor women of color, especially native women, leverage the resources of the Ms. Foundation to promote vital economic development projects on Indian reservations. Though Huerta was initially suspicious of women's liberation, her view on middle-class feminists changed during the grape boycott when she worked directly with Gloria Steinem and other white feminist leaders.[62]

As feminist organizations helped to rally the power of women consumers behind the farm worker cause, Huerta became more comfortable identifying herself as a feminist. She also began to speak more openly about challenging sexism within the farm workers' union. As the 1970s gave way to the 1980s, Huerta became increasingly involved in advocating for women. She traveled around the country for two years in the late 1980s and early 1990s for the Feminist Majority Foundation, helping to organize campaigns for Latinas running for elected office. Her work contributed to a dramatic increase in the number of Latina elected officials on the local, state and federal levels.[63]

Welfare rights activist Ruby Duncan served for a long time on the national Board of Directors of NOW. Through that position she worked on the feminization of poverty, job training for poor mothers to help get them into male dominated trades, building resources for victims of domestic violence and increasing access for all women to affordable, safe birth control. Duncan came to believe that her sex, even more than her race and class, had constrained her from achieving all that she wanted to. She wanted to ensure that younger women did not face the same constraints.

These women found places for themselves within feminist organizations dominated by white, middle-class women. In so doing, they changed those movements from within. If most histories of 1970s feminism have written poor women out of the story, it is not because they were unimportant to the movement. They were, on every level.

Notes

1   Richard A. Garcia, "Dolores Huerta: Woman, Organizer, and Symbol," *California History*, Vol. 72, No. 1, Spring 1993, pp. 56–71.

2   Duane Noriyuki, "The Women of Wounded Knee," *Hearts Not on the Ground*, http://www.dickshovel.com/lsa21.html.

3   Johnnie Tillmon, "Welfare is a Women's Issue," *Ms. Magazine*, Spring 1972, pp. 111–116.

4   "Indian Tribes and Tribal Communities in California," *Research Update: Administrative Office of the Courts: Center for Families, Children and the Courts*, http://www.courts.ca.gov/documents/TribalFAQs.pdf.

5   Troy Johnson, "The Alcatraz Indian Occupation," *We Hold the Rock, Alcatraz Island* (U.S. National Park Service), http://www.nps.gov/alca/historyculture/we-hold-the-rock.htm; Donna Hightower Langston, "American Indian Women's Activism in the 1960s and 70s," *Hypatia*, Vol. 18, No. 2, 2003.

6   Payne, Diane. "Each of My Generations Is Getting Stronger: An Interview with Janet McCloud," *Indian Truth: Special Issue on Native Women* 239, May/June, 1988, pp. 5–7.

7   Mark Trahant, "The Center of Everything: Native Leader Janet McCloud Finds her Peace," *Seattle Times*, July 4, 1999.

8   ibid.

9   Janet McCloud, Yet Si Blue, 1934–2003, *Indian Country Today*, December 5, 2003.

10 Hightower Langston, op. cit.; Sam Howe Verhovek, "Wilma Mankiller, Cherokee Chief and First Woman to Lead Major Tribe is Dead at 64," *New York Times* April 6, 2010.

11 Mary Brave Bird with Richard Erdoes, *Lakota Woman* (New York, Grove Press, reprint 2011).

12 *New York Times*, November 3, 1972. "500 Indians Seize U.S. Building," Peter Osnos, "Indians First, Always," *Washington Post*, November 4, 1972; Donald Baker and Paul Ramirez, "Officials, Indians Parley on Protest," *Washington Post*, November 5, 1972.

13 PBS American Experience, "We Shall Remain: Episode 5, Wounded Knee," http://www.pbs.org/wgbh/amex/weshallremain/the_films/episode_5.

14 Emily Chertoff, "Occupy Wounded Knee: A 71 Day Siege and a Forgotten Civil Rights Movement," *The Atlantic*, October 23, 2012.

15 Noriyuki, op. cit.; Paul C. Rosier, "Women of All Red Nations (WARN)" in Lynne E. Ford, ed., *Encyclopedia of Women and American Politics* (New York: Facts On File, Inc., 2008) American Women's History Online, http://www.fofweb.com/activelink2.asp?ItemID=WE42&iPin=EWAP0564&SingleRecord=True.

16 Agnes Williams, "The Great Janet McCloud," *Indigenous Women Magazine*, March 29, 2006, http://indigenouswomen.org/index.php?option=com_content&task=view&id=5&Itemid=46; "Indians Complete Walk," *Spokane Spokesman-Review*, August 22, 1978.

17 History of IWN, http://indigenouswomen.org/index.php?option=com_content&task=view&id=22&Itemid=60.

18 "History of IWN" December 24, 2006. Indigenous Women's Network, op. cit.

19 Esther Uranday, "'Quite a Wake Up Call,' Veterans of Historic Delano Grape Strike Mark 40th Anniversary," *El Malcriado*, Special Edition, September 17–18, 2005, http://www.ufw.org/_page.php?menu=research&inc=history/05.html.

20 Hortensia Mata, "The day my life was changed forever," *Veterans of Historic Delano Grape Strike Mark 40th Anniversary*.

21 Richard Worth, "Strike in Delano", *Dolores Huerta, The Great Hispanic Heritage,* (New York: Chelsea House Publishers, 2006) *American History Online.* Facts On File, Inc. http://www.fofweb.com/activelink2.asp?.

22 Worth, op. cit.; Margaret Rose, "Traditional and Nontraditional Patterns of Female Leadership in the United Farm Workers of America, 1952–1980," *Frontiers: A Journal of Women's Studies,* Vol. 11, No. 1, 1990, pp. 26–32.

23 Dolores Huerta, "Surmounting Obstacles With Faith and Belief in Justice," *Veterans,* op. cit.

24 David Harris, "The Battle of Coachella Valley," *Rolling Stone,* September 13, 1973.

25 ibid.

26 ibid.

27 "The Fight in the Fields," PBS *American Experience,* http://www.pbs.org/itvs/fightfields/timeline.html; Dolores Huerta biography, Huerta Foundation, doloreshuerta.org.

28 "Workers' Voices," The Official Web Page of the United Farm Workers of America, http://www.ufw.org/_board.php?mode=list&b_code=org_wv&field=&key=&page=2#2927.

29 Sherna Berger Gluck, "5 Interviews with Johnnie Tillmon, 1991," California State University Long Beach Digital Library, http://symposia.library.csulb.edu/iii/cpro/DigitalItemViewPage.external;jsessionid=5190B5DE1C4C84325FBF6BC3B031B7C5.?lang=eng&sp=1001810&sp=T&sp=1&suite=def.

30 Gluck Interviews, op. cit. There is little written on Johnnie Tillmon's early life. For what there is see Guida West, *The National Welfare Rights Movement: The Social Protest of Poor Women* (New York: Praeger, 1981).

31 Nick Kotz and Mary Lynn Kotz, *A Passion for Equality: George Wiley and the Movement* (New York: Norton, 1977), p. 220; for material on ANC Mothers see George Martin, "The Emergence and Development of a Social Movement Organization Among the Underclass," (Ph.D. dissertation, University of Chicago, 1972).

32 West, op. cit., p. 92.

33 Felicia Kornbluh, *The Battle For Welfare Rights: Politics and Poverty in Modern America* (Philadelphia: University of Pennsylvania Press, 2007).

34 Author's interview with Maya Miller and Marty Makower, September 2–3, 1992. Carson City, Nevada.

35 *New York Times,* July 1, 1966; *New York Daily News,* June 29, 1966; *National Guardian,* July 9, 1966; *Christian Science Monitor,* June 29, 1966, cited in Annelise Orleck, *Storming Caesars Palace: How Black Mothers Fought Their Own War on Poverty* (Boston: Beacon, 2005, p. 112).

36 Kotz and Kotz, op. cit. p. 199.

37 Mary Childers, "A Spontaneous Welfare Rights Protest by Politically Inactive Mothers," Alexis Jetter, Annelise Orleck and Diana Taylor, eds., *The Politics of Motherhood; Activist Voices from Left to Right* (Hanover: University Press of New England, 1997).

38 Hobart Burch, "A Conversation with George Wiley," cited in Orleck, *Storming,* p. 113.

39 *New York Times,* August 29, 1967.

40 See Orleck, *Storming,* p. 114; *New York Times,* September 20, 1967; author's interview with Ruby Duncan, Las Vegas, Nevada, September 5, 1992.

41 Orleck, Storming, pp. 111–115.

42 Deborah Gray White, *Too Heavy a Load: Black Women in Defense of Themselves 1894–1994* (New York: Norton, 1999).

43 Minutes of Meetings between Citywide and labor groups, Moorland-Spingarn Archives, Howard University, NWRO Papers, Box 2093.

44 *New York Times*, May 28, 1969; *New York Times*, July 4, 1969; Kotz and Kotz, op. cit. p. 236; for the most complete account of the New York City welfare rights struggle see Kornbluh, *The Battle For Welfare Rights,* op. cit. Credit card campaign detailed in Chapter 5.

45 Orleck, *Storming,* p. 123.

46 "Statement by Beulah Sanders before the Presidential Commission on Income Maintenance," June 5, 1969. George Wiley papers, Wisconsin Historical Society, Box 17, Folder 3.

47 *The Day,* May 14, 1970, http://news.google.com/newspapers?nid=1915&dat=197005 14&id=J_IgAAAAIBAJ&sjid=UnQFAAAAIBAJ&pg=958,2168442.

48 Orleck, *Storming,* pp. 123–125.

49 ibid., pp. 206–207; 227.

50 See Orleck, *Storming,* op. cit; and Ruby Duncan, "I Got to Dreamin'," Alexis Jetter, Annelise Orleck and Diana Taylor, eds., *The Politics of Motherhood: Activist Voices From Left To Right* (Hanover: University Press of New England, 1997).

51 See Vicki Ruiz, *Cannery Women, Cannery Lives: Mexican Women, Unionization and the California Food Processing Industry, 1930–1950* (Albuquerque: University of New Mexico Press, 1987).

52 Margaret Rose, op. cit.; Matthew Garcia, *From the Jaws of Victory: The Triumph and Tragedy of Caesar Chavez and the Farm Worker Movement* (Berkeley: University of California Press, 2012).

53 Orleck, *Storming,* op. cit, pp. 98–105.

54 Statement of Yvonne Swan at the American Indian Movement Conference, Women Support Network Panel Discussion, November 23, 2010, http://www.youtube.com/ watch?v=eSjg4VM0-q0.

55 Noriyuki, op. cit.; AIM Conference Women Panel," op. cit.

56 Margaret Rose, op. cit.

57 ibid.

58 Johnnie Tillmon, "Welfare is a Women's Issue," *Ms. Magazine,* Spring 1972: pp. 111–116.

59 ibid.

60 Winona Laduke, Interviewed by Annelise Orleck and Alexis Jetter, May 17, 1993, Hanover, New Hampshire. In Jetter, Orleck and Taylor, eds., *The Politics of Motherhood,* op. cit.

61 Dolores Huerta biography, "The Feminist Seed is Planted," Dolores Huerta Foundation, http://www.doloreshuerta.org/dolores-huerta; PBS News Hour, May 30, 2012, "Dolores Huerta Calls Herself a Born-Again Feminist," http://video.pbs.org/video/2240859912/.

62 Verhovek, op. cit.; Wilma Mankiller, "Womanhood," from Wilma Mankiller, *Every Day is a Good Day,* p. 98.

63 ibid. Huerta biography; PBS interview.

7

LESBIAN LIVES, LESBIAN RIGHTS, LESBIAN FEMINISM

Back in those days (the 1950s and 60s) we realized that we were considered illegal, immoral and sick. So those were the three issues we took on.

Del Martin, anti-domestic violence activist, co-founder of
the first national lesbian rights organization and the first
openly lesbian board member of NOW[1]

It is the primacy of women relating to women, of women creating a new conscious-ness of and with each other, which is at the heart of women's liberation and the basis for the cultural revolution.

The Woman Identified Woman by
RADICALLESBIANS, 1970[2]

As a forty-nine-year-old Black lesbian feminist socialist mother . . . I usually find myself a part of some group defined as other, deviant, inferior, or just plain wrong.

Audre Lorde, *Sister Outsider*, 1984[3]

The kind of woman I am attracted to is invariably the kind of woman who embarrasses respectably middle-class, politically aware lesbian feminists.

Dorothy Allison, "A Question of Class," 1994[4]

Lesbians, Feminism and the Tensions Between

New York City – May 1, 1970: On opening night of the Second Congress to Unite Women, organized by NOW and other women's groups, 300 delegates from across the country filled the auditorium of a Manhattan junior high school. Some of them noticed that the program did not include a single speech or workshop dealing with lesbian issues. Most did not. They would soon be made aware. As the first speaker mounted the podium, the room went suddenly dark. Through the darkness, delegates heard women laughing excitedly and the drumming of feet as they ran down the aisles.

In a few minutes, the lights came back on, illuminating a phalanx of women stretched across the front of the room wearing dyed purple t-shirts emblazoned with the words *Lavender Menace*. From the audience, authors Karla Jay and Rita Mae Brown theatrically pulled off their button down shirts to reveal that they too proudly wore *Lavender Menace* t-shirts. "Yes, Yes, Sisters," Jay shouted. "I'm tired of being in the closet because of the women's movement." Brown shouted to the audience. "Who wants to join us?" More than a few shouted back, "I do."[5]

The name *Lavender Menace* was drawn from a jab at lesbian activists made by Betty Friedan and published in a 1970 *New York Times Magazine* article. Friedan was worried that association with lesbians and lesbian rights groups threatened NOW's standing as a serious and respectable political organization. She didn't want feminism to be equated with lesbianism. Friedan had gone so far as to delete from the program for the First Congress to Unite Women, held in New York in 1969, all references to lesbian organizations. In 1970, New York NOW leaders had fired lesbian author and activist Rita Mae Brown from her job as editor of the group's newsletter. Many lesbian members of New York NOW had resigned in protest. Together they planned the *Lavender Menace* action and wrote a manifesto they called "The Woman Identified Woman."[6]

Lavender Menace activists passed out the manifesto at the conference. It began provocatively: "What is a lesbian? A lesbian is the rage of all women condensed to the point of explosion." The authors felt angry and betrayed by the organized feminist movement. They now sought to educate and reach out to heterosexual feminist allies – "because we are all women."

Lavender Menace challenged heterosexual feminists to resist the impulse to distance themselves from their lesbian friends and political comrades. "As long as the label 'dyke' can be used to frighten wom[a]n into a less militant stand, keep her separate from her sisters, keep her from giving primacy to anything other than men and family," the manifesto argued, "then to that extent she is controlled by the male culture." The manifesto went farther, claiming lesbianism as a revolutionary stance.

> Until women see in each other the possibility of a primal commitment which includes sexual love . . . they will be denying themselves the love and value they readily accord to men, thus affirming their second-class status . . . It is the primacy of women relating to women, of women creating a new consciousness of and with each other, which is at the heart of women's liberation, and the basis for the cultural revolution.[7]

The women of *Lavender Menace* insisted that they had not come to disrupt the conference, but to open up a discussion of lesbian issues, which had been erased from the official program. Kate Millett, chair of New York NOW, who had known in advance about the action, urged delegates to join in. Some women left, but most stayed. For two hours, they talked about lesbianism as a personal choice and as a political stance and about heterosexism in the women's movement. They held consciousness-raising discussions for women who had never publicly acknowledged attraction to other women. They hammered out pro-lesbian rights resolutions which passed the Congress easily. And they concluded with a women-only dance party. The Second Congress to Unite Women became a coming out party for radical lesbian feminism, and most who were there recalled having a pretty good time. But this attempt at claiming visibility for lesbian concerns was far from the first.[8]

An earlier generation of women, who came of age after World War II, had waged a painful campaign for decades to integrate lesbians into mainstream feminist groups. Their experience and expression of lesbian politics was different from that of the 1970s generation. However, their relationship with Betty Friedan and some of the more conservative women in NOW was no less contested.

One of the lesbian organizations whose sponsorship of the First Congress to Unite Women Betty Friedan had attempted to hide from the public was the Daughters of Bilitis, the nation's first openly lesbian civil rights organization. Founded in 1955 by San Francisco activists Del Martin and Phyllis Lyons, Daughter of Bilitis (or DOB as it was known) had at first made alliances primarily with gay male groups. They were particularly close to the pioneering Mattachine Society, founded in Los Angeles in 1950 by former Communist Party activist Harry Hay. Martin and Lyons were excited by the founding of NOW in 1966 because they saw an opportunity to broaden their coalition, to make common cause with heterosexual feminists as well as with gay men. DOB's focus on overturning laws that discriminated against gay people was very similar to NOW's strategy of challenging laws that discriminated on the basis of sex. DOB activists wanted to be part of NOW's feminist work and they asked NOW to take on lesbian struggles against employment discrimination, laws that criminalized gay and lesbian sex acts, and police brutality against lesbians and gay men. During the late 1960s, DOB's overtures were met by NOW leaders with a cold shoulder.

In 1967, Martin and Lyons signed up for a couple's membership in NOW. Martin later recalled:

> Betty Friedan had decided there should be this couple's membership because she wanted to get more men involved (with NOW) but it didn't occur to her that lesbians could be couples too . . . It was cheaper and we had already decided we weren't going to go back into the closet . . . But of course Betty Freidan had a fit and there was all the to-do about it . . . the couple's membership disappeared.[9]

When Aileen Hernandez became NOW's second President she decided to change policy toward lesbian members, announcing her stance at a meeting in Washington Square Church in Greenwich Village in December 1970. As a woman of color who had worked since NOW's beginnings to make the organization more multi-racial and economically diverse, Hernandez was not comfortable with those who sought to exclude lesbians. "We do not prescribe a sexual preference test for applicants," she said. "Let us – involved in a movement that has the greatest potential for humanizing our total society – spend no more time with this sexual McCarthyism. We need to free all our sisters from the shackles of a society which insists on viewing us in terms of sex."[10]

This turn-around was dramatic for NOW. On one hand, Hernandez succeeded in broadening the group's membership, but she also identified NOW with some of the more radical trends of the era. Women in many local chapters, especially NOW Los Angeles, had been arguing for some time that the national organization needed to make lesbian rights part of the group's political agenda. The 1971 national NOW convention finally did that – passing a resolution that recognized "the oppression of lesbians as a legitimate feminist concern." Building on that sea change, Del Martin campaigned for a seat on the national NOW board. She was elected in 1973.

Still, the issue continued to divide NOW, and Betty Friedan led the charge against associating feminism with lesbian rights. Martin recalled:

> Betty Friedan was such a homophobe. She was so afraid of the stigma that lesbians might bring to the organization . . . As soon as I was on the board she was on the phone to the *New York Times* saying that lesbians are ruining the movement and that some of them had tried to seduce her.

Friedan knew that NOW needed to make alliances with other progressive organizations, Martin says. But she resisted attempts by lesbian groups to affiliate. "Fear of the lesbian taint and refusal to cope with it is what can be disastrous to the women's movement," Martin wrote her. "This is not an unholy alliance."[11] Lesbians and heterosexual feminists shared many concerns, Martin argued – employment discrimination, lack of research in women's health care, affordable child-care and more.

Many NOW members agreed with Martin and Hernandez, but more than a few remained leery of "the lesbian taint." When Martin tried to convince the NOW board that the national organization should fight to repeal laws criminalizing gay sex, board member Kay Clarenbach turned her down flat. For NOW to do that, Clarenbach wrote, would be a "disastrous blunder." It would not only provide enemies with ammunition against NOW but would "destroy the decade of advance in the women's movement." NOW had to choose its battles. Taking up lesbian causes would be distracting, Clarenbach told Martin, and a drain on resources. NOW members might believe that environmentalism was important, but that didn't mean the group should spend its limited resources lobbying for clean air and water legislation. The same was true of lesbian rights, she said.[12]

These alternately icy, sarcastic and hysterical responses to lesbian activists' overtures to NOW unpleasantly echoed the National Woman Party's refusal to support the struggles of African-American and working-class women activists half a century earlier. And battles over lesbians' place in NOW were not only taking place on the national level. Local chapters – in Memphis, Philadelphia and other cities – split over the issue of lesbian rights in the 1970s. Some members left NOW to pursue electoral politics and government appointments. Others left NOW to devote themselves to organizations focused on a range of women's issues. But their actions still felt like rejection. And it was. Some local NOW chapters continued struggling over the issue into the early 1980s and beyond, the tone of the debates shaped by local cultures and political coalitions.

The dramatic turning point in NOW's relationship to lesbian rights came at the 1977 National Women's Conference in Houston. An outgrowth of the 1975 International Women's Conference in Mexico City, and part of the United Nations Decade of Women, the gathering was funded by the U.S. government and mounted with a great deal of ceremony. The funding grew out of a bill introduced by two feminist Congresswomen – New York's Bella Abzug and Hawaii's Patsy Mink. Two thousand delegates from 50 states and six territories participated and an additional 15,000 people observed. Every state held preliminary meetings to work through their state agendas and to elect delegates. Three First Ladies – Roslyn Carter, Betty Ford, and Lady Bird Johnson – as well as members of Congress, Coretta Scott King and women Olympians attended the Houston meeting.[13]

Lesbian rights activists had lobbied President Jimmy Carter intensively to appoint an open lesbian to the President's Commission on Women. In the end he agreed, appointing Jean O'Leary, leader of the new gay civil rights organization, the National Gay Task Force. O'Leary and activist Charlotte Bunch worked with lesbian groups across the U.S. in 1976 and 1977 to build local coalitions with heterosexual feminists and to elect some lesbian activists as delegates to the Houston conference. Evangelical Christian and conservative women's groups also organized to elect their own as delegates.[14]

Delegates to the conference were empowered to make recommendations to Congress and the President on issues of women and poverty, women and health, employment discrimination, immigration, welfare, child-care and more. They discussed all of these in Houston. Perhaps not surprisingly, given the range of views that delegates held, the issues of abortion rights and whether or not to include a plank opposing discrimination against lesbians were the most divisive. Charlotte Bunch, representing the District of Columbia, put forth a plank calling for an end to employment discrimination against lesbian women and for repealing laws that criminalized non-procreative sex. "We come here to you as sisters to say that lesbians have been in the closet too long, too many centuries. And we ask that you do not deny lesbians those rights" that all American citizens are entitled to. The response by Oklahoma delegate Winnie Matthews sent the meeting into an uproar: "We would never advocate a stoning or a burning at the stake, or a throwing in the river of a homosexual," Matthews said, "as long as homosexuals keep their sexual preferences in private, the same as adulterers and adulteresses."[15]

The furor was not calmed, nor the tide fully turned, until Betty Friedan asked for permission to address the gathering. Everyone at the conference knew where Friedan had always stood on the question of lesbian involvement in the women's movement. Tension filled the room as she began to speak. What she said surprised almost everyone there. It was a sign of how much had changed in just a few years.

"I am known to be violently opposed to the lesbian issue in the women's movement, and in fact I have been," Friedan began.

> As someone who has grown up in Peoria, Illinois, and who has loved men – perhaps too well – I have had trouble with this issue. I now see that there is nothing in the ERA that will give any protection to homosexuals. We must help women who are lesbians win their own civil rights.[16]

"I was dumbfounded," Houston lesbian activist Pokey Anderson recalled.

> She'd reversed herself! When the vote was taken, an overwhelming majority rose to confirm the lesbian rights resolution. As our 1,000 helium-filled balloons proclaiming 'We Are Everywhere' floated to the ceiling, pandemonium broke out. We cried, we jumped on the chairs, we danced in the aisles.[17]

Gloria Steinem believed that this was the moment that *Lavender Menace* had called for. Heterosexual feminists had finally decided that they would not be cowed by the threat of being called lesbian.

> Everybody came together and said . . . issues of sexual orientation that oppress . . . women who are lesbian, who are bisexual – those are absolutely crucial issues, and any rebellious woman will be called a lesbian until the word lesbian becomes as honorable a word as any other.

Charlotte Bunch recalled that afternoon in Houston as "one of the most unifying moments in the history of the women's movement and a high point for lesbians, marking both a maturity in our organizing and mainstream feminist acceptance of our presence and power."[18]

By the mid-1980s, NOW and other mainstream feminist organizations had come down firmly on the side of advocating lesbian rights. NOW co-sponsored gay and lesbian marches on Washington, worked to overturn sodomy laws, and advocated for marriage equality long before there was widespread national support. Tensions between straight and gay feminists had finally been replaced by a lasting sense of solidarity.[19]

Butch-Femme Courage in the 1950s and Homophile Courage in the 1960s[20]

> Unlike many other groups in the 1950s, there were no color bars in DOB. There were not just African-Americans, but Asians, Latinas . . . the driving force was that we were gay women.
>
> Billye Talmadge, one of the early members of the Daughters of Bilitis.[21]

If the militant young women who came out in the late 1960s and the 1970s were successful at bridging gaps between lesbian and heterosexual feminists, they remained resistant themselves to recognizing the courage and contributions of an older generation of lesbian activists. These women had come out in the 1940s, 1950s and early 1960s and did not necessarily identify as feminists. Still, they had fought their own painful battles for recognition and respect.

For many in that older generation, their lesbian identities were shaped more by desire than by politics. They rebelled by transgressing and playing with gender norms rather than by issuing revolutionary manifestos. And they built alliances more easily with gay men than with heterosexual women.

There were also lesbian rights activists in the 1940s and 1950s. But they were rarely acknowledged or honored by the young radicals of the 1970s, who dismissed them as too conservative, too timid, too assimilationist. In many ways, it was these women, not 1970s lesbian feminists, who were the true pioneers of gay liberation. But, it was only in the 1990s and afterwards that they began to take their place in histories of the movement.

In truth, there were subcultures of woman-identified women in the U.S. throughout the 20th century. Even before World War I, some of these women openly challenged gender taboos. One photograph of a Women's Trade Union League gathering in 1913 shows women wearing suits, ties, mustaches and slicked back hair standing alongside women with unbound long hair clad in demure white dresses. Cross-dressing lesbian couples thrived in the cross-class Women's Trade Union League though they would never in those years have used the "l" word. Elite women couples abounded in Eleanor Roosevelt's circle of political women friends as well and in the labor feminist networks that occupied state capitals and Washington, D.C. in 1930s, 1940s and 1950s. These were not women who ever adopted the label "lesbian". But, because that label had not yet been politicized or attached fully to sexual desire, they could live in what one might call a glass closet, accepted by heterosexual friends, family and colleagues.[22]

More explicitly "lesbian" public cultures – often created by working-class women, immigrants and women of color – began to appear in American cities during World War II. They were different from those that came before in that they were openly romantic and expressly sexual. As women joined sex-segregated military units, as they worked together in defense plants and shared housing in crowded boomtowns where they had come to find jobs, women began to be open about feeling sexual attraction to other women. It was, as we've seen, dangerous in a time of red-baiting when "perversion" was thought to equal "subversion." Many lost their jobs, or were shamed by arrests and loyalty investigations. But these sub-cultures continued to grow, in part due to the courage of women with little or no economic and political clout.

Working-class white, Native-American and African-American lesbians began to gather in run-down bars in Buffalo, New York in the 1940s and 1950s. They claimed public space as a way of finding one another because they often lived with parents and other disapproving family members, unlike more affluent women who could gather in private homes and apartments. There were more women's bars in Buffalo in the 1940s and 1950s than there were in the 1980s when lesbianism was far more open and widely accepted. Women came to these bars not only from inside the city but also from surrounding areas. The bars drew factory workers, taxi drivers, clerical workers, hospital technicians, and a few middle-class women as well – teachers, business owners, librarians.

The more visibly butch of these women braved physical and verbal abuse for coming out in public, as did their more traditionally feminine partners when seen together with them. As denizens of the Buffalo bar culture later recalled, certain rough and ready lesbians cast themselves as the defenders of this new lesbian community. Oral histories recount the existence of this new character they called a "street dyke." She was, they said, a full time "queer" ready at any time to fight for "space and dignity." Women like these made lesbians visible in urban neighborhoods, in labor halls, and on city streets in the 1940s. And – in part as a result of their fierceness – a group identity began to emerge.[23]

In the early years, most bars where lesbians and homosexual men gathered were segregated by race. Arlette, an African-American lesbian, recalled when her friends decided to desegregate a Buffalo bar called Bingo's.

> The gay kids . . . at the time, Black ones, had no bar to go to. Most of the time somebody would give a house party and we would go to that, but as far as a bar, there was none that I knew of in Buffalo until I ran across Bingo's. So a whole bunch of us got together and went to that place. And it ended up we just kept going. We made friends with quite a few.

When black and white women began dating, there was some pushback, said Arlette. But, that was not the norm in the working-class gay and lesbian bar scene.

Far more than other Americans at that time, gay and lesbian bar goers in Buffalo embraced multi-racial community.[24]

In Albuquerque, New Mexico, similar dynamics unfolded. There was a thriving bar scene that emerged in the 1950s and early to mid-1960s. There were five bars in Albuquerque where lesbians went to meet in that era, one that was for women only. That was run by a Native-American lesbian. The rest, as was the norm in those years, welcomed both men and women. These bars were patronized by men and women who'd grown up together in Albuquerque, who knew and trusted one another. Lesbian women socialized with and made close bonds with homosexual men. Sometimes gay men and lesbians gave each other heterosexual cover, appearing together at family or at job-related functions, helping each other to "pass."[25]

For working-class lesbians of that era, especially in smaller cities like Buffalo and Albuquerque, going to bars helped them forge a collective and public identity. They enjoyed nights out where they could be themselves. Still, they understood that this was risky on many levels.

Speaking decades later to historians, one butch woman from Buffalo proudly described the bruises she had earned in the 1940s. She saw them as combat medals in the struggle for gay liberation. She was not a writer. She had not developed political theories or written militant manifestos like some of the more famous lesbian activists who came after her. But she had won some fierce fistfights and she had endured brutal beatings.

"Things back then were horrible," she said,

> and I think that, because I fought like a man to survive I made it somehow easier for the kids coming out today . . . I'm not a rich person. I don't . . . have a lot of money. I don't even have a little money. I would have nothing to leave anybody in this world but I have that that I can leave to kids who are coming out now . . . Even though I was getting my brains beaten up I would never stand up and say, "No. Don't hit me. I'm not gay" . . . I wouldn't do that.[26]

Despite these acts of bravery and sacrifice, working-class butch-femme couples who came of age in the 1940s, 1950s, and 1960s were often dismissed by lesbian feminists a generation later. These young women saw the butch-femme style of older lesbians as a retrograde emulation of heterosexual norms. Claiming androgyny as the style of the 1970s feminist revolution, young lesbians missed the ways that the butch-femme gender play of the older generation had been radically transgressive at a time when masculinity and femininity were fetishized and strictly enforced. By the late 1970s, many lesbians who did not easily fit into the lesbian-feminist mold felt marginalized and stigmatized. Eventually they rebelled.

Joan Nestle published a ground-breaking article in 1982 in the feminist journal *Heresies* entitled "Butch Femme Relationships: Sexual Courage in the 1950s."

After a decade of lesbian-feminist organizing, she felt that she needed to speak out. She knew she "needed to come home but what was home to me was an anathema to others." For that reason, it had taken her a long time to articulate what bothered her about the lesbian feminist 1970s.

"Silences haunted me then," she wrote,

> the invisibility of my working-class butch-femme community, the muting of the sexual and the dissociation of desire from history. I wanted to tell another story, one of historical and personal reclamation . . . I did know that some pieces would be unsettling to the prevailing lesbian-feminist positions of the mid-seventies, but I wanted to keep complexities alive in a time of rhetorical sternness. This more complicated portrait of a lesbian's life, I believed, could only strengthen the insights of feminism.[27]

In the 30 years after Nestle's article was published, many young lesbians rediscovered butch-femme as a public identity and embraced it. Fusing politics and desire, as so many lesbian feminists had done in the 1970s, was not interesting or attractive to some lesbians who came of age in the 1980s and 1990s. They admired the sexually aggressive, role-playing butch-femme couples of the 1940s. Their bravery was, argued Laura Harris and Elizabeth Crocker in their 1997 book *Femme*, "central to the formation of a sex-radical position, out of which the queer movement grew."[28]

Still it would be inaccurate to suggest that political lesbian activism emerged only in the 1970s. The butch-femme bar world was not the only lesbian public culture before the 1960s; there were lesbian women in those years who were explicitly political and whose refusal to be closeted was as important in shaping a queer future as the bravery of the street-fighters. No one did more to galvanize that post-World War II lesbian political culture than Del Martin, born Dorothy Talifierro, and her partner Phyllis Lyon.

Martin and Lyon were children of the 1920s, born and raised in the San Francisco Bay area. Talafierro was briefly married in her late teens, during which time she gave birth to a daughter. By the early 1950s, she was divorced and going by the name Del Martin. Fresh from a B.A. program in journalism, Martin moved to Seattle to write for a construction trades journal. There she met Phyllis Lyon. The two fell in love, moved to California and rented an apartment on what would soon become the main vein of gay San Francisco – Castro Street. "We only really had problems our first year together," Lyon recalled. "Del would leave her shoes in the middle of the room and I would throw them out the window." Once they resolved that issue, the two did everything together.[29]

In 1955, Martin and Lyons started Daughters of Bilitis (DOB), the first lesbian civil rights organization in North America. They originally conceived it as both a social and a political organization. It was, from the beginning, a cross-class, multi-racial group. The founding members of DOB included a Filipina, a Chicana, two lesbian mothers, two white-collar and two working-class women. And its members were interested in the concerns of lesbian mothers as well as lesbians who did not have children. (It was not uncommon for lesbian women in those years to have married for a time and borne children before coming out and leading more open lesbian lives.)[30]

Martin and Lyon were, from the start, interested in making DOB a tool for gaining political and civil rights for lesbians, but they also wanted to create social environments where lesbians could gather outside of bars. They organized barbecues, picnics and trips to the beach as well as protests and picket lines. After a time, women who had joined DOB primarily to socialize began to drift away. As they formed other structures for lesbian socializing, DOB became more political. And DOB leaders began to conceive of their lesbian community as national and even international in scope.[31]

In 1956, Martin and Lyon began publishing the first lesbian magazine – *The Ladder*. They printed 175 copies of the premier issue and mailed them to women they thought "might be interested." By 1957 there were 400 subscribers. Playwright Lorraine Hansberry, whose play *Raisin in the Sun* was the first script by a black woman to be produced on Broadway, was a longtime correspondent for the magazine. She called it her lifeline and many isolated lesbians, especially those living in small towns and rural areas, saw it that way. Even if they could not physically contact other lesbians, they could find a sort of virtual community through the articles and letters in *The Ladder*.

Barbara Gittings, a decade younger than Lyon and Martin, took over editorship in 1963 and modernized the magazine. She added the subtitle *A Lesbian Review* and began publishing photographs (taken by her partner Kay Taubin Lahusen) of actual lesbian women on the cover. Gittings saw these photographs as one way of increasing lesbian visibility. Instead of line drawings representing an iconic lesbian, *The Ladder* would broadcast the experiences and images of actual people. Gittings also began to sell the magazine through bookstores. One Greenwich Village bookstore alone sold 100 copies a month in the early 1960s. By the mid-1960s, bookstores in many major cities had begun to sell *The Ladder*. Purchasing it publicly was a political act. Women came out of the woodwork, walked right up to store counters, and purchased their copies without shame. The Daughters of Bilitis had opened the closet door and a few brave women were now walking out into the sunlight.

The Ladder continued publishing until 1970, quietly disappearing at the dawn of the lesbian-feminist cultural renaissance, an era that spawned a veritable flood of short-lived lesbian magazines, newspapers and publishing houses. But, in its 14-year run, *The Ladder* had been a trailblazer and a transformative force for a generation of lesbians who had never before seen positive reflections of themselves in media. "No woman ever made a dime for her work," Barbara Grier (who took over as editor after Gittings) later recalled. "And some worked themselves into a state of physical and mental decline on behalf of the magazine . . . Most of the editors believed that they were moving the world with their labors and I believe they were right."[32]

Gittings was a *Ladder* alumna who worked tirelessly to move the world, with some notable successes. She organized a New York City chapter of DOB in 1958 at a time when, as she recalled, "homosexuality was shrouded in complete silence. There were no radio talk shows or TV documentaries. In all the United States there were maybe a half dozen groups, 200 people in all." After listening to numerous medical experts pronounce homosexuality a sickness, Gittings vowed to convince medical and psychiatric professionals that same-sex love was healthy and natural. Her campaign to educate the medical establishment on lesbian lives, ultimately successful, would consume her for the next decade. A librarian by profession, Gittings also worked to bring literature by gay and lesbian writers into public libraries across the country. It was another subtle form of activism with deep impact. Through the late 1960s, young gay people could find no books about same-sex love except for medical texts that pathologized and stigmatized them. Gittings brought literature by gay and lesbian novelists, essayists, poets, historians and journalists onto the shelves of libraries across the country.

She also threw herself into activities that were more conventionally political. Influenced by Frank Kameny of the Mattachine Society, Gittings helped organize the first gay civil rights picket lines in Washington, D.C. In 1965 – after a decade of lavender scare witch hunts that cost thousands of gay men and lesbians their jobs in federal agencies – Gittings, Kameny and a small group of other gay men and lesbians started regular pickets in front of the White House and the State Department to demand fair treatment for gay and lesbian federal employees.

Determined to present themselves as suitable candidates for federal jobs, the organizers directed male protesters to wear suits and ties and women to wear dresses and heels. This staid business attire would earn them derision from 1970s militants who labeled "homophile" activists as assimilationist because they reinforced prevailing gender norms. Younger "radicals" who dismissed these groundbreaking protests as timid and conventional completely ignored how dangerous it was for gay people to demonstrate in those years. "It was risky and we were scared," Gittings recalled. "Picketing was not a popular tactic at the time. And our cause seemed outlandish even to most gay people."[33]

As tens of thousands of gay people migrated to cities like San Francisco and New York, activism, at least there, became a bit less risky. Where there were significant concentrations of gay and lesbian residents, it became possible in the mid-1960s, to begin transforming local urban politics. Lyons and Martin were particularly active in San Francisco around issues of police violence. They created the Council on Religion and the Homosexual, through which local clergy pressured police to stop beating gay and transgendered people on the streets. Lyons and Martin also founded the Alice B. Toklas Democratic Club in San Francisco, the first political organization to run openly gay and lesbian candidates for office. These efforts paved the way for Harvey Milk to be elected to the San Francisco Board of Supervisors in 1977, one of the first openly gay elected officials in the world. Gittings and Kameny were similarly active in New York and Philadelphia.

But, even within the homophile movement there were differences over strategy and where lesbians' primary political and emotional allegiances should lie. Gittings had found her community among gay men. Lyons and Martin felt more at home among feminists – straight and gay. Despite her conflicts with NOW leaders in the late 1960s, Martin was fiercely feminist and there were aspects of gay male culture that she found difficult to live with. Though Martin would work many times after that with gay male allies, in 1970, she publicly chastised male homophile groups, publishing her own version of Robin Morgan's "Goodbye To All That" called "Goodbye My Alienated Brothers." It was every bit as sarcastic and angry as Morgan's famous rant.

"Goodbye to male chauvinists of the homophile movement . . . to washroom sex and pornographic movies . . ." she wrote. Martin put her gay brothers on notice that she was no longer willing to serve either as "your nigger" or "your mother." Playing on the homophile slogan of the time – Gay is Good – she argued that the movement had become too insular, too white, too privileged. "Gay is good," she wrote, "but it is not good enough so long as it is limited to white males only."

Martin's biting sarcasm reflected the depth of her alienation.

> As I bid you adieu I leave each of you to your own device. Take care of it. Stroke it gently. Mouth it. As the center of your consciousness it's really all you have . . . It is a revelation to find acceptance, equality, love and friendship, everything we sought in the homophile community – not there but in the women's movement.[34]

Barbara Gittings felt quite differently. She would later say that she had "no patience with those who said that women, as women, had to stick together because, frankly, most women don't care about lesbians." And she, for her part,

> couldn't care less about day care and abortion rights and the other things that women were concerned about . . . I feel more strongly as a lesbian than as a feminist . . . As long as prejudice continues to exist against my people, my primary identification will be with them.[35]

Most later gay and lesbian activists have seen Gittings as the more radical, the more visionary activist of the two. They have agreed with criticisms of the Daughters of Bilitis as too cautious, too conservative, too willing to indulge members who wanted to remain closeted. They have derided the women who, in the early 1960s, still insisted on receiving their copies of *The Ladder* in plain brown wrappers.

Age and generation can partly explain the differences in style between the two factions. Lyon and Martin were older than Gittings and quite a bit older than the militant activists of the lesbian-feminist generation. And that mattered. But it was not the most important factor in the choices they made. There was a crucial part of their identity and politics that has rarely been considered. They, and many in their constituency, were mothers who faced the dangers and self-doubts of lesbian parenting in that era.

Martin had given in when her ex-husband told her that he and his second wife would be better able to parent her seven-year-old daughter than she and Lyons could possibly be. Though she and her daughter remained close, that decision haunted her. She had done what others convinced her was best for the child. She had doubted herself and her relationship. But, after founding DOB, she became determined to help other lesbian mothers avoid such devastating losses. Through Daughters of Bilitis, Martin and Lyon began creating groups for lesbian mothers in 1956. These were the first public acknowledgements that lesbian families even existed. A 1963 survey of lesbian women, many of whom were DOB members, found that 20% were mothers. Theirs was a different kind of rights movement than that of lesbians without children.[36]

Unlike Gittings and gay activists who were not parents, lesbian mothers did share with heterosexual feminists concerns about education, child care, adoption, and women's parental rights. Well into the 1970s and 1980s, lesbian mothers had more to lose by coming out than did women who had no children. Long before lesbian parenting became a topic of national discussion, Martin and Lyon publicly argued against the prevailing view that lesbians were unfit mothers. Having experienced firsthand the loss of custody, they understood why lesbian mothers might choose to remain closeted.

They were also keenly aware of the recriminations that lesbian mothers turned on themselves at a time when their relationships were seen almost universally as deviant. In the 1950s and 1960s, Lyon and Martin recalled, many lesbian mothers worried that it would damage their children to grow up in a lesbian home. They feared that the children might be more likely to become homosexual themselves. Lesbian mothers wrote letters to *The Ladder* expressing their desires for "happiness and acceptance in society being what I am." DOB brought in child development experts who reassured the mothers that their children would be all right as long as they lived in stable, loving homes. Lyon and Martin knew that stability and safety could only be assured when lesbian mothers and gay fathers were no longer seen as dangers to their own children.[37]

The two collected data from lesbian mothers to help them in their battles with the courts and medical establishment. In 1970, members of the San Francisco chapter of DOB met with mental health professionals and told them that gay and lesbian parents needed "family counseling . . . wherein the parent's homosexuality would not be treated as the catch-all cause" of the family's problems. In 1971, Lyon and Martin founded the Lesbian Mothers Union – the first political organization for lesbians with children. They also raised funds to cover legal costs for women who were in danger of losing custody of their children because they were lesbian.

Finally, they urged lesbian activists without children to recognize that theirs was a movement that included women of all classes and races. It also embraced women who were mothers as well as those who were not. At one 1971 lesbian convention in Los Angeles, Lyon and Martin criticized the lack of child care, explaining that the decision not to provide any meant that women who couldn't afford to pay extra for someone to watch their children would be unable to attend.[38]

In the final analysis, Lyons, Martin and Gittings were fighting the same battle: to end stigmatization of lesbians as sick, and to help lesbians achieve legal and political rights that were denied them on the grounds that they might spread their sickness to children. Martin, Lyon and Gittings met with psychiatrists and therapists innumerable times, urging them to remove homosexuality from the official list of mental disorders. Lyon and Martin also published books and articles affirming lesbian sexuality as healthy and vibrant. "The charge of sickness is perhaps our greatest problem," Gittings wrote in 1967.

> We can't really progress in other directions until the unsubstantiated assumption of sickness . . . is demolished! It's almost always there, however slyly or covertly or even unconsciously, however "sympathetic" the person . . . And in our society sick people, by any definition of sick, just DO *not* get equal treatment. Equal treatment – no more, no less – is what we want![39]

Gittings would go on to co-found the National Gay and Lesbian Task Force, one of the two most important national gay civil rights groups of the late 20th century and to serve on its board into the 1980s. She was crucial in the 1973 decision of the American Psychiatric Association to take homosexuality off its list of diagnosable illnesses. She co-founded the Gay Nurses' Alliance and the gay and lesbian caucus within the American Library Association. In 1997, she convinced the American Association of Retired Persons to recognize her 40-year relationship with photographer Kay Taubin Lahusen. One of Gittings' final political acts was, in 2007, to come out as a lesbian in the newsletter of the Philadelphia assisted living facility where she and Kay spent their last years.

Lyon and Martin also remained active into the 21st century, their politics as broad and multi-faceted as ever. Martin's 1976 book *Battered Wives* launched a national conversation about domestic violence and battering. She personally co-founded several local, state and national organizations that advocated for victims of domestic violence, opened shelters and ran educational programs. Martin founded the San Francisco based Casa De Las Madres – for mothers and their children fleeing violence. And she served on the San Francisco Human Rights Commission and chaired the city's Commission on the Status of Women.

At the end of Martin's life, she and Lyons became two of the best-known faces in the marriage equality movement. San Francisco mayor Gavin Newsom married them on the steps of City Hall in 2008, the first same-sex couple in San Francisco to be legally wed. Senator Diane Feinstein named them to the White House Conference on Aging. And, when they were in their eighties, House leader Nancy Pelosi showed their picture around to colleagues in Congress saying: "Their relationship doesn't threaten anyone else's marriage."[40]

These long campaigners for lesbian rights understood that there is always tension around struggling for equality in a world marked by difference. Equality meant different things for lesbian mothers and non-mothers, for white middle-class educated gay men and for poor, working-class lesbians of color. Martin said as much in her infamous 1970 essay. Gittings acknowledged as much in the mid-1960s, picketing the White House with a sign that said "Homosexuals should be treated as Individuals." But it is challenging to form a movement out of a crowd of individuals.

The *Lavender Menace* manifesto, "Woman Identified Woman," argued that romantic commitment and sexual love between women were, in themselves, revolutionary acts. Maybe they were. Maybe they still are. But love between women did not wipe away differences in class, race, education, geography or sexuality. As they had bedeviled women's movements of all kinds, these differences ran electrically through lesbian activist struggles in the 1970s and long afterwards.

Lesbian Feminism and the Politics of Difference in the 1970s

No lesbian activist articulated the complexities of human identity and the challenges of community more eloquently than the self-described "black, lesbian, feminist, poet, warrior, mother" Audre Lorde. Born in 1934 of Caribbean immigrant parents, the product of New York City public schools, Lorde grew up in a variety of New York communities in the 1950s and 1960s. She joined circles of political radicals in a time of political conservatism and repression. She hung out at Greenwich Village lesbian bars, though her black community in Harlem strongly disapproved. She became a star in the world of poetry journals, though they would not publish her words of love for other women. And she took jobs as varied as factory work and teaching English to make ends meet. Finally, she became one of the most famous names of the lesbian-feminist era, even as she challenged the very idea that the sisterhood its leading activists preached was fully possible.

Always a bit apart from whatever community she engaged with, Lorde began to articulate a theory of strength in difference. In the 1950s, Lorde's community of women lovers was so stigmatized that some of its unrepentant daughters were given shock treatment to "cure" them. One of Lorde's lovers bore the scars of those attempted "cures," going through life with blank spots cutting apart her memory. Still Lorde championed erotic connection between women as resistance to the oppression of the time.

In the 1960s, Lorde lived a heterosexual life for a while, marrying a white man and bearing two children. When the black college students she taught poetry challenged her, Lorde defended her inter-racial family and told her students they needed to interrogate their discomfort. As a lesbian feminist, she defended her choice to marry and mother children. In the early 1970s, Lorde again generated discomfort, becoming life partners with a white psychology professor named Frances Clayton with whom she lived for the next two decades. Finally, at the end of her life, Lorde took as her romantic partner Gloria Joseph, another black woman writer. Through it all she asserted her right to be different.

Audre Lorde lived on the edge of every community she might have been more fully part of, if she had been willing to subsume pieces of her complex and fluid identity. She wasn't. Instead, Lorde became a living critique of the very idea of identity politics, publishing searing critiques of any attempt to label human beings as simply one thing or another. We are all, she challenged, far more complicated and changeable than identity-based ideologies can ever acknowledge. The strength of movements, she fiercely asserted, lies not in the sameness of their members but in celebration of their differences. When lesbian feminists called for a cultural revolution wrought by "sisters," Lorde challenged the homogenizing notion of sisterhood.

Refusing to accept the comfort of being fully inside any one group – the black community, the lesbian community, the women's movement, the world of poets, or feminist academe – Lorde named herself a "Sister Outsider." Claiming difference as a dynamic, energizing reality, she called on feminists to do the hard work of communicating and building alliances. At the end of *Zami*, a fictionalized memoir that she published in the 1980s, Lorde wrote: "We realized that our place was the very house of difference rather than the comfort of one particular difference."[41]

Along with her militant embrace of difference, Lorde challenged feminists from all backgrounds to give up the comfort of silence. Speaking out was essential to change, she argued. "Perhaps for some of you," she wrote, "I am the face of one of your fears. Because I am woman, because I am Black, because I am lesbian, because I am myself – a Black woman warrior poet doing my work – come to ask you, are you doing yours?" The work she wanted to see was for women to transform silence into language, and so to shatter invisibility. "Your silence will not protect you," she famously wrote.

Lorde made common cause with women and men, young and old, straight and gay, people of every kind. Still, she understood that being allies did not remove differences in power and privilege. As she explained to one Jewish feminist mother she was close to:

> Some problems we share as women. Some we do not. You fear your children will grow up to join the patriarchy and testify against you. We fear our children will be dragged from a car and shot down in the street and you will turn your back on the reasons they are dying.

In the 21st century, a time of Stand Your Ground laws and a rash of shootings of young black men and women, Lorde's words echo hauntingly. Audre Lorde called on women and men, lesbian feminists, poets, black college students, black and white mothers to break the silence about differences among those who struggle for social justice. The challenges, fears and pleasures of doing so remain as real in the 21st century as they were in the 1970s.[42]

A generation younger than Lorde, Dorothy Allison became an equally eloquent chronicler of how difference played out among lesbian feminists. She was born to a poor, white single teenage mother in Greenville, South Carolina in 1949. A survivor of poverty, domestic violence and sexual abuse, Allison won a scholarship to college and found refuge in a lesbian-feminist collective in Tallahassee, Florida in the early 1970s. She earned her living there as a photographer's assistant but remembered that "the real work of my life was my lesbian-feminist activism, the work I did with the local women's center and the committee to found a women's studies program at Florida State University. Part of my role, as I saw it, was to be a kind of evangelical lesbian feminist, and to help develop a political analysis of this woman-hating society."

Allison's relief was profound at finding a world in which she could be open about her lesbianism. And yet, she soon began to feel that she still had to hide parts of herself from other lesbian feminists. "I did not talk about class, except to give lip service to how we all needed to think about it, the same way I thought we all needed to think about racism. I was a determined person, living in a lesbian collective – all of us young and white and serious – studying each new book that purported to address feminist issues, driven by what I saw as a need to revolutionize the world."[43]

Allison never talked about the poverty she came from, about her white, rural Southern family, or about the butch-femme working-class lesbian bar world that still attracted her. She knew that many white Southerners in the world she came from hated her for being a lesbian. Some of them were members of her own family. But it was crushing to realize that she was also "hated or held in contempt (which is in some ways more debilitating and slippery than hatred) by lesbians" because

> the kind of woman I am attracted to is invariably the kind of woman who embarrasses respectably middle-class, politically aware lesbian feminists. My sexual ideal is butch, exhibitionistic, physically aggressive, smarter than she wants you to know . . . Most often she is working class, with an aura of danger and an ironic sense of humor.

Allison survived because, she wrote, "one of the strengths I derive from my class background is that I am accustomed to contempt." But being judged by the women who were her political comrades and chosen family was deeply hurtful. Like Lorde, Allison argued that lesbian feminists needed to reject the tunnel vision of white middle-class privilege. For there to be social and political change, she believed, there would also have to be personal transformation. "I grew up poor, hated, the victim of physical, emotional, and sexual violence," she wrote,

> and I know that suffering does not ennoble. It destroys. To resist destruction, self-hatred, or lifelong hopelessness, we have to throw off the conditioning of being despised, the fear of becoming the *they* that is talked about so dismissively, to refuse lying myths and easy moralities, to see ourselves as human, flawed, and extraordinary. All of us – extraordinary.

"What I know for sure," Allison wrote, summing up her complex vision of human identity,

> is that class, gender, sexual preference, and prejudice – racial, ethnic, and religious – form an intricate lattice that restricts and shapes our lives, and that resistance to hatred is not a simple act. Claiming your identity in the cauldron of hatred and resistance to hatred is infinitely complicated, and worse, almost unexplainable.[44]

Sisterhood was indeed powerful in the lesbian-feminist era. It spawned an extraordinary array of institutions – community centers, cafés, women's bookstores, women's music festivals, feminist publishing companies, record labels, battered women's shelters, feminist health clinics and other movement institutions to which lesbian feminists gave their time and energies with incredible depth and generosity. But, like radical feminism itself, lesbian-feminist collectives across the country experienced utopian burnout. The movement sometimes demanded too much from those who belonged or who worked hard to try and belong.

Psychologists and members of a lesbian carpenters' collective in Los Angeles, Maureen Hicks and Sherry McCoy wrote in 1979:

> Communities of oppressed people are typically torn from within by the anger and pain that seek an outlet in the closest targets – their own members. Thus, the fact that the contemporary lesbian community has frequently taken on the aspect of a battleground is not particularly surprising. What is disturbing, however, is how the sometimes visionary politics of feminism have contributed to our making unrealistic demands on each other, which have often resulted in disappointment. The concept of "sisterhood" at times seemed to evaporate as we watched.[45]

In some ways, the notion of lesbian-feminist revolution began to fray almost as soon as it was articulated. There were so many differences, so many pressures from outside as well as from within. And then there was the problem of how quickly change was happening.

Blanche McCrary Boyd, another white Southern lesbian writer who found refuge in 1970s lesbian collectives, described people changing their lives so dramatically and suddenly that they lost any sense of solidity in their identities. "In 1970," she began a partly autobiographical novel,

> I realized that the Sixties were passing me by. I had never even smoked a joint, or slept with anyone besides my husband. A year later I had left Nicky, changed my name from Ellen to Rain, and moved to a radical lesbian commune in California named Red Moon Rising.

Based loosely on Boyd's experiences in the lesbian-feminist 1970s, the protagonist of the novel left a steady job in publishing to go on a wild ride that introduced her to underground radical politics, a rapid succession of lesbian lovers and the vicissitudes of collective living. There was, she makes clear, both exhilaration and damage. Boyd would grow up, settle into a lesbian marriage, raise children and become an English professor. But, as she explained at a reading years later, it took a long time before she could recall anything light or funny about the 1970s.[46]

The passion, the sudden identity shifts that so many people underwent in those years, generated a great many positive changes very quickly. Homosexuality was removed from the list of mental illnesses. The federal government stopped firing people for having same-sex partners. Lesbian couples in many states could live openly without fear of losing their children. Lesbian health needs began to receive attention from the medical profession and the National Institutes of Health. And in literature, film, music and television – lesbians became more visible than ever before – even "chic" for a brief time in the 1990s. But the speed of change also left people feeling scarred. "I was determined to reach terminal velocity," Boyd's protagonist Rain recalled, describing her experiences in the 1970s by using the skydiving term for falling as fast as it is possible to fall. For many lesbian activists who fell to earth as the 1980s dawned, reality brought a hard landing.[47]

Lesbian Activism in the 1980s and 1990s: The AIDS Crisis

The AIDS epidemic brought lesbians back into coalition work with gay men with an overwhelming sense of urgency and grief. Between 1980 and 2013, 636,500 Americans died of AIDS. Most of those deaths – over 400,000 – came during the 1990s. Approximately half of these were gay men. New York was one of the epicenters of the epidemic. In the 1980s, it had nearly half the cases diagnosed in the United States. By the 21st century, 100,000 New Yorkers had died of AIDS.

Though the demographics of the disease would shift to other parts of the world, and in the United States to poor people of color, especially women, in the 1980s more than two-thirds of cases were gay men. The gay community in New York was being devastated.[48]

By 1987, ten thousand New Yorkers had been diagnosed with AIDS. Half had already died and the streets of the West Village were filled with exhausted caregivers and young men wasting away from a disease that, at that point, had no cure and no effective life-extending treatments. That Spring, writer and activist Larry Kramer spoke at the Gay and Lesbian Community Services Center in the West Village and issued a call to activism: "I have never been able to understand why we have sat back and let ourselves literally be knocked off man by man without fighting back. I have heard of denial, but this is more than denial – it is a death wish." He called on his audience to create a new organization. Hundreds came to the organizing meeting. The AIDS Coalition to Unleash Power (ACT-UP) was born.

Within days, new posters and stickers began to appear across New York City. In one weekend, two dozen ACT-UP members pasted more than 1,500 posters and stickers throughout Lower Manhattan and Brooklyn. The stickers became the icons of the epidemic: Pink Triangles on a black background. The triangle was an allusion to the patch that the Nazis forced homosexuals to wear, and to a suggestion the year before by conservative columnist William F. Buckley that people with AIDS be tattooed to protect others. On the triangles were emblazoned a new slogan that expressed rage at President Ronald Reagan's failure to even mention the disease publicly, though 25,000 Americans had by died of it by 1986. "Silence = Death," the stickers said. Audre Lorde's admonition that silence will not protect you became the rallying cry of a new gay and lesbian movement. Its members would be anything but silent.[49]

Building on the media-savvy protests of women's and gay liberation groups from the 1960s and 1970s, New York activists launched the direct-action group – ACT-UP. Jean Carlomusto, one of the early women in ACT-UP, was a 27-year-old film and video-maker when she became politicized by the homophobia rampant in early news reporting on AIDS. She recalls the "horror of seeing homophobia manifested when people were sick and dying. That's what really galvanized me to the issue." Before ACT-UP was founded, Carlomusto was one of the few women working at a new organization called Gay Men's Health Crisis, which tried to educate gay men about AIDS transmission and safer sex and which was one of the only groups at that time caring for the sick and dying.[50]

The women involved in AIDS politics were born a generation earlier than the lesbian-feminist activists. These younger women were born in the late 1950s and 1960s. Some had been involved in reproductive rights protests as young women. Some had not. But, like the women activists who came before them, they were media savvy, motivated to change prevailing views by changing media coverage. A few of the women in ACT-UP were older and had experience in earlier feminist protests. ACT-UP member Lei Chou, then a 19-year-old Taiwanese immigrant gay man, recalled that "the feminists – particularly the lesbians in the group – provided a lot of the driving force for the whole organization – and leadership."[51]

The group's actions drew attention to the urgency of their cause – stenciling bloody hand prints and painting white body outlines on the streets. Their "zaps" echoed the work of feminist artists a decade before who had similarly stenciled bodies on the spots where women had been raped. ACT-UP political theater, going in drag to the Republican National Women's Club, invading a Republican fund-raiser sporting Lesbians for Bush signs, clearly emulated earlier protests by Redstockings, WITCH and other feminist direct-action groups.[52]

In March 1987, ACT-UP New York staged its first march on Wall Street to demand that drug companies speed up testing and provide access to treatment at affordable prices. Activists also demanded government funding for educational programs to fight the spread of the epidemic, and an end to discrimination against people with AIDS. That June, ACT-UP members got themselves arrested at the Reagan White House, breaching security barriers to demand coordinated government action against the disease.

The activists knew that image was crucial. Carlomusto and other film-makers began shooting video for ACT-UP. They publicized footage of police wearing masks and rubber gloves as they arrested the protesters. At a New York Gay Pride Day march, ACT-UP members rode on a concentration camp float. On it stood people with AIDS dressed in black, surrounded by barbed wire and guarded by rubber-glove-wearing police. Soon afterward, activists plastered stickers on thousands of products in drug stores throughout the country branding pharmaceutical companies: "AIDS PROFITEERS." Their use of shocking visuals earned ACT-UP immense media coverage which, in turn, attracted more members. By 1988, the movement had spread to cities across the U.S. By the early 1990s, there were chapters in 147 cities around the world.[53]

ACT-UP staged protests that included symbols easy to decipher on television. Their purpose was simple: to change public opinion about people with the disease, whose treatment had been hampered by homophobia and hysteria. ACT-UP also used civil disobedience to disrupt government and corporate business in ways that attracted attention from powerful politicians and drug purveyors.

In 1988, 1,000 activists took over the Food and Drug Administration, calling for speedier approval of AIDS drugs. The FDA responded by setting new regulations to bring treatment to sick patients more quickly than previously. But nothing could happen quickly enough when thousands, and then tens of thousands and eventually hundreds of thousands in the U.S. alone were dying of AIDS. And so the civil disobedience intensified.

In the late 1980s and early 1990s, activists staged die-ins at the FDA, the White House and the summer home of President George H.W. Bush. They staged political funerals for people who had died of AIDS, carrying the remains of friends and loved ones in the coffins they brought to these political sites. They snuck into and disrupted television broadcasts. They handed out condoms to homeless people and distributed clean needles to intravenous drug users. And they filmed every protest.

ACT-UP's women were angry and vocal and they ensured that the group did not only focus on men. Keenly aware of the rising numbers of women contracting HIV through heterosexual contact and IV drug use, in January 1988, ACT-UP women staged the first protest to highlight dangers of the disease for women. Jean Carlomusto recalls sitting in a New York diner when Maxine Wolfe, Rebecca Cole and Denise Ribbel, other young ACT-UP women, came in carrying a copy of *Cosmopolitan* magazine with a story called "Reassuring News About AIDS." Astonishingly, the article, written by a physician, advised heterosexual women that they did not have to worry about becoming infected with HIV through vaginal intercourse. Vaginal skin, the author assured readers, was "resilient."

Sensing a good opportunity for a media zap, the young ACT-UP women called Dr. Robert Gould, author of the article, and asked for an interview. They brought a video camera with them and recorded him saying that only women who had anal sex had to worry about HIV. Vaginal tissue would slough off the virus, he said on camera. Women were contracting AIDS in Africa, he said, because men there treated women roughly.[54]

On January 15, 1988, 300 ACT-UP women stopped traffic in front of the offices of *Cosmoplitan* on Manhattan's West 57th St. Over the next days and weeks, they delivered hundreds of condoms daily to the magazine's editor Helen Gurley Brown, until she printed a retraction and ran articles documenting safe sex practices for women. Carlomusto and Maria Maggenti edited footage from the interview and the protest into a film called "Doctors, Liars and Women AIDS Activists: Say No to Cosmo." The film was shown around the country and purchased for the permanent collection of the Museum of Modern Art. That Spring ACT-UP women went to a New York Mets baseball game where they distributed condoms to amazed baseball fans and held up signs that said "No Glove, No Love," and "AIDS Kills Women."[55]

They made television talk shows their next target. ACT-UP women snuck into the Phil Donahue show and another television talk show and stormed the stage to ask why there were no women being interviewed about AIDS. Along with smaller women's AIDS organizations like Gran Fury artist collective, ACT-UP women protested narrow federal definitions of AIDS that excluded information about transmission and symptoms experienced by women. "Women Don't Get AIDS," said one poster intended to dispel a common myth. "They Just Die From It." On the poster was printed information about heterosexual transmission from men to women. In 1991, the U.S. Centers for Disease Control finally expanded its definition of AIDS to include symptoms experienced by women.[56]

A new ACT-UP affinity group was formed, focused on the concerns of people of color, poor and homeless people with AIDS in the city – the Majority Action Committee. There were an estimated 8,000 homeless people with AIDS in New York in the early 1980s, out of a total homeless population of 40,000. ACT-UP members protested in front of the luxury high-rise Trump Tower, which had gotten tax abatements while the city failed to allocate sufficient funding to house the homeless. ACT-UP also protested tax abatements for the Catholic Church, which fought attempts to distribute condoms and blocked a safer sex curriculum in New York public high schools.

To protest, ACT-UP women held safer sex demonstrations in front of nine New York high schools in all five boroughs. "We gave out all our information in about 20 minutes flat," they recalled. "Students were hungry for it." In 1991, New York City acceded to ACT-UP, and began distributing condoms in public high schools.[57]

All of this activity around safer sex and around women's mistreatment by hospitals and federal health officials generated a group within ACT-UP interested in doing more political work around women's health issues, especially reproductive rights. Their organizing was speeded up after the Supreme Court's 1989 Webster decision banning abortions and even abortion counseling by employees of any organization receiving federal funds.

In the aftermath, a group of ACT-UP women formed Women's Health Action Mobilization (WHAM). WHAM's first action was a boycott of Domino's Pizza for its successful attempts to get several state governments to end public funding for abortions. The group was founded and sustained by yet another generation of women activists, lesbian and heterosexual, mostly born in the late 1960s and early 1970s.[58]

WHAM's most famous – and definitely its most controversial – demonstration was organized together with ACT-UP against the Catholic Church's policies around AIDS, homosexuality and reproductive rights. In December 1989, 4,500 protesters surrounded, and several hundred marched into, St. Patrick's Cathedral, the heart of the Catholic Church in New York City. While mass was being conducted, lesbian couples hugged and kissed in front of shocked parishioners. They then staged a die-in, collapsing on the floor of the cathedral. Protesters threw condoms at Cardinal John Francis O'Connor as he preached his homily, and one threw a consecrated communion wafer to the floor. Outside on Fifth Avenue, protesters lay down in front of traffic under a 20-foot balloon labeled "Cardinal O'Condom." As they did, protesters, including men dressed in nun's habits, chanted, "Racist, Sexist, Anti-Gay, Cardinal O'Connor Go Away."[59]

After a second "Stop the Church" protest, a year later, WHAM and ACT-UP members who were photographed in the newspapers received death threats, bomb threats and, extremely rough treatment by police. They responded by launching a new campaign against police brutality that, like needle exchanges and activism for the homeless, gave WHAM and ACT-UP street credibility in poor communities of color.

In the early 1990s, as a conservative Christian direct-action group called Operation Rescue blockaded abortion clinics, and attacked providers, WHAM and ACT-UP members staged counter-protests. Political theater was once again their strongest weapon. This time they created a group called "Church Ladies for Choice." Church Ladies was launched after the Supreme Court decision in *Rust v. Sullivan* upheld a presidential gag order preventing abortion counseling in federally funded clinics. Dressed as nuns, WHAM founder Elizabeth Meixell, "altar boy" Karen Ramspacher, and ACT-UP's Steve Quester picketed St. Patrick's Cathedral singing "This Womb is My Womb/It is not your Womb" and "God is a Lesbian" to the tune of "God Save the Queen."[60]

In a time when so many were dying, protest could not be all fun and games, however. The proportion of women with AIDS in the U.S. had tripled since 1985. Most were contracting it through heterosexual intercourse and, though African-American and Hispanic women represented a little over a quarter of the country's women, they accounted for, and still account for, 79% of American AIDS cases among women. In 1990 and 1991, ACT-UP women wrote and distributed "The Women's Research and Treatment Agenda."

Translated into several languages and distributed at two International Conferences on AIDS, the Women's Research and Treatment Agenda sought to push scientists and medical providers to develop treatment protocols specific to women. In 1991, women AIDS activists gathered at the National Institute of Allergy and Infectious Diseases, demanding that the federal government establish a Women's Interagency HIV Study that would prioritize community-based clinics in the distribution of federal funding. These clinics saw the greatest numbers of HIV positive women but they had received very few federal research or treatment dollars.[61]

ACT-UP and WHAM intensified their protests in the 1992 election season. The groups staged actions at both Democratic and Republican candidate stops and, at the two major party conventions, inviting themselves to parties thrown by the state delegations with the worst records on AIDS. In one of the most dramatic protests ever held in Washington, one month before the election, 8,000 men and women carried the ashes of loved ones who had died of AIDS and spread them on the South Lawn of the White House. While the air filled with ash, they read the names of the thousands of people whose remains they were delivering. Just as dramatically tragic, on the eve of the election, 300 New York ACT-UP members carried the body of activist Mark Fischer in an open coffin from Washington Square up 5th Avenue to Republican headquarters on 42nd St. There they convened a mock Grand Jury and, in sight of Fisher's corpse, indicted President George H.W. Bush for "political assassination" of AIDS patients.[62]

The protest did not let up under President Bill Clinton. In 1993, as part of a march of 1,000,000 gay women and men, activists staged another die-in at the White House, and hung artistic representations of people who had died of AIDS from the front of the Pharmaceutical Manufacturer's Association building. The next year, ACT-UP members scaled New York's City Hall, hanging banners renaming it the AIDS Hall of Shame. And in 1995, at the height of AIDS mortality in the U.S., they formed a human barricade, blocking the Mid-town tunnel between Manhattan and Queens, to protest Mayor Rudolph Giuliani's cuts in funding for AIDS treatment and patient services.

In 1996, a second "ashes action" was held in Washington. Activists silently carried the cremated remains of loved ones "murdered by neglect," and scattered them on the White House lawn as they demanded increased funding for research and treatment. Finally, in 1999, at the close of the most deadly decade in the U.S. AIDS epidemic, ACT-UP and WHAM returned to St. Patrick's Cathedral for a tenth anniversary protest against the church's role in fighting distribution of condoms and blocking women's access to birth control and abortion.[63]

With the development in the late 1990s of a drug treatment regimen that has allowed Americans with AIDS to live near-normal lifespans, ACT-UP protest shifted to focus on the epidemic abroad. In the 21st century, ACT-UP has protested pharmaceutical companies' failure to provide affordable treatments to people with AIDS in China, Brazil, Thailand and South Africa. In 2007, the 20th anniversary of ACT-UP, the group organized protests across the country calling for universal health care. In 2013 more than 35 million people around the world were living with AIDS, two-thirds of them in sub-Saharan Africa. Activists' struggle against the disease continues.[64]

The Lesbian Avengers: Playing With Fire

Even as ACT-UP and WHAM were continuing their protests, some women activists decided to split off from those groups to form a lesbian-specific direct-action civil rights group. They called themselves *The Lesbian Avengers*. The Avengers were created initially by Ana Simo and some of ACT-UP's older women, including Maxine Wolfe and Sarah Schulman, who were frustrated by how lesbian activists and their issues had faded quickly from sight in the larger women's, AIDS and gay rights movements.

Their first action came in 1992 in support of an embattled multi-culturalism initiative of the New York State public schools. The state-sanctioned "Children of the Rainbow" curriculum proposed to make learning about gay and lesbian families a part of every child's education in New York City. The curriculum included information about the diversity of New York's families. It did not focus on gay and lesbian parents but it did acknowledge and celebrate the state's gay families. The curriculum had been developed in response to the murder of a black teenager in Brooklyn and was intended to promote respect for differences among New York's young people. Still, the "rainbow curriculum" sparked fierce backlash.

Mary Cummins, a school board president in Queens, promised to block the new curriculum in her district. She believed that it contained "dangerously misleading lesbian/homosexual propaganda" and that it was her responsibility to the children to see that it never reached their classrooms. The Avengers protested in her district on the first day of school. Their theme was straightforward: no child is too young to learn about lesbian families. A lesbian marching band played loud, cheerful music. Members wore t-shirts proclaiming: "I was a lesbian child." Women handed out balloons that said: "Ask About Lesbian Lives." Television news coverage showed some delighted children reaching out for balloons. More than a few parents looked profoundly uncomfortable. The Avengers felt their action had been a success. Visibility was their goal.[65]

In October 1992, Avenger visuals took a more somber and dramatic turn. Politics in Oregon had taken an ugly turn as the state prepared to vote on whether to amend the state constitution to ban gay rights ordinances. In late September, African-American lesbian Hattie Mae Cohens, and white disabled gay man Brian Mock were burned to death when four white supremacist teenagers threw a home-made explosive through the window of their apartment. Many viewed them as martyrs to hatred. The Avengers decided to hold a public memorial for the two in New York's Bryant Park.

At the emotional night-time gathering, the Avengers began literally playing with fire. Avenger Jennifer Monson, a choreographer and dancer, trained the members to safely "eat fire." They did so that night and at every Avengers protest afterward. "The fire will not consume us," they chanted. "We take it and make it our own."[66]

Soon after the memorial, the Avengers marched down New York's 5th Avenue to call attention to the link between anti-gay rights initiatives and anti-gay violence. The statistics were clear. Carrying torches and eating fire as they marched down Manhattan's most famous thoroughfare, the Avengers set aflame signs with the names of anti-gay ballot initiatives in various states that had given rise to homophobic violence. The group and its tactics were going to spread beyond New York.

Visibility was the Avengers' watchword and they were skilled at finding ways to get it. When Colorado passed Amendment 2, banning gay rights laws in the state, members of a Colorado chapter of the Avengers chained themselves to the fence of the governor's mansion. They also invaded a victory party for the amendment's proponents cheerfully throwing water on the celebration.

In 1993, the Avengers organized a "Dyke March" the night before a massive gay and lesbian rights gathering in Washington, D.C. to ensure that lesbian issues did not get lost in the larger gay protest. Twenty thousand lesbians marched that evening, eating fire and chanting in front of the White House. Holding separate

Dyke Marches the night before, larger gay-lesbian-bisexual-transgender events became a tradition throughout the 1990s, spreading to Mid-West cities, the far West, and abroad to Mexico City and other cities around the world. By the mid-1990s there were 60 Lesbian Avenger chapters in the U.S., Europe and Latin America.

In 1994, the Avengers launched their most daring project – the Lesbian Avengers Civil Rights Organizing Project. To the chagrin of many, the Avengers dubbed the campaign "Freedom Summer," an intentional allusion to the voter registration campaign that had taken place in Mississippi 30 years earlier. The Avengers intended to organize in locales across the U.S. where anti-gay initiatives were on the ballot. Organizers fanned out across Arizona, California, Idaho, Maine, Michigan, Missouri, Nevada, Ohio, Oregon and Washington. One purpose of their actions was to provide support for lesbians and gay men who lived in isolated rural areas.

Like Freedom Summer volunteers, Avengers from across the country flooded into Ovett, Mississippi that summer. This time their purpose was to protect Camp Sister Spirit, a rural lesbian retreat that had received death threats. Local police had paid little attention until a letter-writing campaign organized by the Avengers convinced the state attorney general to investigate. That same year Avengers carried a faux Olympic torch 35 miles into rural Cobb County, Georgia, infamous for homophobic violence. The march was to protest the International Olympic Committee's decision to hold events of the 1996 Summer Olympic Games there. Avengers extinguished the flame on the symbolic Olympic torch by eating it, chanting once again, "The fire will not consume us. We take it and make it our own."

Avengers' Freedom Summer was intended to forcefully reject the argument made by some mainstream LGBT organizations that lesbians and gay men in conservative regions should lay low during the election season. That way, the argument went, they would not antagonize conservatives into coming out and voting for anti-gay initiatives.[67] The Avengers believed such a strategy was counter-productive on several levels.

> When their messages are about 'the homosexual agenda' and we respond with de-gayed messages like 'no government intervention in private lives' or 'no censorship', we look not only ashamed, but dishonest. Voters are unlikely to stand up for the rights of an invisible community.[68]

The Lesbian Avengers were determined to be anything but invisible. Even their fund-raising campaigns were geared toward increasing lesbian visibility. To fund their 1994 Freedom Summer activities, the Avengers held flamboyant parties across the country, and distributed 5,000 copies of a book of articles by lesbian activists who described fighting anti-gay initiatives in their states. Finally, they made a million phone calls to lesbians in six states which then had anti-gay initiatives on the ballot, urging them to organize, vote and build broad coalitions with working-class movements and people of color groups.

> We will not accept superficial legal rights for some lesbians and gay men at the expense of real human rights for all of us. Butch, femme, and androgynous dykes, lesbians and gay men of color, drag queens, lesbian and gay youth, transsexuals, people with AIDS, lesbians and gays with disabilities, and rural lesbians and gay men will not be sacrificed in the name of "campaign strategy."

Always in your face, the Avengers began a door-to-door canvassing effort to get out the vote to defeat anti-gay ballot initiatives. They called the campaign, "Put A Lesbian on Your Doorstep." It took courage to knock on doors in remote regions of Idaho where violent white supremacist groups had built communities. And it required equanimity to door-knock even in less dangerous areas, where the Avengers still had to deal with slammed doors and homophobic slurs. Still, they persisted with verve and humor.

Idaho was the center of activity in summer 1994. The Avengers organized a dance-in at a Moscow nightclub where gay and lesbian patrons had been violently ejected. Lesbians and gay men held "freedom picnics" at rural county fairs, square dancing together as astonished onlookers gawked. And at one fair, they handed out Hershey's kisses along with two-sided cards. On one side the cards said: "For the last 12 years lesbians and gay men have been threatened, harassed, and beaten at the Latah County Fair. Stop the Violence, Stop the Hate." On the other side the cards asked, "How about a kiss instead?" The use of chocolate built on a successful Valentine's Day event by the Avengers earlier that year at New York's Grand Central Station. Smiling volunteers had handed out chocolate kisses to thousands of harried commuters, saying "Happy Valentine's Day." When they unwrapped the foil to pop the chocolate in their mouths, they saw the words: "You have just been kissed by a lesbian." In the heart of Manhattan, this was an amusing zap. In rural Idaho, volunteers recalled, it was nervy, dangerous and just a little bit earth-shaking.[69]

Lesbian Activism in the New Millennium

After more than 50 years of continuous political and social struggle, lesbians had, by the turn of the 21st century, achieved some measure of legal recognition and visibility in American public culture. Many states recognized the custodial rights of lesbians who were biological mothers and also protected the rights of non-biological mothers who had helped to conceive and raise their children. Coming out, being out, no longer made it impossible for women to have careers in politics, the arts or even teaching. There were lesbian talk show hosts on television and even a dramatic series about an inter-racial lesbian family. Still, coming out as lesbian was not without its risks.

For low-income women and for women of color who faced multiple prejudices, the risks of coming out at work were still considerable. Forty years after it was first introduced, employment non-discrimination legislation for lesbians and gay men had not passed the U.S. Congress. Despite conservative arguments that gay, lesbian, bisexual and transgendered people were more afflu-ent than average Americans, in 2012, lesbian couples earned considerably less than heterosexual couples and faced discrimination at work. (Gay men also earned more than either lesbians or heterosexual women, though less than het-erosexual men.) The battles over workplace discrimination continue.[70]

Still, lesbian political activism hit one memorable peak in the summer of 2013, when the U.S. Supreme Court, in *United States v. Windsor*, recognized the mar-riage of 84-year-old Edie Windsor to another woman, Thea Spyer. The two had been together for more than 40 years when Spyer died in 2007. They were out at work and out to their families. They shared a life and a home. But Windsor and Spyer could not legally marry in the U.S. As a result, the Internal Revenue Service treated Windsor as a stranger to Spyer, and levied estate taxes that threat-ened to force the old woman to sell her apartment in order to pay her tax bill. Windsor sued and, six years later, the U.S. Supreme Court overturned the pre-mier obstacle to equal federal rights for lesbian and gay couples – the 1996 Defense of Marriage Act. Passed by Congress to prevent lesbians and gay men from receiving over 1,000 federal benefits, even if they could be legally married in their home states, it had been signed into law by President Bill Clinton. "I cried. I cried," Windsor said after the decision. "We won everything we asked and hoped for. Wow."[71]

The legal ramifications of the decision would take years to sort out but some changes happened quickly. Almost immediately, the Defense Department ordered military commanders to allow same-sex marriages among active service-people and to accord them the same benefits as heterosexual married couples received. Federal financial aid forms began to consider same-sex marriages as equal to het-erosexual. And companies that offered medical coverage to married employees had to include same-sex marriages.

Through fierce and varied forms of activism, lesbians in the U.S. fought their way out of invisibility and harsh stigma in the decades since World War II. The history of their activism challenges the commonly held view that the 1950s, 1980s and 1990s were apolitical decades for American women. It also forces rethinking of 1960s and 1970s radicalism. To write the history of women's activism in the 20th century without incorporating lesbian struggles impoverishes understand-ings of feminism and obscures insight into evolving norms of gender, sexuality and the American family. Lesbian activists waged a multi-generational struggle through all those decades that drew in women of every race and class. They often struggled to build communication and trust across their many lines of difference. But they engaged those challenges with openness and intensity. These struggles also continue.

Notes

1 Del Martin interviewed in the film documentary *No Secret Anymore*, directed by Joan Biron, 2007.

2 "The Woman Identified Woman," by RADICALESBIANS, 1970. Documents from the Women's Liberation Movement, An Online Archival Collection. Special Collections Library, Duke University. http://library.duke.edu/rubenstein/scriptorium/wlm/womid/.

3 Audre Lorde, "Age, Race, Class and Sex: Women Redefining Difference," A Paper Delivered at Amherst College, 1980, reprinted in Audre Lorde, *Sister Outsider* (New York: Crossing Press, 1984).

4 Dorothy Allison, "A Question of Class," in *Skin: Talking about Sex, Class and Literature* (Ithaca: Firebrand Books, 1994).

5 Karla Jay, *Tales of the Lavender Menace: A Memoir of Liberation* (New York: Basic Books, 2000), p. 143; Susan Brownmiller, *In Our Time: A Memoir of Revolution* (New York: Dial Press, 1999).

6 Alice Echols, *Daring to Be Bad: Radical Feminism in America, 1967–75* (Minneapolis: University of Minnesota Press, 1989), pp. 212–214.

7 The Woman Identified Woman," op. cit.

8 Linda Rapp, "Lavender Menace," GLBQ – online encyclopedia. Cited in "Metawatershed: Feminism Unadulterated." http://maggiesmetawatershed.blogspot.com/2008/03 feminism-unadulterated-woman-identified.html

9 Stephanie Gilmore and Elizabeth Kaminski, "A Part and Apart: Lesbian and Straight Feminist Activists Negotiate Identity in a Second-Wave Organization," *Journal of the History of Sexuality*, Vol. 16, No. 1, January 2007, pp. 95–113.

10 Aileen Hernandez, Press Release, December 17, 1970. Cited in Gilmore and Kaminski, op. cit., p. 106.

11 Gilmore and Kaminski, op. cit., p. 105.

12 ibid.

13 Charlotte Bunch and Claudia Hinojosa, *Lesbians Travel the Roads of Feminism Globally* (New Brunswick, New Jersey: Rutgers University Center for Women's Global Leadership, 2000).

14 ibid.

15 "Opposing Voices Heard at Women's Conference," NBC Today Show, Aired November 21, 1977, http://archives.nbclearn.com/portal/site/k-12/flatview?cuecard=5835.

16 "Opposing Voices Heard," op. cit; "Battles Loom at Women's Conference," *New York Times News Service*, November 16, 1977, http://www.livablehouston.com/good/articles/anderson.html.

17 Pokey Anderson, "An Idiosyncratic Tour of Houston," *Livable Houston Magazine* archive 2000, http://www.livablehouston.com/good/articles/anderson.html.

18 Bunch and Hinojosa, op. cit., p. 8.

19 *Sisters of 77*, directed by Cynthia Salzman Mondell and Alan Mondell, PBS Independent Lens, http://www.pbs.org/independentlens/sistersof77/film.html; Gilmore and Kaminski, op. cit.

20 The phrase comes from the ground-breaking 1981 article by Joan Nestle, "Butch Femme Relationships: Sexual Courage in the 1950s," *Heresies*, 12, 1981 pp. 100–109.

21 Marcia Gallo, *Different Daughters: A History of the Daughters of Bilitis and the Rise of Lesbian Rights* (Seattle: Seal Press, 2007), p. xxii.

22 See Annelise Orleck, *Common Sense and A Little Fire: Women and Working Class Politics in the United States, 1900–1965* (Chapel Hill, NC: University of North Carolina Press, 1995).

23 Elizabeth Lapovsky Kennedy and Madeline Davis, "Oral History and the Study of Sexuality in the Lesbian Community: Buffalo, New York, 1940–1960," *Feminist Studies*, Vol. 12, No. 1 Spring 1986, pp. 7–26.

24 Elizabeth Lapovsky Kennedy, "Introduction" to excerpts from their book *Boots of Leather, Slippers of Gold*, in Laura Harris and Elizabeth Crocker, eds., *Femme: Feminists, Lesbians and Bad Girls* (New York: Routledge, 1997), p. 19.

25 Trisha Franzen, "Differences and Identities: Feminism and the Albuquerque Lesbian Community," *Signs*, Vol. 18, No. 4, Summer 1993, pp. 891–906.

26 Kennedy and Davis, op. cit., pp. 8–9.

27 Joan Nestle, "Introduction" to the second edition of *A Restricted Country* (London: Pandora and Oram Press, 1996), http://www.joannestle.com/RCintro96.html.

28 Laura Harris and Elizabeth Crocker, eds., *Femme: Feminists, Lesbians and Bad Girls*, (New York: Routledge, 1997) p. 2.

29 Anne Hull, "Just Married, After 51 Years Together; Activist Gay Couple Accepts Leading Role," *The Washington Post*, February 29, 2004. p. A.01.

30 William Grimes, "Del Martin" obituary, *New York Times*, August 28, 2008; Marcia Gallo, op. cit.; Joan Biron, *No Secret Anymore*, op. cit.

31 Grimes, op. cit., Biron, op. cit.; "Harvey and Our Vision," milkfoundation.org.

32 Manuela Soares, "The Purloined Ladder: Its Place in Lesbian History," *Journal of Homosexuality* Vol. 34, No. 3/4, 1998, pp. 27–49; Rodger Streitmatter, *Unspeakable: The Rise of the Gay and Lesbian Press in America* (London: Faber & Faber, 1995), p. 153.

33 "Homosexuals Stage Protest at the Capital," *New York Times*, May 30, 1965.

34 Del Martin, "Goodbye," *The Advocate*, 1970; cited in Marc Stein, *City of Sisterly and Brotherly Love: Lesbian and Gay Philadelphia, 1945–72* (Chicago: University of Chicago Press, 2000) p. 343.

35 ibid. p. 350

36 Daniel Winunwe Rivers, *Radical Relations: Lesbian Mothers, Gay Fathers and Their Children in the United States Since World War II* (Chapel Hill, NC: University of North Carolina Press, 2013).

37 Letter from an African-American lesbian mother to DOB headquarters, 1965, cited in Rivers, op. cit., p. 51.

38 Biron, *No Secret Anymore*, op. cit.

39 Barbara Gittings letter, 1967. Barbara Gittings and Kay Tobin Lahusen gay history papers and photographs, New York Public Library, Manuscripts Division.

40 *No Secret Anymore*, op. cit.

41 Audre Lorde, *Zami: A New Spelling of My Name* (New York: Crossing Press, 1983), p. 226.

42 Audre Lorde, *Sister Outsider: Essays and Speeches* (New York: Crossing Press, 1984, 2007), pp. 42–43.

43 Dorothy Allison, "A Question of Class," in *Skin: Talking about Sex, Class and Literature* (Ithaca: Firebrand Books, 1994).

44 ibid.

45 Sherry McCoy and Maureen Hicks, "A Psychological Retrospective on Power in the Contemporary Lesbian Community," *Frontiers*, Vol. 4, No. 3, 1979, pp. 65–69.

46 Blanche McCrary Boyd, *Terminal Velocity* (New York: Knopf, 1997) p. 1.

47 Alexis Jetter, "Goodbye to the Last Taboo," *Vogue*, July 1993.

48 "HIV in the United States:" Centers for Disease Control and Prevention, www.cdc.gov/hiv/statistics/basics/ataglance.html.

49 David France, "The Men and Women Who Started ACT-UP," *New York Magazine*, March 25, 2012; Ann Cvetkovich, *An Archive of Feelings: Trauma, Sexuality and Lesbian Public Cultures* (Durham, NC: Duke University Press, 2003).

50 Sarah Schulman, Interview with Jean Carlomusto, December 19, 2002. ACT-UP Oral History Project, http://www.actuporalhistory.org/interviews/images/carlomusto.pdf.

51 Sarah Schulman, Interview with Lei Chou, May 5, 2003. ACT-UP Oral History Project.

52 Tamar Carroll, *Mobilizing New York: Community Activism from the War on Poverty to the AIDS Epidemic* (Chapel Hill, NC: University of North Carolina Press, 2014), Chapter 5.

53 ibid.

54 Sarah Schulman, Interview with Jean Carlomusto, op. cit.

55 Carroll, op. cit. Chapter 5.

56 *ACT-UP New York Capsule History*, http://www.actuporalhistory.org/interviews/images/carlomusto.pdf; AIDS Activism Poster by Gran Fury, 1991, Courtesy Gran Fury Collection. Manuscripts and Archives Division, The New York Public Library, Astor, Lenox and Tilden Foundations; "CDC action flyer, Women's Committee, *ACT UP*," January 8–9, 1990, Courtesy Lesbian Herstory Archives.

57 *Village Voice*, January 9, 1990, p. 41, cited in Carroll; *ACT-UP Capsule History*, op cit.

58 Carroll, Chapter 5.

59 Sarah Schulman, Interview with Ron Goldberg, ACT-UP Oral History Project, October 25, 2003.

60 Carroll, Chapter 5.

61 Am-Far, Making Aids History – "Statistics Women and HIV/AIDS," http://www.amfar.org/About-HIV-and-AIDS/Facts-and-Stats/Statistics--Women-and-HIV-AIDS/.

62 *ACT-UP Capsule History*, 1992.

63 *ACT-UP Capsule History*, 1993–1995.

64 ACT-UPNY Reports, http://www.actupny.org/reports/index.html.

65 Steven Lee Myers, "How A Rainbow Curriculum Turned into Fighting Words," *New York Times*, December 13, 1992.

66 Anna Quindlen, "Putting Hatred to a Vote," *Chicago Tribune*, November 3, 1992.

67 *Out Against the Right: An Organizing Handbook, LACROP: Getting Started* http://www.octobertech.com/handbook/start.html.

68 ibid.

69 ibid.; Sara Pursley, "Gay Politics in the Heartland: With the Avengers in Idaho," *The Nation*, January 23, 1995, pp. 90–94.

70 Crosby Burns, "The Gay and Transgender Wage Gap," Center for American Progress, April 16, 2012, http://www.americanprogress.org/issues/lgbt/news/2012/04/16/ 11494/the-gay-and-transgender-wage-gap/.

71 "I Cried. I Cried," NBC News, June 26, 2013. http://usnews.nbcnews.com/_news/2013/06/26/19155699-i-cried-i-cried-doma-widow-says-on-hearing-of-supreme-court-win?lite.

8

ANTI-FEMINIST BACKLASH AND FEMINISM REBORN: THE 1970S THROUGH 2013

The Backlash Against 1970s Feminism

[Feminists] have given us divorce, millions of fatherless children and the idea that it's O.K. to be a single mom . . . That made the father and husband irrelevant.

Phyllis Schlafly, Founder and President of the Eagle Forum,
leader of the successful movement to defeat ratification
of the Equal Rights Amendment in 1977[1]

It is a philosophy of death . . . Radical feminists are self-destructive and are trying to bring about the death of an entire civilization as well.

Beverly LaHaye, founder and President of
Concerned Women for America, 1984[2]

Perhaps it was inevitable that there would be a backlash against the feminist revolution of the 1960s and 1970s. When it came, it was part of a larger revival of American conservatism in the 1970s and 1980s, funded by Western oil barons and defense contractors, and driven by the fervor of evangelical Christians in the American South, the mid-West and parts of the Southwest. These activists politicized their faith, their values, and their families, arguing that feminism had created chaos and disorder by overturning divinely ordained gender roles. This conservative backlash was in many ways a women's movement – a reaction by women who felt that their identities as wives and mothers were being devalued and diminished by late 20th-century American feminists. And yet, even though conservative women were galvanized and inspired to act in opposition to feminism, in structure and organizing style these movements shared many similarities. And, even more importantly, both movements actively politicized the personal.

Anti-feminists in the 1970s built on and learned from the successes of earlier women activists. Leaders tapped into women's informal networks to build a grass-roots base. Organizing in traditionally female church and parent associations, they mounted effective letter writing campaigns and lobbied elected officials. And they energetically politicized their personal lives, generating a policy vision intended to reinforce "traditional" families, made of wives, husbands and children.

Like the feminists against whom they were rebelling, conservative women activists found themselves riding a wave of emotion and energy far greater than they had ever imagined. Beginning in the early 1970s, conservative Christian women in the U.S. created a vibrant and lasting political movement. It would be a glaring oversight to close this book without, at least briefly, recounting their story. For anti-feminist women organized as well and as widely as their feminist counterparts. And the political organizations they built continue to wield significant influence in the 21st century.

Political organizing by conservative women in the U.S. was not new. From the mid-19th century on, there had been American women's groups that organized against woman suffrage and decried the pernicious influence of "new women," "free love" and mothers working outside the home. White women had organized to commemorate and glorify the Confederacy. They formed a women's Ku Klux Klan in the 1920s with branches across the U.S. And, in the 1950s, conservative women had flocked into patriotic women's federations to fight Communism abroad and radicalism at home.

Late 20th-century anti-feminism was an outgrowth of those strains in American women's politics. But it was distinguished from those earlier movements in a few key ways. One was the stridency of the movement's opposition to feminists and feminism. Another was the sophistication, longevity and scope of its political operations.

Modern anti-feminism began in the early 1970s in response to three political developments that religious Christian women viewed as direct threats to the traditional family. The first was the 1973 Supreme Court *Roe v. Wade* decision which, by a 7–2 vote, guaranteed women's right to legal abortion across the United States. The second was the passage through Congress, more than 50 years after it was first introduced, of an Equal Rights Amendment to the U.S. Constitution banning discrimination on the basis of sex. Finally, as the gay, lesbian, bisexual and transgender rights movement grew stronger, Christian conservatives increasingly focused their attentions on fighting "the homosexual agenda." Activists were particularly incensed by the rising numbers of lesbians and gay men who were having children and by the claim that their families were legitimate and deserving of legal protection. These issues generated strong emotions among millions of women who formed a deep grass-roots base for the social conservative movement.

Attorney and long-time Republican Party stalwart Phyllis Schlafly realized, as soon as the Equal Rights Amendment passed Congress in 1972, that there was great political potential in organizing a "Stop ERA" campaign. Her arguments were simple and emotionally potent. "Since the women are the ones who bear the babies and there's nothing we can do about that," she said in a March 1973 "Stop ERA" speech, "our laws and customs then make it the financial obligation of the husband to provide the support. It is his obligation and his sole obligation. And this is exactly and precisely what we will lose if the Equal Rights Amendment is passed."[3]

For many married stay-at-home mothers, especially those whose lives were centered on church communities, Schlafly's words were a call to arms. They felt alienated by the "selfishness" of feminists who, they believed, sought personal fulfillment at the expense of their husbands and children. They were horrified by the willingness of mainstream feminist organizations to advocate for lesbian rights. Indeed, the increasing closeness during the 1970s between feminist leaders and lesbian rights activists confirmed many Christian activist women in their belief that feminism was, in the words of evangelical leader Beverly LaHaye, "an illness." During the second half of the 1970s, LaHaye and other like-minded women began to create political lobbying organizations with a speed and breadth that rivaled that of their feminist counterparts.

The first test of conservative women's strength as a political force came in the 1977 International Women's Year conference in Houston. After successes on the state level electing representatives to the conference, "pro-family" delegates tried energetically to inject their views on abortion and homosexuality into what one conservative delegate called "a feminist Woodstock." Conservative delegates were determined to try to prevent the conference from passing a Plan of Action for the world's women that they saw as "an undiluted 'womanifesto' for big-government and feminist liberalism taken to extremes." In spite of their best efforts, the Plan of Action was approved by the majority of delegates, leaving conservative women activists frustrated and motivated.[4]

Even before the convention ended, they organized a protest rally across town. Speakers stood in front of stacks of petitions gathered by conservative women across the country urging federal officials to reject the International Women's Year Plan of Action. Fifteen thousand women and their families crowded into the Houston Astrodome to applaud the birth of a new women's movement, while another 2,000 listened outside. By the time they left the rally, they had begun to feel themselves part of something large and lasting.

Their goals were two-fold: to reverse what they saw as the most damaging forces in American life – the left-ward drift of American politics, and the "anti-family" influence of organized feminism. Shaped both by stay-at-home wives and mothers and by career women like Schlafly, this political vision simultaneously exalted the role of wives and mothers and acknowledged the needs of women in the paid labor force. The new movement's advocacy for wage-earning women resulted in one of the movement's only cooperative efforts with feminists – to pass the Pregnancy Discrimination Act of 1978. But, apart from that anomalous collaboration and some brief moments of agreement on the issue of regulating pornography, the two women's movements would remain locked in combat from the 1970s into the 21st century.[5]

A young Catholic firebrand named Connaught "Connie" Marshner was the new movement's organizing genius. Marshner was a Baby Boomer, the same age as the radical feminist organizers she pitted herself against. Through the 1970s and 1980s, she worked hard to pull disparate local conservative women's groups into a national political force. Marshner allied with women 30 years older than herself to promote the cause of "family values" – Schlafly and an evangelical pastor's wife named Beverly LaHaye. Together they organized conservative women against ERA, legal abortion, feminism, gay rights and pornography, and for equal pay and equal rights for wage-earning women.

Fresh out of college, Marshner rocketed to a position of national prominence when she was not yet out of her teens, working as a staffer at the Heritage Foundation in Washington, D.C. Her mentor at Heritage, Paul Weyrich, asked her to critique the Comprehensive Child Development Bill, overwhelmingly passed by Congress in 1971 and the closest that the U.S. ever came to a federally funded early childhood education system. As the bill was worded, it would have provided federal child-care subsidies to single working mothers. That was precisely what Marshner objected to.

Marshner argued that the bill proposed to substitute "communal" child-rearing for the traditional two-parent family. And she circulated her critique widely among church-affiliated women. Her inflammatory memo, warning that the traditional family was in danger, sparked a flood of letters demanding that President Richard Nixon veto the bill. He did and justified his decision by citing Marshner's arguments. Conservative activists celebrated. Marshner would later say that December 9, 1971, the date of Nixon's veto, was "the birthdate of the pro-family movement."[6]

"All over the country," Marshner said,

> were little clusters of evangelical and fundamentalist Mom's groups – it was mainly mothers. They were unstructured. They didn't have an organization; they were just in touch with each other and they were beginning to be aware that there was really a problem here . . . This totally informal network of parents out there in real America . . . those real, true grassroots Americans are the ones who provided the blood and the bones for what became an organized movement.[7]

Marshner's primary tool to reach those groups and unite them in a coherent movement was the *Family Protection Report* – a national newsletter that she edited for the Heritage Foundation. She also reported on the work of other Heritage staff such as Onalee McGraw, who was then organizing conservative mothers to protest "ungodly" curricula in public schools. In a 1976 pamphlet called "Secular Humanism and the Schools: An Issue Whose Time Has Come," McGraw urged mothers to run for school board positions to combat curricula that affirmed feminism, homosexuality or "enforced" desegregation through busing. They did just that, and school board elections became a springboard for the political ascendancy of women in the rising conservative tide.[8]

Perhaps the most important figure in the new movement was Beverly LaHaye, wife of evangelical minister, conservative activist and popular novelist Tim LaHaye. Beverly was moved to begin organizing Christian women while watching newswoman Barbara Walters interview Betty Friedan on television in 1978. As LaHaye would later describe her political epiphany, she jumped out of her TV-watching chair, shouted "Betty Friedan does not speak for me," and began making plans to create a Christian women's political action group. "It seemed like the Christian women of America did not have a voice in any of the women's movement, nothing at all," she told a reporter for a Christian women's newspaper. "The women got so excited, they kept saying, 'We've got to do something, we've got to do something' . . . Christian women seemed to realize they were being shut out of any discussion on women's rights . . ." Soon thereafter, LaHaye convened a mass meeting in San Diego to Stop the ERA that drew 1,200 women.[9]

Less than a year later, LaHaye created the political lobbying group – Concerned Women For America. "We've trained them," she noted proudly on the group's 30th anniversary in 2009. "Today the Concerned Women for America (CWA) have a voice in their city government, their state government and the federal government."[10]

CWA got its start in 1979, when President Jimmy Carter announced three regional White House Conferences on Families, insisting that 30% of delegates to the conferences be democratically elected at the local level. The rest would be appointed by governors and state conventions. LaHaye made common cause with Schlafly and Marshner, and other church-based women activists, and they rallied conservative women's networks across the country to elect some "pro-family" delegates to these conferences. Organizing through churches, Bible study groups and parents' organizations, "pro-family" women secured 22 of 24 elected delegate slots from Virginia as well as the bulk of slots from Michigan, Oklahoma and a sizable number from Oregon. Even in New York State, feminists found they had a battle on their hands. Ultimately the new movement was able to secure 250 of the 1,500 delegate positions.

Not surprisingly, the conferences immediately became embroiled in heated debate over the definition of family. "We saw that homosexuals were driving in because they wanted to be part of the whole definition of the family," LaHaye recalled. "And we objected to that." She and other pro-family delegates were determined to "hold onto the real true meaning of the genuine family, as God intended it to be." Marshner took the floor at the June 1980 Baltimore conference and laid out her vision for the pro-family movement:

> Families consist of people related by heterosexual marriage, blood, and adoption. Families are not religious cults; families are not Manson families [a cult of murderers in the late 1960s who referred to themselves as a family]; families are not heterosexual or homosexual liaisons outside of marriage.

Claiming that they were unable to make themselves heard, Marshner and 30 delegates staged a walkout on the second day of the White House conference. Conservative activists would later recall that this was a play for the media spotlight, pre-planned by the always media-savvy Marshner. She and other conservative women leaders were determined not to cede the label "family" to feminists, single mothers or gay people. They wanted to make it theirs and theirs alone, and to cast their movement as its stalwart defenders.

Even before the White House conferences had ended, LaHaye convened an American Pro-Family Conference in Long Beach, California, attended by 7,000 women. A month later, Marshner, Schlafly and others organized the American Family Forum in Washington, D.C. There they announced the new National Pro-Family Coalition, which claimed 150 conservative women's groups as members.

Energetic as it was, there was a central contradiction inherent in 1970s and 1980s anti-feminist activism that was embodied by the three most powerful charismatic leaders of the movement: Schlafly, LaHaye and Marshner. Fighting to preserve traditional gender roles and heterosexual family norms, the "pro-family" movement politicized the American family, heterosexual relationships and women's bodies. In so doing, it launched political careers for conservative women activists across the U.S. and made anti-feminism a force in American politics that is alive and well in the 21st century.

By 2013, Concerned Women for America, with its more than 500,000 members, chapters in every corner of the U.S. and an army of trained political lobbyists, was only slightly smaller and less influential than the National Organization for Women (NOW). Penny Nance, CWA's post-LaHaye director, has repeatedly been quoted as saying that CWA had passed NOW in size – "the other side, we're very proud." Throughout the 1980s, half a million CWA members, alongside 80,000 members of Schlafly's Eagle Forum, fought against abortion rights, the United Nations, and "the homosexual agenda." They lobbied the U.S Senate to confirm Justices Clarence Thomas and Antonin Scalia. In the 1990s, they campaigned against "pornographic" art, gay rights ordinances and FDA approval of the "morning after pill," RU-486. In the 2000s, they fought against approval of stem-cell research, hate crimes legislation, the Violence Against Women Act and the Affordable Care Act.[11]

In the second decade of the 21st century, Concerned Women for America was operating prayer chapters in nearly every state. Its volunteers monitored local, state and federal legislation. Conservative women activists continued to be trained by Connie Marshner, who created the Leadership Institute to hone the political skills of conservative women. Disciples of Marshner and Beverly LaHaye continued to lobby elected officials in the 21st century with as much energy as they displayed in the 1980s. Their stated priorities continue to be: "family and marriage, sanctity of human life, education, pornography, religious liberty and national sovereignty." Once a month, in 2013, 535 trained volunteers – 100 for the Senate, and 435 for Congress – traveled to Washington, D.C., to lobby members of Congress through CWA's Project 535. The organization also developed e-blasts and e-newsletters to keep its membership informed.[12]

According to conservative columnist and military preparedness expert Elaine Donnelly, Ronald Reagan's campaign for President in 1980 was the moment when conservative women became fullbore political operatives, engaged and embedded in every kind of political institution. "Many conservative women became precinct delegates, worked hard as county and state Republican-party officials, and became voting delegates to the Republican National Convention," she recalled. "In 1980, they provided a comfortable margin of victory for presidential nominee Ronald Reagan." While feminists were marching in the streets, Donnelly argued, "pro-family women . . . were quietly writing and counting the votes for platform language." She believes that women provided the margins of victory that elected Ronald Reagan in 1980 and 1984, and George H.W. Bush in 1988. Conservative women also ran successfully for city, state and federal offices and served in the administrations of Reagan and both George Bushes. "Feminists in 1977 thought that their historic IWY conferences would inspire women to take over the world," says Donnelly. "The irony is that the conferences did have that effect, but those who were motivated the most were admirers of Ronald Reagan."[13]

The local campaign strategy crafted by Marshner and LaHaye in the 1970s proved immensely successful and has had lasting effects. Conservative women and their political allies have won victories on school boards, city councils and in state legislatures. The 2010 elections produced numerous victories for socially conservative Republicans from North Carolina to Texas, many of which were achieved through the volunteer efforts of activists in CWA and other Christian women's groups. Though the candidates were more often men than women, the grass-roots and professional staff who got them elected were die-hards of the conservative women's movement.

In their quest to limit access to abortion, Christian women activists have been quite successful. Pro-life/anti-abortion activists started to chip away at abortion rights beginning in 1976, when the Hyde Amendment banned Medicaid funding for abortion. In the years since that time, they have been able to push through laws requiring parental consent for minors, 24-hour waiting periods, and gag orders for clinic workers whose salaries were paid with federal funds. They have also been able to limit insurance coverage for abortions. The most dramatic changes came between 2010 and 2013, during which time Republican-controlled state legislatures passed more than 130 bills restricting access to abortion – including bans on abortion after 20 weeks, mandatory ultrasounds for women seeking abortions, and requirements that abortion-providing clinicians have hospital admitting privileges.

These successful state-level political campaigns dramatically restricted American women's access to safe, legal abortions. Despite the fact that 77% of Americans in 2013 continued to believe that women should be able to get abortions if they needed them, it was no longer possible to get an abortion in 87% of U.S. counties. Outside the major metropolitan areas, 97% of counties in the U.S. no longer had abortion providers. American women had to travel long distances, take time off from work and endure the expense of travel and lodging, in order to fulfill a right that had been guaranteed them by the Supreme Court for 40 years. Battles between anti-feminist and feminist organizations can reasonably be termed a political civil war between American women. And in 2014, the war showed no signs of ending any time soon.[14]

Feminisms in the 21st Century: "Silence has the Rusty Taste of Shame"[15]

They must have thought that, because rape victims are so ashamed of themselves, none of us would talk to each other and compare notes about how we were treated, and would never go public.

Tucker Reed – University of Southern California student
and one leader of a nationwide movement, born in 2013,
to combat sexual violence on college campuses[16]

It really speaks to how powerful men and women and students in general can be when we all work together . . . I think this is when the change will start to happen. I think people will look back in 20 or 30 years and say, "This is when things started to improve."

Former Amherst College student Angie Epifano –
November 2013 about the movement to
make college campuses safe for all[17]

To me, courage is all of the children who go to school every day wondering if their parents will still be there when they come home at the end of the day. And courage is also my mom, who is here risking arrest today so she can fight for my future, our family's future, and the rights of all families to be together.

Josie Macaraeg, an 11-year old girl in Washington, D.C.
protesting deportation of undocumented immigrants,
September 2013[18]

Four decades after the revolution in women's legal rights that took place in the 1960s and 1970s, Americans continued to battle over abortion, contraception, gay and lesbian rights, and many other issues. Most of the legal and legislative gains of the 1960s and 1970s remained on the books in 2013. Legal rights, once established, are difficult to reverse. And yet, as the dramatic restrictions on women's access to abortion illustrated, state and local governments between 1975 and 2013 significantly eroded women's rights. In the realm of the mass imagination as well, conservative women activists had their impact, contributing to a growing popular discomfort with all things feminist.

In the realm of collective consciousness, though, the most powerful anti-feminist force at the turn of the 21st century was a post-sexual revolution popular culture awash with glossy images of girls and women as bitches and sluts, popular literature that portrayed feminists as angry and man-hating, and media-manufactured crises purporting to show the damage that feminism had done – supposedly leaving too many women unhappy, unmarried and childless. At the dawn of the 1990s, journalist Susan Faludi chronicled these so-called "crises" in a widely read book called *Backlash: The Undeclared War Against American Women*. Faludi described the beginning of the backlash, but it was far from over.[19]

As the 1990s began, Americans watched televised coverage of the intensely hostile questioning by U.S. Senators of legal scholar Anita Hill, who had charged U.S. Supreme Court nominee Clarence Thomas with sexually harassing her when she worked for him at the Equal Employment Opportunity Commission. The televised Hill-Thomas hearings riveted the nation, sparking a national discussion of sexual harassment in the workplace. Americans were sharply divided between those who thought Hill was lying – Thomas called the proceedings "a high tech lynching" – and those who stood behind the soft-spoken law professor, sporting buttons that read "I Believe Anita Hill."

These tensions could also be seen in the coverage of a gang of Los Angeles teenage boys called the Spur Posse who kept a scorecard of their sexual conquests – many of them non-consensual. "Nothing my boy did was anything any red-blooded American boy wouldn't do at his age," said one Posse member's father. He was not outraged at the boys' behavior but at the girls who dared file complaints against them.[20]

The view that women falsely cried rape, unnecessarily subjecting boys and men to scrutiny by law enforcement and media, was reinforced by the "post-feminist" writing of 1990s literary sensations Camille Paglia and Katie Roiphe. The two writers argued that women should stop hand-wringing over date rape and simply protect themselves. The outrage on college campuses over rape was disingenuous, they insisted. Paglia said it was nothing more than "feminism hitting the wall of its own broken promises." Too much discussion of rape was promoting fear rather than strength. Young women could protect themselves by not being "fools" or "idiots." Masculinity, Paglia posited, is "aggressive, unstable, combustible . . . The only solution to date rape is female self-awareness and self-control."[21]

All of this post-feminist consciousness was interrupted in the early 1990s by a new resurgence of feminism among young women – who described themselves as "The Third Wave." Asserting that they were more concerned with difference than with sisterhood and with individual freedom rather than collectivity, young women in the 1990s accepted the notion that feminist activism had occurred in two prior waves: from the mid-19th century to the early 20th, and from the 1960s through the 1970s. They saw themselves as a third wave of feminism – less likely to express themselves through protests or zaps than through writing and art. Their focus on creativity spawned a very in-your-face expression of feminism that took the form of raw, angry punk rock music and self-produced, intentionally non-slick woman-run "zines."

"Riot Grrrl" activism was born in the Pacific Northwest and Washington, D.C. Its first sparks were lit by feminist musician Kathleen Hanna, a student at The Evergreen State College in Olympia, Washington, an alternative state school opened in the early 1970s and staffed by radical faculty, some of whom had been purged from other colleges and universities. In the 1970s, Evergreen had been a bastion of feminist activism and lesbian separatism, of independent punk music and early grunge rock. By the early 1990s, the music and feminism had evolved into a new sort of political-aesthetic fusion. Hanna and other Evergreeners created a band called Bikini Kill and joined forces with University of Oregon students Allison Wolfe and Molly Neuman, who had started another girl band called Bratmobile and a "zine" they called *Girl Germs*.

When one of the zine's founders landed an internship at the U.S. Congress, the whole group of feminist punk rockers decided to relocate to Washington, D.C. There they founded a new "zine" they called Riot Grrrl. The name evolved from a comment that what this new musical scene needed was to start a "girl riot." In many ways, the name Riot Grrrl was intended to distance their generation from 1970s feminism, with its focus on "woman-centered" politics and culture. They wanted to reclaim the joy of being "girls." And they liked that the name sounded like "an angry growl" – as did their music, and their lyrics.[22]

Riot Grrrls didn't relate to 1970s feminism as they understood it. They found its insistence on the use of the term woman instead of girl silly. They took women's studies classes, but felt them too dry and academic, said Allison Wolfe. Still, they were at least as angry as the feminist generation who had revolted 20 years earlier. The lyrics to Riot Grrrl songs were far angrier and more sexually explicit than feminist "womyn's" music of the 1970s. But the discussion groups they created had a lot in common with the consciousness-raising groups of the earlier generation.

In the summer of 1991, Riot Grrrl started publicizing times and places for weekly meetings, and ever-growing groups of young women began coming together to talk about body image, sexual harassment, sexual violence and the pressures of being a "girl." Kathleen Hanna later recalled that many of those who attended those early meetings "had never been in a room with only women before, and were blown away by what it felt like: everybody had so much to say." More "girl" bands grew out of these meetings, as chapters of Riot Grrrl spread throughout the U.S., made up of young women who created their own "zines," shared personal experiences and played loud, raucous music. It was a way of building community by consciously attacking the male-dominated world of rock music. In addition to Olympia, Eugene and D.C., vibrant Riot Grrrl scenes could be found in New York, L.A. and Philadelphia in the early 1990s.[23]

The bands that were at the heart of this movement had names like Bikini Kill, Babes in Toyland and 7-Year Bitch. The musicians invited women at their shows to come up close to the stage to dance in a space where they could dance together, free of the unwanted groping too many had experienced at male-dominated punk concerts. And their songs made clear the Riot Grrrl message. Bikini Kill's "We Don't Need You" told men and boys: "Don't need you to say we're cute, Don't need you to say we're alright, Don't need your atti-fuckin-tude boy, Don't need no kiss goodnight. We don't need you, We don't need you. Us girls, We don't need you." Bratmobile promised to "kill Spur Posse boys." And the most lasting band to emerge from Riot Grrrl, Olympia's Sleater-Kinney, which would continue touring through 2006 and would be called by rock critic Greil Marcus "America's best rock band," penned what could only be called feminist anthems. Their 2002 song, "Step Aside," released after much of the fury of early Riot Grrrl had ebbed, gives a sense of what the movement embodied:

> Knife Through the Heart of our exploitation. Ladies can you feel it? Disassemble discrimination. When violence rules the world outside, and the headlines make me want to cry, it's not the time to just keep quiet. Speak up one time TO THE BEAT.[24]

In 2013, a decade after Step Aside, more than 20 years after the beginning of Riot Grrrl, another generation of women college students suddenly erupted in anger over the sexual violence that had become endemic to college life and over the refusal of college administrators to take it seriously. Though the numbers of rapes in the U.S. had declined dramatically since the 1970s, parts of 21st century popular youth culture seemed to positively revel in sexual violence against women. Popular hip-hop artists were selling millions of albums with songs that depicted raping, beating and killing women. Eminem – the most "liked" person on Facebook (with 60 million fans) – rapped about raping women with umbrellas and promised "all I got for these hoes is dick, duct tape and a stapler." By 2011, one out of four college women in the U.S. had experienced rape or attempted rape while on campus, and one out of five American women at some point in their lives.[25]

Though many had questioned the idea of "rape culture" when 1970s activists first coined the term, by the 21st century, "rape culture" had come roaring back. Even mainstream media began to use the term. In 2013, a series of gang rapes of teenagers by high school football heroes made national news when images of an unconscious girl, carried by her assailants, were posted on the Internet alongside a video of a laughing eyewitness. Victims who dared bring charges were viciously bullied on social media sites. When a gang rape/murder on a private bus in

Mumbai provoked outrage in this country at what journalists called India's "rape culture," American activists pointed out that there was a serious problem right here at home that cried out for immediate attention.[26]

A 2011 survey by the U.S. Department of Justice found that 1.3 million women were being raped annually in the U.S., 80% of them before they turned 25. And, rather than those statistics sparking general outrage, victim blaming was common, not just among young people but also among adults. From Connecticut to Missouri to Ohio, adults were involved in covering up rapes, getting charges against accused rapists dropped and challenging the victims' credibility online and in the mainstream media.[27]

In Marysville, Missouri, a 14-year-old rape victim's family was driven out of town by intense harassment after they dared seek justice. The home they left burned mysteriously to the ground. Repeatedly hospitalized, the victim attempted suicide several times after being bullied online for daring to name her assailant. The perpetrator – a popular high school football player and grandson of a powerful state legislator – faced no charges of rape, only charges of child endangerment for leaving the unconscious girl on her mother's lawn on a freezing January night. He was sentenced to community service. The case was closed in January 2014, when the county prosecutor announced that the perpetrator had taken responsibility for his actions by issuing a public apology. Two weeks later, in response to a two-year ESPN investigation, police in Columbia, Missouri, finally began investigating charges of rape that had been brought three years earlier by a member of the University of Missouri women's swim team. The university had not investigated her report or notified her parents that she had been assaulted. The young woman committed suicide in 2011.[28]

These tragedies helped fuel a movement by college students to combat sexual violence. That movement spread rapidly across the country in 2013, putting an unprecedented degree of pressure on campus administrators. By the end of the year, college women had filed 1,300 Title IX cases with the Department of Education arguing that sexual assault and harassment on campus constituted a form of sex discrimination. Title IX, passed in 1972 as part of the Education Amendments of 1972, mandated that: "no person shall, on the basis of sex, be excluded from participation in, be denied the benefits of, or be subjected to discrimination under any educational program or activity receiving federal financial assistance . . ."[29]

How college and university administrations responded to complaints of sexual assault was almost as big a problem as the assaults themselves, student activists argued. Campus judicial systems did not consider most acts of sexual misconduct crimes. Some campuses had a one-year statute of limitations on assault charges, even though the legal statute of limitations was 15 years. One former Wesleyan professor recalled being in a meeting with deans who insisted that a series of confirmed campus assaults, harassment and threats did not constitute crimes. They were corrected by the Middletown, CT, police chief. Activists began to see a pattern of willful ignorance and intentional cover-up.[30]

A reflexive effort by administrators to downplay sexual assault, harassment, stalking, rape and death threats on campus made survivors reluctant to report their assailants. Fewer than 5% of campus rapes were being reported. Even when survivors did report their assailants, campus administrators ignored the safety of their students by failing to expel rapists found guilty by the university. Studies of campus violence showed that a small minority of male students were responsible for the assaults and that these perpetrators raped an average of six women each. If reported rapes resulted in expulsions, all students on campus would be safer.[31]

By early 2014, these complaints had triggered full-scale federal investigations of 55 colleges and universities, including some of the most elite colleges in the country: Amherst, the University of California at Berkeley, the University of Colorado at Boulder, Dartmouth, Georgetown, the University of Montana, the University of North Carolina at Chapel Hill, Notre Dame, Occidental, Princeton, Swarthmore, the U.S. Naval Academy, the University of Virginia, Wesleyan, the U.S. Military Academy at West Point, the College of William and Mary, and Yale.

The federal government's willingness to investigate colleges as major sites of sexual violence began in the Spring of 2011, after 16 Yale students and alumnae filed a Title IX complaint with the Department of Education's Office of Civil Rights, claiming that the University's failure to confront sexual assault and harassment on campus created a hostile environment for women students. The move was spearheaded by Alexandra Brodsky and several other students. Although it specifically addressed Yale's failure to expel campus rapists, the decision was sparked by two incidents that illustrated the very meaning of "hostile environment". In the first, fraternity members carried signs around campus saying "We Love Yale Sluts." In another, a group of fraternity brothers chanted "No Means Yes and Yes Means Anal" in front of a dormitory where women students lived. Yale administrators took no action against the fraternities.

Outraged, a group of students reported Yale to the federal government for failure to properly report incidents of sexual violence on campus as required by the 1990 Clery Act. Passed after intense lobbying by the parents of slain Lehigh University student Jeanne Clery, the Clery Act requires that colleges and universities annually release statistics documenting the incidence of violent crime on and around campus.[32]

The DOE opened an investigation of Yale around the same time that Vice President Joseph Biden, who had made violence against women one of the signature issues of his career, announced new executive branch guidelines for how the DOE must handle Title IX complaints. Noting that sexual violence had become "epidemic" on campuses, the DOE wrote a 19-page letter to every campus receiving federal funds, outlining their legal obligations around sexual assault. Campuses were ordered to operate under a "preponderance of evidence" standard in adjudicating sexual assault charges, meaning that the evidence suggests that "more likely than not sexual violence occurred." Administrators were told by federal authorities that, under Title IX, they must make accommodations for assault survivors with PTSD who were having trouble in classes. They were legally bound to do whatever it took to ensure that students who reported assaults would be able to comfortably continue their education on campus. Finally, campus officials could no longer legally try to dissuade students from going to the police to report assaults by other students, a practice that was common.[33]

In 2012, Yale was fined $155,000 by the Department of Education under the Clery Act for failure to report incidents of sexual violence on campus. Despite this, punishments for students convicted of sexual assault remained almost non-existent. In the first half of 2013, Yale found six students guilty of "non-consensual sex." Only one was suspended. The others were given written reprimands.

This was not unique to Yale. In October 2012, Amherst College sophomore Angie Epifano, an independent student who had survived a childhood of brutal abuse, published a searing article to explain why she was leaving the college. She had been raped by an acquaintance in May 2011. Like most student survivors of sexual assault, she had not at first reported it, figuring she could tough it out and move on. But, as is so often the case with post-traumatic stress, memories of the trauma began to ambush her. "Some nights," she wrote a year later, "I can still hear the sounds of his roommates on the other side of the door, unknowingly talking and joking as I was held down."

When she reported her rape in 2012, what ensued sounded more like a story from the 1950s than from the 21st century. Campus authorities told her that she should "forgive and forget," because "maybe it was just a bad hookup." They advised her not to attend a support group for assault survivors because it would be better to stop dwelling on what had happened. She was denied a room change that would have moved her away from her attacker. And she was told not to press charges because she had no proof. To commemorate the one-year anniversary of her assault she created an exhibit of 20 photographs depicting herself before, during and after the rape. Fellow students told Epifano they could not understand why she seemed so angry.

When she went to the counseling center to talk about how sad and isolated she felt, counselors derided her for the photographs, calling the exhibit "unhealthy, delusional and inaccurate." She was ruled a suicide risk, involuntarily detained in a psychiatric facility for five days where she was drugged, kept behind locked steel doors and treated by a doctor who told her that he didn't believe a school like Amherst would allow her to be raped. Amherst administrators tried at first to prevent her from returning to campus. Her attacker was not even suspended. Epifano was ultimately allowed to return but Amherst rescinded permission for her to participate in a foreign study program she had been excited about. As Epifano recalled in her essay, an administrator explained that she would have to be kept under close supervision for the remainder of her time in college if she chose to continue at Amherst.

"I was made to feel like the perpetrator," Epifano wrote, "like a broken piece of trash who was of no use to anyone, like an outcast from society, but most damaging of all, I was treated like a liar." Epifano left the college shortly thereafter. Her rapist graduated with honors. At the conclusion of her article, Epifano vowed to be quiet no longer. She closed with a quote she had first read in a pamphlet for survivors and that she credited with starting her process of healing: "Silence has the rusty taste of shame." With that slogan, she tied herself and her movement, consciously or not, to Audre Lorde, ACT-UP and generations of women activists who believed that their silence would not protect them.[34]

Her article sparked an upwelling of anger that spread like wildfire throughout the country. Ninety-five percent of campus assaults are never reported. Alexandra Brodsky argues that this is because students expect that their colleges will do nothing to punish their attackers. Indeed, they are more likely to punish the complainants. Even among the few students found guilty of rape by college disciplinary boards, only 10% to 25% are expelled. Frustrated and angry, survivors of campus sexual assaults began filing Title IX and Clery Act suits by the hundreds and, eventually, the thousands.[35]

In January 2013, five students at the University of North Carolina Chapel Hill, including Annie Clark and Andrea Pino, filed Title IX complaints against the campus administration. The suit was joined by a former dean who testified that she was pressured not to report sexual assault cases. Clark and Pino pinned a map of the U.S. to the wall of their room, on which they printed: "For the 'bigger picture,' we need to prove that rape, sexual assault, violence and discrimination are not isolated to one campus. This is not about UNC. This is about a nationwide culture . . . and the time for CHANGE is now."

In February 2013, University of Southern California student Tucker Reed posted the name and photograph of the male student who had raped her. Other survivors flocked to her and they formed a new group called SCAR – Student Coalition Against Rape. At Tufts University, former student Wagatwe Wanjuki began coordinating a network of assault survivors. Wanjuki described the sudden growth of this new student movement as "a perfect storm of people who are more willing to speak out." Together these students formed the Know Your IX network to link rape survivors from more than 50 colleges seeking justice from the federal government.[36]

In March 2013, in response to this new wave of activism, Congress passed, and President Barack Obama signed, the Campus SAVE – Sexual Violence Elimination Act – of 2013. This act gave the federal government authority to enforce the 2011 DOE letter to colleges. It mandated that all colleges and universities receiving federal funds create training programs for students, faculty and staff that define and condemn sexual violence, harassment and stalking, that enhance support for survivors by informing them of their legal rights to report incidents, to police protection and to be free of stalking and threats. Campuses must take the sexual assault complaints of GLBTQ students seriously. The act changed definitions of rape to include assaults on men. Finally, all campuses were now legally bound to report annually to the federal government on their efforts to reduce sexual violence. The passage of new federal legislation encouraged student activists but they knew that they would have to organize to enforce the law.[37]

In July 2013, Alexandra Brodsky and other student leaders staged a protest in front of the Department of Education in Washington, D.C. wearing their college t-shirts. The women then marched into the building to deliver a petition with 112,000 signatures calling on the federal government to enforce Title IX prohibitions against hostile environments for women on campus. The petitioners met with a dozen federal officials, demanding that colleges be forced to resolve assault complaints within a semester, that the government fine non-compliant colleges and that assault survivors have a voice when the Department of Education is deciding on fines.

Because the federal government at first offered "all carrot and no stick," anti-rape activists encouraged more students to file complaints. Clark and Pino formed End Rape on Campus (EROC) to help students seeking to file claims. In August 2013 they, along with Brodsky, created a website called Know Your IX. The site contained photographs and testimonies from students who had filed Title IX suits, information about Title IX and the Clery Act and advice on how to harness media in their favor. "Is your school mistreating survivors?" the site asked. "Does it not do enough to prevent assault and harassment? Do you want to improve your administration and campus? Welcome to the movement against campus sexual violence."[38]

By the end of 2013, students from Vanderbilt and the University of Connecticut had filed their own suits. At Arizona State, students sued the university for tolerating sexual harassment by faculty and sexual assault by students. At Dartmouth, transgender students, queer students and students of color added their own experiences of violent harassment to the sexual violence testimonies, in a 38-person Title IX and Clery Act suit.[39]

Why did they need to do all this? Alexandra Brodsky argued that the federal government has been slow to enforce the law on campuses. Corporatization of higher education have made colleges even more reluctant to crack down on rapists in their midst. "When colleges become a market," Amherst College rape survivor Dana Bolger says, "there is no incentive to teach what customers would rather not know." Activists in the still-growing movement to make campuses truly equal for all students have taken it on themselves to do what their elders in higher education will not. Epifano says that 2013 was a watershed year: "I think this is when the change will start to happen. I think people will look back in 20 or 30 years and say, 'This is when things started to improve.'"[40]

As 2014 began, President Barack Obama decided to highlight campus activism across the U.S. and activism by women in the military to protest cover-ups of the epidemic of sexual assault. He gave military leaders one year to reduce rates of sexual assault in the military, where an estimated 1 in 3 servicewomen have been victims of sexual assault at the hands of military colleagues and commanders. On January 22, the President announced a White House Task Force to Protect

Students from Sexual Assault. Throughout February 2014, its members met with student activists, college officials, and experts on sexual violence prevention to develop recommendations for federal action to reduce rates of rape, harassment, stalking and physical abuse on college campuses.[41]

Vice President Joe Biden spoke emotionally about the issue:

> Our daughters, our sisters, our wives, our mothers, our grandmothers have every single right to expect to be free from violence and sexual abuse. No matter what she's wearing, no matter whether she's in a bar, in a dormitory, in the back seat of a car, on a street, drunk or sober – no man has a right to go beyond the word 'no.' And if she can't consent, it also means no. Men have to take more responsibility; men have to intervene. The measure of manhood is willingness to speak up and speak out, and begin to change the culture.

Changing the culture has been a complicated, emotionally fraught and end-lessly difficult endeavor. But activist survivors on campuses across the country and military bases around the world broke open the deadly silence on issues of sexual violence in 2013. They moved federal authorities to pass new laws, and to make military commanders and campus administrators enforce them. Campus leaders and military commanders had often said that stricter sanctions would not reduce sexual violence; only education would. As Martin Luther King Jr. said in 1963 in answer to the argument that a tougher civil rights law wouldn't reduce racism – "While it may be true that morality cannot be legislated, behavior can be regu-lated. It may be true that the law cannot change the heart but it can restrain the heartless." For sexual assault survivors that is an essential first step.[42]

2013 was also a year of intense activism by women and children seeking to end a virtual tidal wave of federal government deportations of undocumented immi-grants. In September 2013, 104 women from 20 states, including 20 undocu-mented women, were arrested for blocking an intersection in front of the House of Representatives in Washington D.C. to protest Congress's failure to pass immi-gration reform that addresses the needs of women and children.

The protesters sought to draw attention to the fact that three-quarters of immi-grants to the U.S. since 2000 have been women and children. And yet two-thirds of employment visas were given to men. 70 percent of women immigrants during the 21st century have been forced to seek entrance to the U.S. on family visas. But that system has been so backlogged that some women seeking visas have been waiting decades.

"Immigration reform is not just legislation but the ability to take care of our families," said Premila Jayapal of We Belong Together: Women For Common Sense Immigration. "Women contribute every day to our families, our economy and our country. Immigration reform is about being able to live, breathe free, and remem-ber the values that brought us all here in the first place: democracy, freedom, and justice." Terry O'Neill, president of the National Organization for Women, saw the women's civil disobedience action in Washington, D.C. as just another stage of the long tradition of American women's activism and protest. "Women have fought for centuries to be recognized," she said, "to have the right to vote, to work and be paid for it, to realize their full potential. We must continue to fight for millions of immigrant women to get that same recognition."[43]

If college student protesters against sexual violence in 2013 impressed observers with their youth, the immigration rights movement generated even younger leaders – some of them still small girls. Among the protesters on Capitol Hill in Fall 2013 was Josie Molina Macaraeg, who found her political voice in the Tennessee Immigrant and Refugee Rights Coalition. Macaraeg was one of a group of children who delivered red heart-shaped cookies to members of Congress, urging them to vote for immigration legislation that would help keep their families together. Macaraeg told her elected officials:

> I am 11 years old, and I am a U.S. citizen, but I cannot live my life because my father is in deportation proceedings. To me, courage is all of the children who go to school every day wondering if their parents will still be there when they come home at the end of the day. And courage is also my mom, who is here risking arrest today so she can fight for my future, our family's future, and the rights of all families to be together.[44]

The young and old, women and men, who joined together to fight for a living wage at the end of 2013 felt that they too were fighting for their families. On Black Friday 2013, the day after Thanksgiving when retailers dramatically cut their prices and shoppers mob the stores, workers picketed across the country. They walked off the job at Walmart, the nation's largest private employer, and at fast-food restaurants in cities across the U.S., to remind consumers that they could not keep body and soul together on the little they are paid. Despite working full time, these low-wage workers reminded a shopping-obsessed nation during Christmas season that they and their children live below the poverty level. Because women of color and immigrants remain concentrated in the lowest-wage jobs, they were in the majority in the living-wage protests that swept the nation's cities at the close of 2013.

Fifty-nine-year-old Mary Coleman, a long-time server at Popeye's chicken in Milwaukee, decided to join the one-day strike because she was tired of trying to support herself and an ailing adult daughter on $7.25 an hour. "If we sit back and leave everything to the younger generation," she explained, "we'll never get any-where. At this point it seems like the majority of the younger generation thinks that their voices don't matter. I want to let them know their voice does matter."

Young women seemed to sense that. In many parts of the country, they joined the strike wave. Twenty-three-year-old Naquasia LeGrand, a Kentucky Fried Chicken worker in Brooklyn, New York, explained that she just could not pay her bills on

$7.70 an hour. "Why do you think these corporations are an over $200 billion a year business?" she said. "Off our hard work." It took a long time for her to make up her mind. "In the beginning I was afraid," she said. And "I was skeptical. I didn't even know what a union was." To anyone who has studied women workers' uprisings at the beginning of the 20th century, LeGrand sounded very much like one of the young immigrant garment workers who had launched their own strike wave 100 years earlier. Just like them, she had become empowered and emboldened by her experiences on the picket line. Just like them she had begun to feel a sense of class consciousness.

To those who had been telling her that fast-food workers will never get their hoped-for living wage, LeGrand answered:

> Look where we started . . . On November 29, 2012, it was 127 workers who decided to walk out on their jobs to make a statement and say we want $15 an hour and a union. Now 200 cities are about to have actions. This is spreading around the whole country.[45]

American women's activism has had its cycles, its peaks and its troughs since the early 19th century. Feminism and anti-feminism, subsistence activism, labor and consumer activism, protests for reproductive rights, for equity in the workplace, consciousness raising, civil disobedience. One thing that has not happened in the nearly two centuries this book chronicles is quiescence – a time when American women were not active. If it is true that American women's activism has come in waves, the movement has been ceaseless. There have been bigger and smaller waves. But, as in the ocean, the waves have kept on coming.

Notes

1 Q&A: Phyllis Schlafly, Antifeminist – TIME, Interviewed by Andrea Sachs, April 7, 2009, http://content.time.com/time/nation/article/0,8599,1889757,00.html#ixzz2lOOFjVDD.
2 Beverly LaHaye, *The Restless Woman* (New York: Zondervan Publishing House, 1984), p. 54.
3 "Phyllis Schlafly: Still Championing the Anti-Feminist Fight," NPR, March 30, 2011, http://www.npr.org/templates/story/story.php?storyId=134981902.
4 Elaine Donnelly, "What Women Wanted," *National Review*, June 7, 2004.
5 Susan Faludi, *Backlash: The Undeclared War Against American Women* (New York: Vintage, 1989; 15th anniversary edition Broadway Books), p. 252.
6 William Martin, *With God On Our Side: The Rise of the Religious Right in America* (New York: Broadway Books, 2005), p. 174.
7 ibid., p. 175.
8 Onalee McGraw, *Secular Humanism and the Schools: The Issue Whose Time has Come*, pamphlet (Washington, DC: Heritage Foundation, 1976); "Christian Right Roots: Marshner and McGraw," PRA: Public Eye.Org. The Website of the Political Research Association, http://www.publiceye.org/christian_right/values-voters/Values%20Voters-09-19.html#TopOfPage.

9   Concerned Women for America Timeline, http://www.cwfa.org/history.asp.

10 Lori Arnold, "Beverly LaHaye marks three decades of promoting traditional values through CWA," *Christian Examiner,* December 2009.

11 Martin, op. cit., pp. 178–182; Connaught Marshner, C-Span Interview, December 19, 1984, http://www.c-spanvideo.org/program/Marshn; Concerned Women for America timeline; "Penny Nancy Discusses Social Issues on Life Today," CWA Legislative Action Committee web page, http://www.cwalac.org.

12 Concerned Women for America Legislative Action Committee, http://www.cwalac.org; Arnold, op. cit.

13 Donnelly, op. cit.; Adam Clymer, "How to Win Elections: Moral Majority Looks to 1982," *New York Times News Service,* June 20, 1981.

14 "Expanding Civil Rights: Landmark Cases," http://www.pbs.org/wnet/supremecourt/rights/landmark_casey.html; National Abortion Federation – The Professional Association of Abortion Providers in North America, "Abortion Facts – Access to Abortion: Legal Abortion is Not Widely Accessible to Women in the U.S.," http://www.prochoice.org/about_abortion/facts/access_abortion.html; David Crary, "Roe V. Wade After 40 Years: Deep Divide is the Legacy," *Huffington Post,* January 19, 2013.

15 Angie Epifano, "An Account of Sexual Assault at Amherst College," *The Amherst Student,* October 17, 2012.

16 Callie Beusman, "Title IX Network Takes Colleges to Task for Mishandling Rape," *Jezebel,* November 19, 2013.

17 Callie Beusman, "Title IX Network Takes Colleges to Task for Mishandling Rape," *Jezebel,* November 19, 2013.

18 "America's Voice: The Power to Win Common Sense Immigration Reform," http://americasvoiceonline.org/blog/104-women-including-more-than-20-undocumented-immigrants-arrested-for-protesting-houses-inaction-on-immigration-reform/ September 12, 2013.

19 Susan Faludi, *Backlash: The Undeclared War Against American Women* (New York: Broadway Books, 1991).

20 "Anita Hill Reflects on 20 Years Since Clarence Thomas Hearings," PBS News Hour, October 10, 2011, www.pbs.org/newshour/bb/law/july-dec11/anitahill_10-10.html; "Sex With a Scorecard," *Time,* April 5, 1993.

21 Camille Paglia, "It's a Jungle Out There," *New York Newsday,* 1991, http://users.ipfw.edu/ruflethe/itsajungleoutthere.htm; Katie Roiphe, *The Morning After: Sex, Fear and Feminism* (Boston: Back Bay Books, 1994).

22 Hilary Belzer, "Word and Guitar: The Riot Grrrl Movement and Third Wave Feminism" (M.A. Thesis, Georgetown University, 2000).

23 Kathleen Hannah, cited in Belzer, op. cit., p. 44.

24 www.lyricsfreak.com, lyrics to Bikini Kill, Bratmobile, Sleater-Kinney.

25 TSS Crew, "32 Overlooked Rape Lyrics in Rap," *The Smoking Section,* April 1, 2013, http://smokingsection.uproxx.com/TSS/2013/04/50-absurd-rape-lyrics#page/6; Rabin, op. cit.; Sexual Violence Report 2012, Centers for Disease Control, www.cdc.gov/violenceprevention.

26 Neha Therani Bagri, "Gang Rape in India, Routine and Invisible," *New York Times,* October 26, 2013.

27 Jessica Valenti, "America's Rape Problem: We Refuse to Admit There Is One," *The Nation,* January 4, 2013.

28 Matt Pierce, "The Case is Closed: No Charges in Marysville, Mo Case," *Los Angeles Times,* January 9, 2014. Rabin, op. cit., George Howell and Paul Vercammen, "Police

Investigate Alleged Rape of Swimmer Who Died in Suicide," CNN, January 28, 2014, http://www.cnn.com/2014/01/27/us/missouri-suicide-rape-allegations/.

29 Title IX, Education Amendments of 1972, U.S. Department of Labor, www.dol.gov/oasam/regs/statutes/titleix.htm.

30 Claire Potter, "It's Friday Night. Is Your Kid at a Frat?" *Tenured Radical, Chronicle of Higher Education* blog, February 21, 2014.

31 John Lauerman, "College Serial Rapists Evade Antiquated Campus Responses," *Bloomberg News,* June 13, 2013.

32 Ken Gross and Andrea Fine, "After Their Daughter is Murdered in College, Grieving Parents Mount a Crusade for Campus Safety," *People,* February 19, 1990; Caroline Tan, *Yale Daily News,* April 9, 2012 "Title IX, One Year Later," http://yaledailynews.com/blog/2012/04/09/up-close-title-ix-one-year-later/.

33 Aaron Liu, October 26, 2013, "National Push to Confront Colleges That Mishandle Sexual Assault," *Neon Tommy.* Annenberg Digital Media, USC; Emanuella Grinberg, "Ending Rape on Campus: Activism Takes Many Forms," February 12, 2014. CNN, http://www.cnn.com/2014/02/09/living/campus-sexual-violence-students-schools/.

34 Angie Epifano, "An Account of Sexual Assault at Amherst College, *"The Amherst Student,* October 17, 2012; Rosemary Kelly and Shaina Mishkin, "Angie Epifano: How One Former Amherst Student Sparked a Movement Against Sexual Assault," *Huffington Post,* June 2, 2013.

35 Tyler Kingkade, "Yale Fails to Expel Students Found Guilty of Sexual Assault," *Huffington Post,* August 1, 2013.

36 Liu, op. cit.; Libby Sander, "Quiet No Longer, Rape Survivors Put Pressure on Colleges," *The Chronicle of Higher Education,* August 12, 2013.

37 Sander, op. cit.

38 "Know Your IX, Empowering Students to Stop Sexual Violence," http://knowyourix.org.

39 Callie Beusman, "Title IX Network Takes Colleges to Task for Mishandling Rape," *Jezebel,* November 19, 2013.

40 "Know Your IX, Empowering Students to Stop Sexual Violence," http://knowyourix.org. Bersman, op. cit.

41 Jackie Calmes, "Obama Seeks to Raise Awareness of Rape on Campus," *New York Times,* January 22, 2014; http://www.whitehouse.gov/blog/2014/01/22/renewed-call-action-end-rape-and-sexual-assault.

42 ibid.

43 *America's Voice: The Power to Win Common Sense Immigration Reform,* http://americasvoice online.org/blog/104-women-including-more-than-20-undocumented-immigrants-arrested-for-protesting-houses-inaction-on-immigration-reform/September 12, 2013.

44 ibid.

45 Allison Kilkenny, "Fast Food Strikes Hit 100 Cities Thursday," *The Nation,* December 2, 2013.

INDEX

abortion: activism against rights to 190, 201–202, 204–207; activism for rights to 98, 111, 189–190; illegal 119, 120, 132; legislation 95, 189, 200; and radical feminism 132

ACT-UP *see* AIDS Coalition to Unleash Power (ACT-UP)

Adkins v. Children's Hospital of Washington 33–34

advertisements: in *Ms. Magazine* 120–121; sexist and segregated 91

Affirmative Action programs 91

African-Americans: AIDS epidemic 190; anti-rape movement 126; birth control 95; civil rights movement 65–73; labor unions 41–42, 46; lesbians 173; sterilization abuse 96–97; suffrage 9; women's activism 81–84; women's labor movement 38, 55, 78–79; women's suffrage 30–31, 34 *see also* black men; black women

Against Our Will: Men, Women and Rape (Brownmiller) 124–125

agricultural workers 37, 40, 147–148 *see also* farm-workers movement

AIDS Coalition to Unleash Power (ACT-UP) 186–191

AIDS epidemic 185–191

AIM *see* American Indian Movement

airline industry, sex discrimination 90–91

Albuquerque, New Mexico, bar scene 174

Alcatraz Island, San Francisco, California, Native-American women's activism 138–140

alcohol ban, and women's suffrage 30

Alice B. Toklas Democratic Club 177–178

Allison, Dorothy 183–184

AMC *see* American Mothers Committee

American Civil Liberties Union Women's Rights Project 87

American Equal Rights Association 9–10, 11

American Indian Movement (AIM) 140–143, 157, 159

American Mothers Committee (AMC) 57

American Woman Suffrage Association (AWSA) x, 12–13

Amherst College 212–213, 214

ANC Mothers Anonymous 149–150

Anthony, Susan B. 9–15, 18

anti-Communism 47–48

anti-feminist movement 199–206, 207

anti-gays 192–194

anti-lynching activism 15–19

anti-rape movement 122–126

Anti-Slavery Convention of American Women 3

anti-slavery movement 2, 3–4, 14

"Arn't I A Woman" speech (Truth) 6–7

AWSA *see* American Woman Suffrage Association

Backlash: The Undeclared War Against American Women (Faludi) 207

Baird v. Eistenstadt 94–95

Baker, Ella 38, 68–69, 72–73, 82, 106

Battered Wives (Martin) 127–128, 180

battered women's movement 127–131, 180–181
Bikini Kill 208, 209
Bird, Mary Brave 141, 142
black men: suffrage 10–13, 16–17; and white women 15–17, 124–126
black women: activism 16–18; anti-rape movement 125–126; civil rights movement 65–73; discrimination in workplace 39–40, 55, 78; suffrage 10–13, 16, 31–32; welfare rights movement 153, 155; and white men 16–18, 124–125
Blatch, Harriet Stanton 30
Bomefree, Isabella *see* Truth, Sojourner
books, feminist 116–118
Boston: anti-slavery movement 4, 14; feminist self-defense classes 122; housewives movement 46; welfare rights movement 151; women's labor movement 2, 21
Boston Women's Health Collective 132
boycotts: Domino's Pizza 189; grape 145–148, 158, 159–160, 162; meat and milk 44–47; Montgomery Bus Boycott 1955 66–69
Boyd, Blanche McCrary 185
bra burners myth 108
Braniff Airlines 91
Bratmobile 208, 209
Britain, women's suffrage 30
Brodsky, Alexandra 211, 213, 214
Brotherhood of Sleeping Car Porters and Maids 18, 39
Browder, Aurelia 67
Brown, Rita Mae 167
Brown v. Board of Education 66, 83
Brownmiller, Susan 115, 123–125
Buck v. Bell 96
Buffalo, New York, women's bars 173–174
Bunch, Charlotte 170–171
Bureau of Indian Affairs occupation 141
Bush, George H.W. 148, 190, 205
butch-femme lesbians 173–175, 183

California: anti-gay initiatives 193; anti-rape movement 123, 126, 213; Chinese-American women's activism 19–20; conservative women's movement 204; domestic violence bill 131; farm-workers movement 144–148, 158–160; Japanese communities 55–56; lesbian activism 175; Native-American women's activism 138–140; sterilization abuse

97–98; welfare rights movement 148–150
California Agricultural Labor Relations Act 1975 147–148
Campus Sexual Violence Elimination Act (SAVE) 2013 213–214
Carlomusto, Jean 186–187, 188
Carter, Jimmy 43, 155, 156, 170, 203
Carter, John Mack 115
Carter, Roslyn 170
Catholic Church, and AIDS epidemic activism 189–191
Chacón, Juan and Virginia 62–63
Chavez, Cesar 145, 147–148, 158, 162
Chicago: abortion 132; battered women's movement 129; domestic labor 38; domestic violence 129; housewives movement 46–47; radical feminism 109, 111–112; welfare rights movement 151, 154, 158; women's labor movement 21
Chicago Women's Liberation Union 112
Chicana *see* Mexican-Americans
"Children of the Rainbow" curriculum 191–192
Chinese-American women: American Mother of the Year 57; immigrants activism 19–20; numbers of immigrants 56; opposition to in suburbs 58; post-war employment 56–57
church communities, conservative women's movement 200–203
"cities of women" 40–41
Citizenship Schools 71
Civil Rights Act 1964, Title VII 80, 83–85, 87, 90–94
civil rights movement: labor support for 42–43; and welfare rights movement 153, 158–159; as a women's movement 65–73; and women's rights 78–87
Clark, Annie 213, 214
Clark, Septima 68, 70–73, 106
Clery Act 1990 211–212, 213, 214
Cleveland Board of Education v. LaFleur 92
Coachella Valley, California, farm-workers movement 146–147
Coalition to End Sterilization Abuse (CESA) 98
coalitions: shifting xii–xiii, 29; and women's suffrage 25–26
college students, and sexual violence 209–215
Colorado, gay rights laws 192

Committee for Abortion Rights and to End Sterilization Abuse (CARASA) 98
Communism: and conservative women's movement 200; fear of 57–61; and housewives movement 47–48
Communist Party USA 46, 58–59, 64–65
Comprehensive Child Development Bill 1971 202
Concerned Women for America (CWA) 203–205
Congress of Racial Equality (CORE) 68, 83, 106
"consciousness raising": impact of 121–133; for women's liberation 110–111
conservative women's movement 199–206
consumers, and women's activism 44–48, 145–146, 158
contraception legislation 94–95, 97, 100
CORE see Congress of Racial Equality
Corning Glass Works v. Brennan 91–92
Cosmopolitan, and ACT-UP protest 188
cost of living protests 44–48
Cottier, Belva 138
Council on Religion and the Homosexual 177
credit in welfare rights movement 153–154
cross-dressing lesbians 172
CWA see Concerned Women for America (CWA)

Daughters of Bilitis (DOB) 42, 168, 175–179
Davis, Caroline 85
Declaration of Independence 5, 22
Declaration of Sentiments 5, 6
DeCora, Lorelei 141, 143
defense industries: discrimination against black women 55; employment of women 39–44
Delano, California, United Farm Workers strike 144–146, 148, 157–158
Democratic Party 10–11, 41
Detroit: housewives movement 46–47; post-war layoffs 41
Dialectic of Sex, The (Firestone) 117
die-ins 187–188, 189, 191
difference: fear of 58–59; politics of lesbian feminism 181–185; women riven by xii
discrimination: on college campuses 210–213; defense industries 55; families on welfare 153, 155; lesbians and gay men 61–62, 168–170, 177, 195; people with AIDS 187; pregnancy 91–93, 101, 201; race 31, 39–40, 63; sex 31–32,

78–94, 200, 215–217; workplace 39–42, 55–56, 78–87, 90–94, 195
diversity in activism ix–x, xiii
DOB see Daughters of Bilitis (DOB)
"domestic containment" 58
domestic violence: Del Martin's activism 180–181; legislation against 100–101, 121; and Native-American women 142–143; politicization of 127–131
domestic workers: and Montgomery Bus Boycott 66–68; and women's labor movement 37–38, 40
Domino's Pizza 189
Douglass, Frederick 5, 8, 9, 12, 14–15, 18
Duncan, Ruby 95, 155–156, 162

Eastwood, Mary 79, 83–84
Economic Opportunity Act 1964 73, 150, 155, 159
education: access for immigrant women 19–23, 55; for black freedom struggle 70–73; garment workers 23; sex discrimination 86, 88–89
Eisenhower, Dwight 58, 59–60, 61
Elementary and Secondary Education Act 1972, Title IX 88–89, 211–212, 213–214
Eminem 209
Empire Zinc mine 62
employment: discrimination against lesbians and gay men 61–62, 177, 195; race discrimination 39–40; sex discrimination 78–87, 91–93, 215–217; of women immigrants 215–217; of women outside the home 79; and women's activism 38–39; World War II and post-war 54–55
End Rape on Campus (EROC) 214
Epifano, Angie 212–213, 214
Equal Employment Opportunity Act 1972 91
Equal Employment Opportunity Commission (EEOC) 80–81, 84–85, 90–91, 93, 207
Equal Pay Act 1963 79–80
equal pay legislation 40, 43, 79–80
Equal Rights Amendment to US Constitution 32–34, 84, 200–201
Equality League for Self-Supporting Women 30
ERA see Equal Rights Amendment to US Constitution
ethnocentrism, and women's activism 12–15

Eveleth Taconite mine 93–94
Evergreen Sate College 132, 208
Exodusters 9

Fair Employment Practices Commission 39
Fair Labor Standards Act 1938 34, 37
families, importance of traditional 57–58, 200–205
Family Assistance Plan 1969 154
farm-workers movement 144–148, 157–160
Federal Housing Authority 57–58
Felker, Clay 118, 119, 120
Feminine Mystique, The (Friedan) 53–54, 77–78, 130
feminism: backlash against 199–206; diversity of 137–138; idea of ix–x; impact of women's suffrage 29–30; industrial 2–3, 22; labor 34–39, 41–42, 77–78; and the law 77–101; lesbian 181–185; and poor women's activism 157–162; radical 105–116, 121–127; resurgence 207–208; tensions with lesbians 166–172
feminist books 116–118
Feminist Majority Foundation 162
feminist media 113–116, 118–121
fire safety, in garment industry 23–24, 35
Firestone, Shulamit 106–107, 111, 112–113, 115, 117
First Congress to Unite Women 167, 168
First Wave (of American feminism) 1–6, 9, 29, 43
Food and Drug Administration 187
Ford, Betty 170
Freedom Schools 71
Freeman, Jo 109, 111–112
Friedan, Betty: attitude towards lesbians 167–171; *Feminine Mystique* 53–54, 77–78, 130; founding of National Women's Political Caucus 119; founding of NOW 85–86; television interview 203; union activist 64
Frontiero v. Richardson 89

gang rape 209
garment workers movement 21–25
Garrison, William Lloyd 8, 10–11
gay men: AIDS epidemic 185–186; employment 61–62, 177, 195; and Lesbian Avengers 193–194; and lesbians 172, 174, 178; mistrust of 60–62
Gay Men's Health Crisis 186

gender norms xii
gender roles: 1950s America 52–57; Mexican-American mine workers' families 62–65; trust of normativity 59
Ginsburg, Ruth Bader 87–90, 92, 95
Gittings, Barbara 176–181
Goldberg v. Kelley 155
Goldstein, Betty *see* Friedan, Betty
Goon, Toy Len 57
Graham, Richard 84–85
grape boycott campaign 145–148, 159–160
Green, Edith 89
Griffiths, Martha 78, 85
Grimké, Sara and Angelina 3–4
Griswold v. Connecticut 94
Grove Press 115–116

Head Start nursery programme 71
health care for women 131–133
Hernandez, Aileen 84–85, 169
Highlander Folk School, Tennessee 70–71
Hill, Anita 207
homemakers rights 42
homophobia, and AIDS epidemic 186–187
homosexuality: mental health 180; mistrust of 60–62; women's activism against 200, 203–204 *see also* gay men; lesbians
housewives movement 44–48
Huerta, Dolores 144–147, 148, 158, 159, 162

Idaho, Lesbian Avengers 194
immigrants: Chinese women's activism 19–20, 56–57; Korean women's activism 20; lobbying for labor reforms 35; meat boycotts 44–48; and "slave markets" 38; women's activism 19–22, 215–217; women's suffrage 22–26
immigration reform, activism for 215–217
Indigenous Women's Network 139, 144, 161
industrial feminism 2–3, 22
industrial labor movement: mill workers 2–3; women's activism 2, 20–26, 34–39
industrial trades, employment of women 39–44
International Tribunal on Crimes Against Women 128
International Women's Year conferences 201, 205
Irish immigrant workers 10, 21
Italian Catholic women immigrants 21

Jane Collective 132
"Jane Crow and the Law: Sex
    Discrimination and Title VII"
    (Murray) 83–84
Japanese-American women 55–56
Jenkins, Esau 70–71
Jewish women immigrants 21–23, 38
Jim Crow segregation 15, 66
Johnson, Lady Bird 170
Johnson, Lyndon B. 71, 73, 80, 91
journalism, and radical feminism 113–116

Kelley, Florence 33, 35
Kennedy, Florynce 107–108
Kennedy, John 78, 79, 80
Kennedy, Robert F. 145
Kennedy, Senator Edward 97, 99
Kenyon, Dorothy 88
Khrushchev, Nikita 58
King Jr., Martin Luther 65, 68–70, 153
King v. Smith 155
Know Your IX Network 213, 214
Korean women immigrants 20
Ku Klux Klan 30–31, 200

labor feminism 34–39, 41–42, 77–78
labor legislation: and domestic workers
    38; ERA threat to 32–34; and women's
    activism 34–39
labor unions *see* trade unions
Ladder, The 176–177, 179
Ladies Home Journal 115
LaDuke, Winona 144, 161
Lahausen, Kay Taubin 176, 180
LaHaye, Beverly 201, 202–205
Las Vegas, welfare rights movement
    155–156, 158
Latina women, and anti-rape movement
    126
Lavender Menace 167–168, 181
Leadership Institute 205
legislation: feminism 77–101; and labor 38;
    rape 126; sex discrimination 87; welfare
    rights movement 155; women's rights
    206–207
LeGrand, Laquesha 216–217
Lemlich, Clara 21, 22–23, 45–46
Lesbian Avengers 191–194
Lesbian Mothers Union 180
lesbians: AIDS epidemic 185–191; butch-
    femme 173–175, 183; campaign for
    rights 175–181; early transgressing and
    cross-dressing 172; as feminists 181–185;

Lesbian Avengers 191–194; mistrust
    of 60–62; mothers 179–180; in New
    Millennium 194–195; public culture
    during World War II 173; publishing
    176; tensions with feminism 166–172;
    working-class 173
Lincoln, Abraham 8, 9
living wage protests 216–217
Lorde, Audre 181–183, 186
Los Angeles: anti-rape movement 123, 126;
    housewives movement 46; sterilization
    abuse 98; welfare rights movement
    149–151
Lowell, Massachusetts, women mill workers
    strike 2–3
lynching: prevention of 25; and women's
    activism 15–19
Lyon, Phyllis 168, 175–176, 177–181

magazines: feminist 118–121; and radical
    feminism 113–116
male domination of women 128
Mankiller, Wilma 140, 162
marriage, same-sex 181, 195
Marshner, Connaught "Connie" 202, 203,
    204–205
Martin, Del 127–128, 168, 169, 175–176,
    177–181
mass media, and radical feminism 113–116
Mattachine Society 168, 177
McCloud, Janet 138–139, 143–144
Means, La Nada Boyer 140
meat and milk boycotts 44–48
media: negative images 87; radical
    feminism 113–121
Media Women 114–115
medicine, women in 133
mental disorder, homosexuality as 180, 185
Meritor Savings Bank v. Vinson 93
Mexican-Americans: anti-rape movement
    126; mine workers strike 62–65;
    opposition to in suburbs 58; sterilization
    abuse 97–98; United Farm Workers
    strike 144–148; women's activism
    157–158
middle-class women: allies of working-class
    women 32, 43, 44, 150, 160, 162; black
    18, 66, 67, 68, 153; opposition to slavery
    3; unhappiness 53, 78
migration of women workers 40–41
military, and sexual violence 214–215
mill workers movement 2–3, 21–22
Miller, Dorothy Lone Wolf 140

Miller, Frieda 43
Miller Sexual Psychopath bill 61
Millett, Kate 117, 121, 168
Mink, Patsy 89, 170
Miss American Pageant, Atlantic City,
  New Jersey 107–108
Montgomery Bus Boycott 1955 65–68
Montoya, Chana 65
Morgan, Robin 106–107, 113–118, 125,
  133
Morrow, Governor Edwin 25
mothers: activism 158, 159–160; and Ethel
  Rosenberg 60; lesbians as 179–180;
  rights 42; uprising against high cost of
  living 44–48; welfare rights movement
  148–157, 160–162; of the year 57
Mott, Lucretia 4–6
Ms. Foundation 162
Ms. Magazine 118–121, 160
Muller v. Oregon 32–33
Murray, Pauli 78–86, 88

Nance, Penny 204
Narrative of Sojourner Truth (Truth) 8
National Abortion Rights Action League
  (NARAL) 100
National Airlines, advertisements 91
National Association for the Advancement
  of Colored People (NAACP) 18, 37, 38,
  68–69
National Association of Colored Women
  16, 18, 33
National Black Feminist Organization
  (NBFO) 125
National Consumer's League 32, 33, 35, 44
National Council of Negro Women
  68–69
National Freedman's Relief Bureau 9
National Gay and Lesbian Task Force 180
National Labor Advisory Board 36
National Labor Relations Act 1935 36
National League of Women Voters 33, 150
National Organization for Women
  (NOW): founding of x, 84–87;
  policy towards lesbians 167–172; and
  sterilization abuse 100; welfare rights
  movement 162; women of color 156;
  women's rights protests 90
National War Labor Board 40
National Welfare Rights Organization
  (NWRO) 152, 161
National Woman Suffrage Association 12, 14
National Woman Suffrage Convention 11

National Woman's Party (NWP): and
  African-American women 31; and ERA
  32–34; and sex discrimination 32–33
National Women's Conference 1977
  170–171
National Women's Political Caucus 73,
  119
Native-American women: activism
  138–144, 157; and legislation for
  violence against 100–101; sterilization
  abuse 97, 99
Nelson, Rose 45
Nestle, Joan 174–175
New Left movement: contempt for
  feminists 112; and women's liberation
  movement 111–113
New Mexico, mine workers strike 62–65
New York: AIDS epidemic 185–191;
  "Children of the Rainbow" curriculum
  191–192; garment workers 21–25;
  lesbian activism in 191–192; welfare
  rights movement 151, 153–155
New York Radical Women (NYRW)
  106–108, 110, 111
New York State Factory Investigating
  Commission 35
Newman, Pauline 22–23, 35–36, 38, 43, 46
newspapers 2, 47, 121
Nisqually River, Yelm, Washington, Native-
  American women's activism 138–139
Nixon, Richard: American democracy
  58; Mexican-American women 63;
  Ms. Magazine 120; Native-American
  women 141; New Left movement 112;
  pro-family movement 202; sterilization
  abuse 96; welfare rights movement 154,
  161
Northampton, Massachusetts 8
Northampton Association of Education
  and Industry commune 8
NOW *see* National Organization for
  Women (NOW)

Obama, Barack 148, 213
O'Leary, Jean 170
Operation Life 156
Our Bodies Ourselves (Boston Women's
  Health Collective) 132–133

Paley, Grace xi
Pankhurst, Emmeline 30
Parks, Rosa 65–67
Paul, Alice 31–32

pensions 36–37
Perkins, Frances 24, 35–37, 158
Peterson, Esther 43, 79, 91
Philadelphia 151
Phillips v. Martin Marietta 91
picketing: farm-workers movement
145–147, 159–160; gay rights 177, 181,
190; housewives movement 45–46; labor
reform movement 21–22, 216; Mexican-
American mine workers 62–63; women's
rights 90, 116
Pino, Andrea 213, 214
*Pittsburgh Press v. the Pittsburgh Commission
on Human Relations* 91
Piven, Frances Fox 150
Plath, Sylvia 60
Playboy 118–119
police treatment 127, 128–129
political organizations: anti-feminist
movement 199–206; Lowell Female
Labor Reform Association 2; sex
discrimination in 86
popular culture: portrayal of 1950s
America 52–53; portrayal of women
207
poverty, and welfare rights movement
148–162
pregnancy, discrimination 91–93, 101
Pregnancy Discrimination Act 1978
92–93, 201
President's Commission on the Status of
Women 78–80
President's Commission on Women 170
Production for Use campaign 47
pro-family movement 202–204
Progressive Friends, The 9
publishing houses, and radical feminism
113–116
Puerto Rican women: brought into labor
unions 38; sterilization abuse 97–98

Quaker community, and Sojourner Truth
7, 9

race discrimination: in defense industries
55; in employment 81, 86; Mexican-
Americans 63; in National Woman
Party 31–32
racism: in defense industries 39–40; and
women's activism 12–17
radical feminism: and health care for
women 131–133; and mass media
113–116; and New Left 111–113;

raising consciousness 105–111; and
redefinition of rape 121–127; and
women of color 125
rape: in colleges and universities 210–216;
culture 209–210; redefinition of
121–127; views of 206–209
Rapid City, South Dakota, Native-
American women's activism 143
Rat newspaper 113
Reagan, Ronald 205
Red Record, A 17–18
Redstockings 110–111
Reed v. Reed 88
Relf family 96–97
rent strikes 44, 46
reproductive rights 94–97, 189
Republican Party 10, 13, 190, 205
restaurant workers 216–217
Revolution, The (newspaper) 10–11, 12
Revueltas, Rosario 63–64
right to vote *see* suffrage
Riot Grrrl 208–209
Rodriguez-Trias, Dr. Helen 97–98
Roe v. Wade 95–96, 132, 200
Roosevelt, Eleanor 35–37, 78, 81–82, 172
Roosevelt, Franklin D. 35–36, 39, 44
"Rose the Riveter" 39, 54
Rosenberg, Ethel and Julius 59–60
Rosset, Barney 115–116
Rust v. Sullivan 190
Rustin, Bayard 39, 83

safer sex, and AIDS epidemic 188–189
safety: in garment industry 23–24; social
37; women's 124, 143, 211; workplace 3,
23–24, 35–38
salaries, and equal pay legislation 40
Salt of the Earth (film) 63–65, 158
same-sex marriages 195
San Francisco: gay migration to 177–178;
Native-American women's activism 138,
139–140
Sanders, Beulah 150–155
SAVE Act *see* Campus Sexual Violence
Elimination (SAVE) Act 2013
Schlafly, Phyliss 200–201, 203, 204
Schneiderman, Rose 22–24, 32–38, 43, 46
schools, for black adult education 70–71
Sears and Roebuck 153
Second Congress to Unite Women
166–168
Second Wave (of American feminism) 43
segregation 15, 65–69, 81–82

self-defence movement 122
Seneca Falls Convention 1848 1, 5–6
sex discrimination: employment 215–217; founding of NOW pressure group 84–87; reproductive rights legislation 94–95; sexual harassment as 210–213; Title VII and workplace legislation 90–94; view of NWP 32–33; workplace legislation 78–84, 87–90
sex slavery 20
sexual harassment 93–94, 101, 207, 210–215 *see also* sexual violence
Sexual Politics (Millett) 117, 121–122
sexual violence, women's activism against 206–216
sexuality, fear of non hetero-normative 60–62
Shapiro v. Thompson 155
Shavelson, Clara Lemlich 45–46, 47, 60
shop workers 216–217
sisterhood xiii, 182, 184
Sisterhood is Powerful (Morgan) 117–118
"slave markets" 38
slavery: anti-slavery movement 2, 3–4, 14; and women mill workers 3
Snodgrass, Carrie 108
Social Security Act 1935 36–37, 158–159
Southern Christian Leadership Conference 68–69, 71–72
Spiritualism movement 9
Stanton, Elizabeth Cady 4, 9–15
State's Law on Race and Color (Murray) 83
Steinem, Gloria 118–121, 171
sterilization abuse 96–100, 143
Stewardesses for Women's Rights 91
Stone, Lucy 9, 10, 12–13
Stop the ERA 203
Stowe, Harriet Beecher, and Sojourner Truth 8
strikes: bread and roses 158; garment workers 21–22; meat 48; Mexican-American mine workers 62–65; rent 44, 46; in stores and restaurants 216–217; women mill workers 2–3
Student Coalition Against Rape 213
Student Non-Violent Coordinating Committee 68, 69, 71–72
students activism 214
suburbs, development of 57–58
suffrage: African-American men 9; black 10–13; different constituencies 29–39; petition for universal 10; universal

11–12; women's 9–15, 19, 22–26; women's activism against 200
support systems, for victims of crime 123–126

"Take Back the Night" marches 123
Talifierro, Dorothy *see* Martin, Del
Taylor v. Louisiana 92
Teamster's Union 146–148
telephone, power of in women's activism 47
television, portrayal of 1950s America 52–53
temperance movement, and women's activism 2
Third Wave (of American feminism) 207–208
Thomas, Clarence 204, 207
Thorpe, Grace 140
Thunderhawk, Madonna 140–143, 159
Tillmon, Johnnie 97, 148–155, 160–161
Title IX *see* Elementary and Secondary Education Act 1972
Title VII *see* Civil Rights Act 1964
trade unions: and domestic workers 38; feminists in 41–42; fired for organizing 115–116; and housewives movement 46–47; and labor laws 32; and National Labor Relations Act 36; organizing drive 38; and post-war layoffs 41
Trail of Broken Treaties 140–141
Train, George Francis 10–11
Triangle Shirtwaist Factory, New York City, fire 23–24, 35
Truman, Harry S. 61
Truth, Sojourner (given name Isabella Bomefree) 6–9

unemployment insurance 43
United Auto Workers' Union 41, 42, 85
United Electrical Workers 64, 77
United Farm Workers' Union 144–148, 157–158
United States v. Windsor 195
universal suffrage 10–12
universities and colleges, and sexual violence 209–215
uprisings, peaks and troughs x–xii
Uranday, Esther 144–146
Uri, Dr. Connie 99
Uribe, Alicia 146
U.S. Constitution: 5th Amendment 89; 14th Amendment 10, 88–89; 15th

Amendment 9, 10, 11, 12–13; 19th Amendment 25, 30–31; Equal Rights Amendment 32–34, 84, 200–201

violence against women: legislation 100–101; politicization of 127–131; redefinition of rape as 121–127; women's activism against sexual 206–216
Violence Against Women Act (VAWA) 1994 100–101, 129, 204

Wage Earner's League for Women Suffrage 24
'wage slaves,' women mill workers as 2–3
Wagner, Robert 35, 36
waitresses, and women's labor movement 37
Walmart 216
Washington, D.C.: AIDS protests 190–191; anti-rape movement 124; gay men and lesbians 61, 177; housewives movement 47; and the Lesbian Avengers 192–193; Native-American women's activism 140, 143–144; suburbs 58; welfare rights movement 150–151
Webb, Marilyn Salzman 112–113
Weinberger v. Weisenfeld 92
Weisstein, Naomi 112
Weixel, Lola 54
welfare rights movement: poor mothers activism 158–159, 160–162; women in the 148–157
welfare state 37, 38
Wells, Ida B. 15–19, 25
West Side Group 111
WHAM *see* Women's Health Action Mobilization
White House Conferences on Families 156, 203–204
White House protests: AIDS 187–188, 190–191; lesbians and gay men 177, 181, 192; suffragists 25, 31
White House Task Force to Protect Students from Sexual Assault 214–215
Wiley, George 150
Willard, Frances 16–18
Williams v. Saxbe 93
Windsor, Edie 195
WITCH (Women's International Terrorist Conspiracy from Hell) 109
Woman Identified Woman 167, 172, 181

women mill workers movement 2–3
Women of All Red Nations (WARN) 143
women of color: discrimination against 39; distrust of anti-rape movement 126; legislation on sterilization abuse 96–100; post-war employment 55; radical feminism 125; women's labor movement 37
women workers: campaign for rights 42; migration of 40–41; numbers of in World War II 40; protection laws for 32–34
women-owned businesses 91
Women's Action Alliance 119
women's bars 173–174
Women's Bureau of US Department of Labor 40, 43, 78
Women's Christian Temperance Union (WCTU) 16
Women's Health Action Mobilization (WHAM) 189–191
women's health movement 131–133
women's labor movement: early 20th century 20–26; feminism 34–39; and World War II 39–44, 55, 78–79, 216
women's liberation: impact of 121–133; and New Left 111–113; raising consciousness 106–111; Tillmon on 161
Women's Liberation Convention 109–110
Women's National Council 14
Women's Research and Treatment Agenda 190
women's rights conventions: first 5–6; idea for 4; National Woman Suffrage Convention 11; Ohio 6; Seneca Falls 1, 5–6
women's role, 1950s America 52–62
women's studies 112
women's suffrage: achieved 25; different constituencies 29–39; and immigrant women 19, 22–26; militancy 31; race and class 9–16; and Triangle tragedy 24–25
Women's Trade Union League (WTUL): campaign for equal pay 40; cross-dressing lesbians 172; and Eleanor Roosevelt 36–37; and ERA 33; and fire safety 23; and labor laws 32; and organizing drive 38; and state government 35
working conditions: protection for men 32; protection for women 32–34

working-class women: allies of middle-class women 32, 43, 44, 150, 160, 162; black 66–67; housewives movement 44–48; and labor laws 32–36; lesbians 63, 173–176; Mexican-American 63–64; post-war employment 54–57; and World War II 40–42
workplace discrimination 39–42, 55–56, 78–87, 90–94, 195
Works Progress Administration 37, 82
World Anti-Slavery Convention 1840 4

World War II, and women's activism 39–44
Wounded Knee, South Dakota, occupation of 141–143

Xue Jinqin 20

Yale, and sexual violence 211–212
Youth International Party (Yippies) 107

zines 208
Zuk, Mary 45, 47